ABITUAL GRUMBLING UNCHECKED

AMING BITTER SINFUL JUDGMENTA

RIDEFUL CHEERLESS MATERIALISTI

ATIVE LORD, CONDEMNING ANGR

ACTIOUS CYNICAL CHANGE MY

ATTITUDE

BEFORE IT'S TOO LATE

ABITUAL GRUMBLING UNCHECKED

MING BITTER SINFUL JUDGMENTA

RIDEFUL CHEERLESS MATERIALISTI

ATIVE LORD, CONDEMNING ANGR

ACTIOUS CYNICAL CHANGE MY

ATTITUDE

BEFORE IT'S TOO LATE

JAMES MACDONALD

FOREWORD BY ERWIN W. LUTZER

MOODY PUBLISHERS

CHICAGO

All Scripture quotations, unless otherwise indicated, are taken from the *New American Standard Bible*®, Copyright © 1960, 1962, 1963, 1968, 1971, 1972, 1973, 1975, 1977, 1995 by The Lockman Foundation. Used by permission. (www.lockman.org)

Scripture quotations marked KJV are taken from the King James Version.

Scripture quotations marked NLT are taken from the *Holy Bible, New Living Translation*, copyright © 1996. Used by permission of Tyndale House Publishers, Inc., Wheaton Illinois 60189, U.S.A. All rights reserved.

Scripture quotations marked NKJV are taken from the *New King James Version*. Copyright © 1982 by Thomas Nelson, Inc. Used by permission. All rights reserved.

Study guide produced with the assistance of Neil Wilson and The Livingstone Corporation (www.LivingstoneCorp.com).

Published in association with the literary agency of Wolgemuth & Associates, Inc.

Edited by Neil Wilson
Interior Design: Erik M. Peterson
Cover design: Nate Baron

Library of Congress Cataloging-in-Publication Data

MacDonald, James, 1960-
    Lord, change my attitude—before it's too late / by James MacDonald.
        p. cm.
    Originally published: Chicago : Moody Press, c2001.
    Includes bibliographical references.
    ISBN-13: 978-0-8024-1319-2
    1. Attitude change—Religious aspects—Christianity. 2. Christian life.
    I. Title.

BV4597.2.M33 2008
248.4—dc22

                                                                    2007052964

We hope you enjoy this book from Moody Publishers. Our goal is to provide high-quality, thought-provoking books and products that connect truth to your real needs and challenges. For more information on other books and products written and produced from a biblical perspective, go to www.moodypublishers.com or write to:

Moody Publishers
820 N. LaSalle Boulevard
Chicago, IL 60610

3 5 7 9 10 8 6 4

Printed in the United States of America

To Rick Donald
and Kathy Elliott,

Partners in ministry who have faithfully chosen
Christ honoring attitudes
and whose joy and contentment
consistently overflow to those who know them

CONTENTS

FOREWORD

If it is true, as the saying goes, that attitude determines altitude, this book will help you "mount up with the wings of eagles"! In his own direct style, James MacDonald has pinpointed those negative attitudes that keep us in the wilderness of our spiritual experience and has given us positive help in developing God honoring attitudes that will bring us in to "Promised Land Living."

This book is not for everyone. Not all people who read books are really interested in changing their attitudes. Some are more interested in learning new "insights" rather than actually letting God change their lives. This book is intended to bring about positive, radical change. Those who are serious will benefit; those who read it with other people in mind, or simply as a primer on human nature, will finish it with the same attitudes with which they began.

Let me suggest that you read the entire text of Israel's adventure in the wilderness in your own Bible. Make the changing of your attitude your number one personal priority. Your family will be delighted, your friends will approve, and most of all, God will be pleased. That, after all, is the goal of personal transformation.

I recommend this book because I believe that the transformation of our attitudes is the key to seeing the world through the eyes of faith; it is the key to the inner work of the Holy Spirit in our lives. The author gives practical illustrations and assignments that will help us view events and people the way God intended us to see them. Since how we live this life determines our rewards in the next, we must begin today to learn from the mistakes of those who have preceded us, and get on with becoming the people God wants us to be.

So fasten your seat belt, as you take this tour of the wilderness, because just up ahead is the Promised Land. And, with the right attitude, you will enter in.

ERWIN W. LUTZER
Pastor Emeritus
The Moody Church, Chicago

ACKNOWLEDGMENTS

A powerful life lesson for me recently has been the power of simplicity. Simple pleasures, simple schedules, and simple expressions of thanks. Writing a book, however, is far from simple. Many people are at work to make it a reality. Thanks to the people of Harvest Bible Chapel who support my preaching ministry from which each of these chapters originated. Thanks to Rosa Sabatino who took each message from tape to transcript with punctuality and accuracy. Thanks to Neil Wilson, who edited each transcript from its verbal style to a written format with creativity and insight. Thanks to Jim Vincent at Moody Publishers, who made the final edits when I was done writing and greatly improved the end result. Thanks to Kathy Elliott, who brokered that process with her usual patience and commitment.

Thanks also to Greg Thornton and all the folks at Moody Publishers who did their part to get this into book form and into the hands of readers like you.

Special thanks to my wife, Kathy, and our three children, Luke, Landon, and Abby, who once again endured with great patience a husband/father who was dealing with deadlines and working on his own attitudes.

Most of all, thanks are due to our faithful God, who has seen us through another important season of life and ministry with His abiding love and sufficient grace.

AN INVITATION

So you've picked up a book on attitudes and now you're trying to decide if you should read it. Let me help by asking a question: How did you get the book?

- Did you pick it up yourself browsing through a bookstore display? Are you considering whether an attitude upgrade might be the very best thing for your life right now?

- Did you receive this book as a gift from someone? Are they trying to tell you that your attitude needs some work? Or perhaps theirs needed some work, they read this book, and now they want you to share in the life change they have found so exhilarating.

- Maybe you received the book from a pastor or small group leader who knows you very well and believes this book will lead you into the kind of life transformation you have been searching for.

Possibly you read my first book on change and are ready to take the next exciting step in life transformation.

However you came to hold this book, I'm glad you did. I have been praying that this would not be "just another book" for you but a marvelous, joy-producing experience between yourself and God.

FIVE IMPORTANT QUESTIONS

Before we get to the introduction (it's really important that you read the introduction), I want to ask you five important questions based on the title of this book to help you decide if this is a book for you. Then I will conclude this invitation to read *Lord, Change My Attitude* by detailing six key features of each chapter. Each of these features is designed to help you pace yourself as you move through the life-changing content that is headed your way.

First the questions. Question one is:

Are you open to considering what the Lord has to say about changing your attitude?

This is not some futile self-help book, and it's not filled with the opinions of pseudo experts. This book is a study of what God has to say in the Scriptures about our bad attitudes. It details the consequences of rejecting God's ways and the benefits of accepting God's ways. Many people do not even believe in God, let alone have an interest in what He has to say about their happiness. To profit from this book, you have to be willing to reflect upon what the Bible says about attitudes and how God wants to change you.

Are you open to considering what the Lord *has to say about changing your attitude?* Yes or No? (Circle one.) If the answer is yes, this book is definitely for you!

Question two is:

Are you willing to be changed?

If change was easy, everyone would be doing it; but the fact is most people are just staying the same. So much so that we are generally pretty skeptical about people who say they have changed. As a pastor for more than fifteen years, I can tell you with confidence that people don't change until they know for a fact that "their thing" is not working. Life change can never begin until some circumstance brings you to the unalterable conclusion that your current course is taking you somewhere you don't want to go. Sometimes it's a tragic event or a relational breakdown. Sometimes it's a profound internal emptiness or a devastating personal failure. Whatever the circumstance that produces your readiness to change, you won't make it through this book without one. In fact, if you think your attitudes are as they should be, might I suggest that you give this book to someone who is ready for it now? Personal transformation is not a leisure sport, so it might be better that you come back to it at a later date.

Are you truly willing to be changed? Yes or No? (Circle one.) If the answer is yes, this book is definitely for you!

Question three is:

Are you willing to change your *attitude*?

The title makes it very clear that this is a book about attitudes. It's not about your actions or your circumstances. It's not about your relationships or your ministry. It's about you, and more specifically it's about your pattern of thinking. It's about the way you look at life. Attitudes are patterns of thinking formed over a long period of time. You can't change your attitudes in a few minutes, but you can admit the wrong ones and decide to begin working on the right ones. You can stop the flow of negativity that causes happiness to hemorrhage, and you can start the flow of good attitudes that causes abundant joy to overflow.

Are you willing to change your attitude? Yes or No? (Circle one.) If the answer is yes, this book is definitely for you!

Question four is:

Are you willing to focus exclusively on *your* attitude?

This is not a book to read with someone else in mind. Of course, you can share it with a friend, but please don't do that until it has had its potential impact upon you. We all need to grow and change, and no one has the attitude thing down 100 percent. Certainly not you or me. Throughout the book I will be sharing my own struggles in the area of attitude and praying that God will give you the capacity to be honest about where you are at. So let's promise now that we won't be focusing on the shortcomings of others but really working on our own attitudes.

Are you willing to focus exclusively on your own attitude? Yes or No? (Circle one.) If the answer is yes, this book is definitely for you!

Question five is:

Are you willing to go after this change of attitude with urgency?

Did the "Before It's Too Late" portion of the book title get your attention? Maybe you see yourself on a pathway that's headed downhill. Maybe you're seeing some of the fallout of bad attitudes in your family or where you work. We would be wrong to assume that there is always time to change. That is why Scripture says over and over again, "Today, if you would hear His voice, do not harden your hearts" (Psalm 95:7–8). In fact, that quote from Scripture describes the exact situation that we will be looking at. It's a fact: Just because God is working in your heart today regarding a specific matter does not guarantee that He always will be. There is an urgency to the message of this book that you would do well to heed.

Are you willing to go after this change of attitude with urgency? Yes or No? (Circle one.) If the answer is yes, this book is definitely for you!

The way you have answered these questions will influence to a great extent what you receive from this book. I invite you to read it prayerfully, expectantly, and fervently. As you embrace attitude change and all that comes with it, you will never be the same!

Helpful Tools

Each chapter has six helpful tools to assist you in the process of attitude replacement. These tools will help you understand key concepts and apply them in your life. Read each section attentively, and expect God to give you guidance and strength for the changing of attitudes in your life.

1. Chapter Couplets. Read the chapters in pairs. Note how the titles for each pair of chapters complete a sentence: "Replace an X Attitude . . . With a Y Attitude." Every two chapters go together. More on this in the introduction (another reason you should read it!).

2. "Say It in a Sentence." Each chapter begins with a summary statement that connects the truth of that chapter to the central theme of the book: Those who choose murmuring as their lifestyle will spend their lifetimes in the wilderness. The purpose of these summaries is to leave no doubt about the subject matter that is on the table in any particular chapter.

3. Bible Time. We will be focusing in on a particular time period where God's Word communicates very clearly how God feels about bad attitudes. The people of Israel will serve as our negative example, particularly the events that occurred in the Old Testament book of Numbers, chapters 11 to 16. For teaching and illustrations of the positive attitudes that replace the ones we are putting off, we will be turning to the New Testament. By taking the truth of God's Word seriously in each chapter, we can confidently anticipate that He will give us the strength to make the changes that are needed.

4. "Up Close and Personal." I own every attitude in the pages of this book—especially the negative ones! I couldn't write about them if I didn't know them from the inside. I will be candid about my own experiences and struggles in these areas. I'm familiar with wilderness journeys—both the way in and the way out. In each chapter, I'll show you how that particular attitude has affected me, and how God continues to help me put the wilderness behind.

5. "Let's Talk Solution." To help you move from thinking about attitudes to doing something about them, I will close each chapter with a series of pointed questions. The "Let's Talk Solution" questions will help you move toward application and action.

6. "Look Up!" Taking time to turn to God in prayer is essential to the process of life transformation. If you are like me, you may sometimes find it hard to express yourself to God in prayer. The prayers near the end of each chapter will help you confirm to God what you are intending to do in applying the truth in your own life. Use these prayers to keep your mind focused on your goal: This is change at the deepest level, attitude change.

Now it's time to read the introduction!

This is now the third time I have exhorted you to read the introduction. I know that it can be kind of boring in some books, but in this one it is essential. The introduction is where I give you the biblical context behind all the studies up ahead and explain why an ancient story has such urgent application for your life. The introduction is the foundation upon which this whole book is built.

Now please turn to the introduction and begin learning how to change your attitudes.

—JAMES MACDONALD

READY FOR PROMISED LAND LIVING?

The Sahara, the Mojave, the Gobi—deserts, all of them. Just the names can make your mouth go dry as they conjure up images of heat that abuses your senses. The sun beats down upon your forehead and into your eyes, forcing you to squint as you scan the horizon in every direction for shelter. Walking and walking but not getting anywhere as you trudge endlessly over identical dunes of desperation. Then you begin to think of water and realize you are thirstier than you have ever been in your life. You try to swallow but can't because your throat is as dry as the wasteland around you. Your skin screams for shade as you feel the burning accelerate and know that you won't be able to last much longer . . .

Welcome to the wilderness! It's a lousy place to visit and a devastating place to live. In fact, I would guess that not a single person reading this book lives in a desert—well, not a physical one. But we often live in a spiritual/emotional desert without realizing it. We feel the dry, lifeless, parched experience but fail to connect with where we really are and how we got there. Let me tell you straight up: It's our attitudes that turn our lives into wilderness experiences.

ATTITUDES *ARE* IMPORTANT

You may be tempted to think that attitudes are not that important, that what really matters in life and to God is our actions, but if you did think that you would be wrong. Back, back, back, hidden in the Old Testament journey from Egypt to the Promised Land is the most radical thing God ever did until Christ and the cross. It's an action that settles once and for all where attitudes are on God's list of priorities for our lives. The children of Israel left Egypt and journeyed to the very edge of the Promised Land. The journey took eighteen months and covered more than three hundred miles. Not a lot of distance except that there were more than two million people, and twelve of the eighteen months were spent at the base of Mt. Sinai getting the Ten Commandments and God's other laws.

There they were on the edge of "the land flowing with milk and honey," as the Lord had called it, meaning that it was a very cool place to live in every way. There they were, finally ready to step into all the blessing and joy that God had promised, and God tells them they are not going in. In fact, He tells them that they must go back into the desert and stay there until everyone over the age of twenty has died. If you're like me, you're thinking, "No way!" Way!

A PROMINENT MESSAGE IN GOD'S WORD

That is such a radical move, isn't it? To kill off an entire generation of Your children. Go figure. Actually, I did. I was so rocked by this move on God's part that I have spent a lot of time examining the precise reason that God would make such a decision. God never gets angry without a good reason. He doesn't just "lose it" and then wonder what happened. So there must be a very important lesson that such a radical move was intended to teach. Apparently the other writers of Scripture thought so, because almost every one of them refers to this incident either directly or indirectly.

This tragic event is referred to over and over in the Psalms (e.g., Psalm 95:8–11), in the Prophets, the Gospels, the Epistles (e.g., 1 Corinthians 10:5; Hebrews 3:17). Three separate times it's referred to in the book of Hebrews (3:7–11, 15–18; 4:1–3). Bottom line: It's the Old Testament event that everyone was talking about. All of God's people all the way through the writing of Scripture were thinking about these wilderness wanderings and the subsequent death of a whole generation of God's children. This is a message that was meant to be emphasized, but for some reason it has been mostly overlooked here in the last one hundred years. If you're like me, you're ready to ask . . .

OK, OK . . . why the big deal about wilderness wanderings?

If you want to know exactly why God killed off a whole generation of His children, you don't have to search very far; just open a Bible and check out Numbers 13–14.

Numbers 13 records the expedition of twelve spies sent by God and Moses into the Promised Land. They were to bring back a report so the people would have the faith to go up and conquer the land. But ten came back full of fear and started whining about the armies, the giants, and the obstacles they would face across the Jordan River. Two of the twelve, however, submitted a minority report (Numbers 13:30; 14:6–9), declaring, **"The land which we passed through to spy out is an exceedingly good land. If the Lord is pleased with us, then He will bring us into this land and give it to us—a land which flows with milk and honey. Only do not rebel against the Lord; and do not fear the people of the land, for they will be our prey"** (14:7–9).

Joshua and Caleb came back with the report of faith and confidence.

How did the people respond to this faith report? According to verse 10, **"But all the congregation said to stone them."** Don't miss the attitude here: No faith. Wrong attitude. "Stone them with stones," the people said. In response, an angry God revealed Himself "to all the sons of Israel" and then said to Moses, **"How long will this people spurn Me? And how long will they not believe in Me, despite all the signs which I have performed in their midst? I will smite them with pestilence and dispossess them, and I will make you into a nation greater and mightier than they"** (verses 11–12). That's when Moses pleaded with God not to wipe them out even for His own reputation. And God relented.

But God was still upset with the people's wicked attitude. Catch this: **"The Lord spoke to Moses and Aaron, saying, 'How long shall I bear with this evil congregation who are grumbling against Me? I have heard the complaints of the sons of Israel, which they are making against Me. Say to them, "As I live," says the Lord, "just as you have spoken in My hearing, so I will surely do to you."'"** And then God amplified: **"Your corpses will fall in this wilderness, even all your numbered men, according to your complete number from twenty years old and upward, who have grumbled against Me"** (verses 26–29). Paraphrased, that means, "All the grumblers—they're going down!"

His pronouncement spared only the God-fearing spies, Caleb and Joshua: **"Surely you shall not come into the land in which I swore to settle you, except Caleb the son of Jephunneh and Joshua the son of Nun"** (verse 30). In essence, God said to the two faithful spies, "You're going in; everyone else is gonna die in the wilderness."

PAYING THE PRICE FOR ATTITUDES

The Lord then told the rebellious people **"Your children, however, whom you said would become a prey—I will bring them in, and** they will know the land which you have rejected" (verse 31). God was saying, "You said I couldn't take care of them. You feared they were going to die. They're not going to die; *you're* going to die." Then He added, **"But as for you, your corpses will fall in this wilderness. Your sons shall be shepherds for forty years in the wilderness, and they will suffer for your unfaithfulness, until your corpses lie in the wilderness"** (verses 32–33). What an awful picture! How long would the people wander outside the Promised Land? **"According to the number of days which you spied out the land, forty days . . . "** (verse 34). So they wandered forty years—one for every day. Every faithless day. Every grumbling, complaining, critical-attitude day. **"For every day you shall bear your guilt a year, even forty years, and you will know My opposition"** (verse 34).

God was sending a message. He was saying, in effect, "I want you to know how I feel about this!" Verse 35 records His words: **"I, the Lord, have spoken, surely this I will do."**

You say, "But God is a God of grace and compassion and loving-kindness. What would push Him to such extremes?" Well, you would think that there must have been sexual impurity. No mention of that. There must have been real serious alcohol abuse or maybe a sudden rash of divorces or idolatry. Or were they abusing their children or some other gross sin to have God react like this? Nope!

THE PROBLEM WAS . . .

The problem was the people's "murmurings," as the old King James Version translates it (Numbers 14:27). The original word is actually an example of a universal language habit. Perhaps you remember from your high school English class the poetry term *onomatopoeia*. That's when a word sounds like what it is: *drip, drip, drip;* or *swoosh,* or *yawn. Murmuring;* that's what God hears. "Murmurmurwhazahazahas-senmurmur. . ." You almost feel like you're doing it when you're saying it! "Murmur, murmur, murmur." Well, if you would forgive the modern parlance, it makes God crazy! God absolutely hates that contrary, doubtful, rebellious attitude. He despises it. And He simply will not tolerate it.

"But," you say, "there are a lot of bad attitudes. I mean, I can think of a lot of bad attitudes that I have. Which attitudes are the attitudes that constitute this murmuring?" By carefully studying the events that surround Numbers 14, *we will discover five specific stories or events that illustrate the attitudes that make up murmuring.*

WHERE WE ARE GOING

It's no different today. God hasn't changed what He does about murmuring. He judges it. So if we decide to live like the Israelites did, then God will treat us like He treated them. Or if we choose murmuring as our lifestyle, then back to the wilderness we go. But you say, "There is no wilderness around me." You're right; God doesn't thrust us into a physical wilderness anymore, but He does cause our lives to become like a wilderness—a desolate, dry place not unlike a barren desert. Bad attitudes are what make life a dry, hard, joyless, parched experience.

Do you ever feel like that? Like your life is lacking the kind of joy and fulfillment that you desire? That you're missing the kind of abundant life that God's Word promises? If you do, then you have come to the right place, because the theme of this book is: *Those who choose murmuring as their lifestyle will spend their lifetimes in the wilderness!*

FIVE PAIRS OF ATTITUDES

Identifying wrong attitudes is only half the job; we have to replace those attitudes with the attitudes God has designed for Promised Land living. The ten chapters of this book are broken down into pairs of attitudes. Each pair begins with the negative attitude that must be put off. The next chapter then goes to the New Testament and presents the positive, life-giving attitude that has to be put on to replace the negative wilderness one. So, for example, chapter 1, "Replace a Complaining Attitude . . .", will be followed by chapter 2, ". . . With a Thankful Attitude." This will be a healthy yet aggressive process of personal change. Identify the bad attitude—put it off; identify the good attitude—put it on! Off with the bad; on with the good. Out with five bad attitudes; in with five good attitudes.

"But, hey, that was then!"

You say, "C'mon. What does this have to do with me? This happened more than three thousand years ago. You don't mean to tell me that God still feels the same way as He felt about their bad attitudes back then." Do! I *do* mean to tell you that God feels the same way about our bad attitudes today.

In fact, the apostle Paul wrote in the New Testament, **"For I do not want you to be unaware, brethren, that our fathers** [he's talking about the nation of Israel] **were all under the cloud and all passed through the sea; and all were baptized into Moses in the cloud and in the sea; and all ate the same spiritual food"** (1 Corinthians 10:1–3). He goes on to describe the application. Verse 6, **"Now these things** [everything in Exodus, Leviticus, Numbers, Deuteronomy] **happened as examples for us . . ."** Why did these things all happen? Why did God send them back into the wilderness? Here's your answer: **"These things happened as examples for us, so that we would not crave evil things as they also craved."** This truth is so important that Paul repeated it in verse 11: **"Now all these things happened to them as an example, and they were written for our instruction."** Verse 7 continues, **"Do not be idolaters." "Nor let us act immorally . . ."** (verse 8). **"Nor let us try the Lord . . ."** (verse 9). **"Nor grumble, as some of them did"** (verse 10). *Ding*—as in, "you today in the year 20??. Don't get a bad attitude like they did back in the wilderness, or you're going to be joining them."

You may think, *No way! God would not do that.* Wanna bet? Read verse 11, **"Now these things happened to them as an example, and they were written for *our* instruction"** (italics added). The reason behind God's action in Numbers was to teach us! The reason these events are recorded in Scripture is for you and me in the twenty-first century. These were written for *our* instruction, especially; verse 11 concludes, for those **"upon whom the ends of the ages have come."** And when is the "ends of the ages"? I believe . . .

This is now!

I believe we may be living in the last days. Most students of Scripture agree that every sign indicates that the return of Christ and the "ends of the ages," might be very near. All the more reason then that we should embrace God's dealings with the children of Israel as directly intended for us. For our attitudes. To get us out of the place where life is like a wilderness. To leave behind wilderness attitudes and embrace Promised Land attitudes.

READY FOR TAKEOFF

I know it has taken longer than normal for you to be ready to head into the content of this book. But we have built a great launchpad.

- You have decided that you believe attitudes are critically important for your life.

- You understand that attitudes are very important to God.

- You understand that there are serious "wilderness" consequences to wrong attitudes.

- You have decided that you want your attitudes to change.

- You have embraced the idea that you can't change your attitudes without God's help.

- You are willing to study God's Word to learn which attitudes need to change and how to begin.

Great job! Thanks for taking time to prepare for personal transformation. Your willingness to take that time has you ready for launching into an adventure of life change. Before we begin, let's take a moment and together ask the Lord to prepare us for change.

Look Up

Lord, thank You for the powerful message that You have preserved more than three thousand years. Thank You for loving me enough to seek me and pursue what is best for my life. As best I know how, I submit all my attitudes to You in this moment and pray that You will begin the process of transformation in me. I want the landscape of my life to change. I want to experience the unhindered joy and blessing that You have promised to those who will leave wilderness attitudes behind and move into the promised land of attitudes that please You.

Change my attitudes for Your own pleasure, and use the truths in this book, which come from Your Book, to do it, I pray. Do that work in me, oh, God, and begin today.

In Jesus' name I pray. Amen!

1

REPLACE A COMPLAINING ATTITUDE . . .

NUMBERS 11:1–3

SAY IT IN A SENTENCE:

Complaining is an attitude choice that if left unchecked will wither my capacity to experience joy and geniune thankfulness.

I hope you aren't one of those people who starts reading the first chapter of a book without reading the introduction, because if you are, things are going to get messed up really bad. In my writing, the introduction is far more than a "Hi, how are ya?"; it's the foundation for all the life-transforming truth to follow. If the foundation is strong, we can build some pretty phenomenal life-changing truth together. If it isn't . . . well, I think you get the picture. So circle back to the introduction if you need to, and I'll wait right here for you . . .

Welcome back. Now that everyone has read the introduction, we know where we are going and how we intend to get there.

Are you upset that I asked you to circle back and read the introduction? Did you complain about that invasion of your freedom, thinking, "I should be able to read as I please?" If not, you are in the minority, because we all complain far more than we like to admit. Wilderness attitude number one is *complaining*. When we express resentment over circumstances that are beyond our control and about which we are doing nothing, we are complaining. God hears it, hates it, and pushes everyone who persists in it toward the wilderness. Remember that those who choose complaining as their lifestyle will spend their lifetime in the wilderness.

Have you ever wondered why complaining is such a battle when we all agree that complaining changes nothing? The reason is that complaining satisfies our sinful natures. Complaining releases negative emotional energy in a way that provides momentary relief from a situation or circumstance that may be frustrating to us. That is why we find it so hard to resist.

Let me be the first to say that in certain situations I really like complaining. In fact, I like it so much that I would never consider eliminating my complaining were it not for what I have learned about how destructive it really is. What we desperately need to learn is how God judges our complaining with emotional fallout that makes our lives like **"a dry and weary land where there is no water"** (Psalm 63:1). Remember the theme of this book:

"Those who choose murmuring as their lifestyle will spend their lifetimes in the wilderness."

That is certainly true in the area of complaining. If you find it hard to believe that God would "make such a big deal" about your complaining, take a moment and come with me to an often-neglected passage in God's Word, Numbers 11:1–3. Note carefully Moses' "journal entry" from one day in the wilderness with his people: **"Now the people became like those who complain . . . and when the Lord heard it, His**

anger was kindled, and the fire of the Lord burned among them, and consumed some of the outskirts of the camp"(Numbers 11:1).

So here's this group of people standing somewhere on the edge of their makeshift city, and they are whining and grumbling about something. Maybe it was Moses' leadership style, or maybe it was the food, or the weather, or a very draining, difficult person. Whatever the subject matter, it was the final straw for God, and He sent fire among the whole group. If that doesn't tell you how God feels about complaining, nothing will. Now before you try to dismiss that as "Old Testament," review 1 Corinthians 10:11, which we covered in the introduction. (You did read that, didn't you?) Remember that what happened to the Israelites was intended by an almighty, unchanging God as an example for us; so let's make sure we don't miss it!

Looking a little closer at Numbers 11:1, it's hard to miss the fact that we choose our attitudes. That's a short sentence and you might be speed-reading, so let me say it again:

We choose our attitudes!

Oh, yes, we do! They don't choose us; we choose them. You should see the looks I get when I teach this truth publicly. People get all uptight and angry looking, like they're going to storm the platform, and I understand why. Nobody wants to be told "Your attitude problem is in the mirror"—but it is. Until we embrace as fact the idea that we choose our attitudes, we will never be able to choose differently, and life will always be a like a wilderness.

Notice what Numbers 11:1 says: *the people!* They couldn't point the finger anywhere but at themselves. Wouldn't that be great if we could say, "Well, it's my mom's attitude I've got," or "It's my dad's fault I'm this way." "It's my boss." "It's my neighbor." "It's my circumstances." Sound familiar? Back to God's Word: **"The people become like those who complain."** Why did they become like that? Because they had to? Because someone forced them, because of the way they were brought up? No; they chose. They had good reasons not to complain; they had more than enough reasons to be thankful. Instead, they chose the attitude of complaining.

God's final judgment on their attitudes clearly held them account- able for their choosing. Later twelve spies went into the land; twelve spies came back. Two spies chose God and faith and a good attitude— and they got the Promised Land. Ten spies chose self and doubt and a bad attitude—they got the wilderness. The people listened to the majority report and the minority report, and then they chose. They voted with their attitude—and they got the wilderness. We choose our attitudes.

I recently received a letter from a man who wrote multiple pages of eloquent persuasion trying to convince me that we don't choose our attitudes, and therefore we're not responsible for them. He wanted to blame circumstances and other people and a host of secondary influ- ences, all of which may play a part, but do not control us. We are the ones in control, and we do choose our attitudes.

At this point, you may be asking, "What exactly do you mean by attitude?" Let's get a definition stated right now, because if we're going to be talking about attitudes for ten chapters, we should all be on the same page.

Attitudes are patterns of thinking.

That's the first thing. Attitudes are patterns of thinking. You develop a way of thinking about things—a way of approaching life. Every sin- gle person, including you, has patterns of thinking; a way that you think about life. It goes back to the time when you were very young.

Imagine for a moment that you and I are observing a toddler who is holding a large, red, rubber ball. Before we can ask any questions, the child speaks.

"What are you looking at? It's my ball. It's not your ball." Wow, what an attitude!

Now that attitude may be influenced by his parents, or the fact that he needs a rest, or a cookie, or whatever, but still he is choosing.

We continue watching that two-year-old and his red ball as he tosses it up in the air and catches it. All of sudden, right in the middle of his nice playtime, he drops the ball, and everyone freezes to see what will happen next. Will he be upset about the fact that he dropped the ball? Will he get angry because he liked it a lot better in his hands than on the ground? We hold our breath and wait to see what attitude he will choose. Over the next few years, he will "drop many balls," and each time he will choose his attitude. Over time, his whole view of life will be shaped by a pattern of thinking—the attitude—he establishes. He has many attitudes to choose from.

1. He could choose to say: "Dumb ball! Who made this cheap, lousy, dime-store ball anyway? It's so slippery!"

2. He could choose to say: "Where's my parents? I can't believe they're not here when I dropped this ball! What kind of parents are they? If they really loved me, they would be here to help me pick up this ball!"

3. He could choose to say: "I'm such a loser. I always drop balls. I've played with other kids. They don't drop balls all the time. I'm the only one who drops balls! What's wrong with me? I'm such a loser!"

4. Or he could choose to say: "It's my fault. I dropped the ball. People drop balls all the time. I'm going to have a positive attitude. I'm going to pick it up and I'm going to go on. Maybe I can grow through this somehow, and stop dropping balls as often as I do now."

These little speeches sound familiar, don't they? But rather than from the mouths of toddlers, too often they come from our mouths, and betray a negative pattern of thinking—an attitude. In fact, they may reflect the way you think most of the time, because we all drop balls, don't we? The key to happiness is in the attitude we choose when we do "drop a ball." Attitudes are patterns of thinking. But here's the second part of the definition:

Attitudes are patterns of thinking formed over a long period of time.

Our attitudes are patterns of thinking—get this now—formed over a long period of time. Trace the career of the children of Israel, and you will know they didn't suddenly become complainers in Numbers 11. Go back to the days when they were making bricks in Egypt. They were constantly whining and sniveling about everything. You say, "Well, their lives were hard." Yes, their lives were hard, but some of them chose complaining and resentment toward God, and others in the exact same circumstances chose thankfulness instead. My point is this: Attitudes are patterns of thinking formed over a long period of time. Wrong attitudes are hard to change because they are habitual, harmful ways of thinking about life and circumstances.

Patterns of thinking are so deeply ingrained in our hearts that we hardly even notice them. We get so used to reacting a certain way that our choices become automatic, and in time we cease to see them as actual choices. We feel like we are trapped, but we are not. *Tragically, the consequences are also automatic,* and that is the cycle that we are trying to break in this book.

CHOOSING YOUR ATTITUDES

It won't be automatic or overnight, but if you stick with it and remain sensitive to what God is teaching you, lasting joy and true "Promised Land living" are not as far away as you might think. Did you know that the whole generation died just a few miles from the land flowing with milk and honey? Do you know why they died without stepping into the Promised Land? They died because they grumbled against God and rejected the call to enter the land. (See Numbers 14:1–4, 22–35, especially verse 29.)

They were so close to the joy of Promised Land living. Like them, you and I are much closer than we think to dramatic, joy-producing life change. Like them, you can make a choice to reject complaining and to trust God. Like them, the barrier is your patterns of thinking—and those patterns can change. Yes, they can!

And you can take the first step when you are willing to say, "I choose my attitudes." You can't change an attitude until you admit you chose it. But if you are willing to say, "I choose my attitude," then a different choice becomes your option. By admitting you made the choice, you put yourself in a position to make a different choice next time.

Perhaps you're not quite there yet. You want to read more before you accept responsibility for your attitudes. If that is your case, I encourage you to say this by faith: "I choose my attitudes. Lord, show me this is true." Pray that out loud. It's a prayer I'm confident God will answer, because He wants you out of the wilderness even more than you do. He wants to give you the fullness of Promised Land living, and He will as you allow Him to change your negative attitudes.

THE TRUTH ABOUT COMPLAINING

OK, back to the specific attitude of *complaining*. Here is one basic truth about complaining we cannot ignore:

Complaining is a sin.

Yes, it is. Complaining is a sin. The word *sin* literally means "missing the mark"; "failing in regard to God's holy standard and just demands." So equating complaining with sin puts complaints in a dangerous category.

Maybe you're thinking to yourself, "Wait a minute; complaining's not a sin. I mean, it may not be a great thing, but a sin? I mean, stealing and lying and blasphemy—sure (because they're obvious sins), but complaining? I mean . . . who am I hurting? Who am I really hurting when I complain?"

Well, first of all, you're hurting yourself! When you complain, you are choosing a response that does you harm rather than good. Our complaints may lead to anger, bitterness, and even depression. God loves you. He doesn't want you hurting yourself. What hurts you, hurts Him; so complaining hurts you both.

Beyond this, when you complain, you're not just hurting yourself but God indirectly. God is directly affected when He hears our complaining and our wrong attitudes, because complaining questions God's sovereignty! To complain is to say in effect; "God, You blew it! You had a chance to meet my expectations, but You couldn't handle it! Nice try, God, close—but not close enough." So complaining definitely injures you and the Lord.

In addition to that, we hurt the people around us. We affect others with our "stinking thinking." Nobody likes a negatron, or a lifetime member in the cold-water brigade, do they? If your friends and family hear you complaining all the time, you are bringing them down.

"But they do the same thing," you say. OK, then, y'all are bringing each other down. My point is only that complaining hurts far more than just you. It hurts God and those who hear it, and that's not right. So, no doubt about it, complaining is a sin.

DEFINING COMPLAINING

Before we go any further, let's get on the table a clear definition of this sin, so we will know when we are damaging ourselves and others and our relationship with God. Here's a key definition: *Complaining is expressing dissatisfaction with a circumstance that is not wrong and about which I'm doing nothing to correct.*

First of all, complaining is about *things that are not wrong*. If the
thing is wrong, and you express dissatisfaction, it's not complaining.
It's not a sin to picket an abortion clinic. That's not complaining. It's
not a sin to say to my spouse, "We need to spend more time with the
children." That's not complaining. Complaining is grumbling about
things that aren't wrong. You're dissatisfied with the meal served on
a trip and ask the flight attendant to rewarm the food, or later write cus-
tomer service suggesting they change caterers or offer different options.
That's not complaining; that's expressing a legitimate grievance.

Second, complaining involves *things that I'm doing nothing to correct*.
I'm choosing to whine about it, but I'm not doing anything to correct
the situation. That's complaining. It is complaining to whine about
abortion, but never pray or picket or vote or give donations or write
leaders. Just do nothing but mumble a lot under your breath, and there
it is—you're complaining. It is complaining to talk about your husband's lack of time with the children. It's not complaining when you
talk with your husband and together try to reach a constructive solution. It is complaining when you tell a fellow passenger, "This food
stinks." It's not complaining when you tell the flight attendant you dislike the beef and politely request a different entrée.

According to our definition, complaining involves *circumstances*.
Please note that complaining doesn't involve people. Criticism involves
people; complaining involves circumstances. We're going to talk about
criticism in chapter 5. Complaining is about circumstances, specific situations that we dislike because of how they affect someone or something
we value.

Finally, complaining involves *expressing dissatisfaction*. This gets a
little tricky. Some people pride themselves on verbal control. "I never
complain," they say. Well, hang on for a minute. Those of us who are
extroverts and often find ourselves saying things that we regret would
plead with those of you who are introverts to recognize that you're not
simply living in victory because you have a piece of duct tape over
your mouth. **"Man looks at the outward appearance, but the Lord**

looks at the heart"(1 Samuel 16:7). So complaining is not just the outbursts of frustration, but it's also those things that we think. That's complaining, too. To express dissatisfaction in any way—not just verbally but even in your thoughts—with a circumstance that is not wrong and about which I am doing nothing to correct . . . that's complaining. In the short term, it separates us from God; in the long term, it becomes a lifestyle, and we spend our lifetime in the wilderness.

HOW COMMON IS THIS PROBLEM?

"Is there a lot of complaining going on?" you may ask. "Are people really complainers?" That's easy to answer; just open the newspaper to the letters to the editor and read complaint after complaint. Or hang around the water cooler at work to hear employees gripe about the boss's latest "bad decision." And then there's the Internet. The number of web sites dedicated to complaining is amazing.

One Internet site is called Iventing.com. "Welcome to Iventing.com, the free place on the Internet to get it off your chest and complain. Go on. It's good for you. Do you want to vent right now? Go right ahead! Look at what others are venting about. Write it all down. Give us your name."

Can you believe that? Here's another site called The Complaint Station: "The king of complaints. Over five million served. We hold the record for the most complaints on any one site and are the pioneers of open complaining." To which I must respond, "Get a life!" But they're not finished: "The purpose of The Complaint Station is to provide you with a central location to file your complaints or research previous complaints. You can complain about issues related to . . . [blah, blah, blah]." How sick is that? Now this next site must have been the first of its kind on the Internet; it has the best name: Complain.org.

Complain about anything. The whole world is here to listen. Complain about your neighbor. Complain about the airlines. Complain about trains. Complain about noise. Complain about your mother-in-law. Complain about high prices. About getting ripped off. About potholes. About the police. Complain about welfare. Complain about work. Complain about your boss. Complain to us or even about us. We'll listen and tell everyone. No exceptions!

As I was reading all this to find out how common the problem of complaining is, I began thinking that these people need some serious, long-term counseling. But then I thought, "Well, surely the body of Christ is ahead in this problem." And then I found a Web site that offers an opportunity to "complain about anything here. Everyone needs to vent sometimes."

This site offers Christians a whole section where they can pick things to complain about. Multiple-choice complaining has arrived! I can just hear people reading this list and thinking, "I wasn't even mad about that, but now that I see it—man, that is kind of lame!" The site lists categories like: Complain that Bible college is expensive; complain about people who cuss; complain about my brother who is a pig; complain about your youth pastor . . ."

Is that twisted or what? Tragically, it's things like this that display the spiritual poverty in the church today. As a pastor, I constantly hear people complaining that the joy and peace of the Christian life is somehow eluding them. They feel frustrated that many of the good things Jesus offers are only concepts to them and not personal realities. When I press them for specifics, they report that their lives have, in fact, become like a wilderness! Well, yeeaaahhh!! Exactly! Just like a wilderness. Are we making the connection? Those who choose complaining as their lifestyle will spend their lifetimes in the wilderness. Complaining is sin that makes life like living in a wilderness.

GOD IS LISTENING

Think of it: God heard every word of every complaint of the children of Israel. Notice the text again: **"Now the people became like**

those who complain . . . and . . . the Lord heard it" (11:1). The
Lord heard it; He was there. The people ignored the pillar of cloud by
day and the pillar of fire by night, right there all the time. Those should
have been awesome and humbling evidences of God's nearness.
Instead, the people took God for granted. This wasn't the first time
they had complained. Look at the complaints recorded in Exodus alone:

> "Is this not the word that we spoke to you in Egypt, saying, 'Leave
> us alone that we may serve the Egyptians'? For it would have been bet-
> ter for us to serve the Egyptians than to die in the wilderness." (14:12)
>
> So the people grumbled at Moses, saying, "What shall we
> drink?" (15:24)
>
> The sons of Israel said to them, "Would that we had died by the
> Lord's hand in the land of Egypt, when we sat by the pots of meat,
> when we ate bread to the full; for you have brought us out into this
> wilderness to kill this whole assembly with hunger." (16:3)
>
> But the people thirsted there for water; and they grumbled against
> Moses and said, "Why, now, have you brought us up from Egypt, to
> kill us and our children and our livestock with thirst?" (17:3)

Over and over we read it: "And the people complained." And,
"Why can't we have more of this . . . and when are we going to get some
of that?" And, "Why don't You see that we need . . . ?" And, "Why
didn't You let us . . . ?" The chorus of complaints rose constantly:
"Can't we know . . . ?" And, "This isn't right!" And, "You should have
. . . " So the complaint chorus continued, and worst of all, the clamor
created a continuous ringing in the very ears of their Creator. God
heard their complaints, and He hears our complaining.

THE WORST KIND OF COMPLAINING

Now, this is an important point. Yes, God hears our complaining
about the weather and the traffic and the taxes and the social decline

and our age and whatever else we complain about. God hears all that. But there is one particular kind of complaining that grates most of all on the ears of God. Look at Numbers 11 again; see if you can pick out the worst kind of complaining from verse 1. **"Now the people became like those who complain of adversity in the hearing of the Lord."** That's the worst kind of complaining there is. Complaining about adversity. "Why do I have to go through that? Why must I endure all this hassle when life goes so smoothly for them? I'm sick and tired of being sick and tired; when will all this end? Why can't my life be more like Bill Jones or whatever?"

It's "My trial. . . . My hardship. . . . My lot in life. . . . My misfortune. " All this nauseating noise rises to the very ears of God until He replies, "Could you get away from Me with that chronic complaining?"

The writer of Hebrews has warned us, **"Do not regard lightly the discipline of the Lord. . . . For those whom the Lord loves He disciplines"** (12:5–6). God has entrusted to every person a measure of adversity. You have a measure of adversity, and so do I. Just the right amount to accomplish the eternal purposes of God in our lives. Your measure of adversity is like no one else's. This is a place in life about which you could say, "Nobody knows the trouble I've seen."

For some people, the adversity is a health situation. And for others, it's a struggling career and continuous job changes. And for others, a family tragedy happened years ago, and now they have to shoulder an incredible weight of responsibility that seems grossly unfair and unbearable. Some made a very poor decision early in life and their marriage fell apart, and now they struggle with blended families and the consequences of those choices. Whatever that measure of adversity is, it's your "cross" to carry.

I hurt for friends who want desperately to be parents, yet God has not allowed them, up to this point, to have children. Some long to be married, yet God has not provided the right mate. I could go on and on with examples. But hear this: Every one of us has a measure of adversity, and God Himself is the one who measured it out. And for that reason, every person has something in his or her life that God doesn't want to hear complaints about.

Instead of rejoicing in all the good things that God has done in our lives, we complain about that one thing—whatever it is. You say, "But it's hard." I know it's hard. It's hard to live with adversity and it's hard not to complain. But listen to me. Hear this pastor's heart. You are forfeiting the grace that could help you through that trial by complaining about it. All the grace and strength you need to experience joy and victory is available to you, but by choosing to complain, by clinging to the idol of a perfect life. . .

You are flushing away the grace of God.

As Jonah wrote, **"Those who worship false gods turn their backs on all God's mercies"** (2:8 NLT). Is that your worthless idol, your false god? Do you feel you are entitled to a perfect life, one without adversity? Realize this: That very adversity that you so often complain about is the thing God wants to use to keep your heart close to His. In His grace, He grants adversity to bring us close to Him.

"But it's so hard," you say. I understand; I am not making light of your adversity. I'm just trying to point out the connection between a life that feels like living in the wilderness and the attitudes of resentment and complaining that put us there. The bad thing isn't the adversity; it's our response to it! It's our attitude! And God simply will not tolerate repeated complaints about adversity. In fact:

God Hates Our Complaining.

Notice God's response to those who complained: **"His anger was kindled, and the fire of the Lord burned among them and consumed some of the outskirts of the camp"** (Numbers 11:1). God's anger was kindled. Again, this was not an isolated occurrence. The people habitually offended God. Verse 10 reports that **"Moses heard**

the people weeping throughout their families, each man at the
doorway of his tent; and the anger of the Lord was kindled greatly." Why? Because the people were crying? No, because of what they
were crying about! They were longing for things that God was not
willing to give them. They had complained so long that they completely lost perspective and started melting down about it.

Later in the same chapter we read, **"While the meat was still
between their teeth, before it was chewed, the anger of the Lord
was kindled against the people, and the Lord struck the people
with a very severe plague"** (verse 33). In subsequent chapters, we see
God's constant response to their complaints: **"So the anger of the
Lord burned against them and He departed"** (12:9). **"The Lord
said to Moses, 'Take all the leaders of the people and execute
them in broad daylight before the Lord, so that the fierce anger of
the Lord may turn away from Israel'"** (25:4). **"Now behold, you
have risen up in your fathers' place, a brood of sinful men, to add
still more to the burning anger of the Lord against Israel"** (32:14).

Now I know what you're thinking: *Well, that was then. This is now.
God doesn't get angry anymore.* But Psalm 7:11 says that **"God is a
righteous judge, and a God who has indignation every day."** Every
day! You say, "But God is a God of love." Yes, He is. And in His infinite transcendence, God can both love us extravagantly and hate our sin
passionately at the same time. God can embrace us and forgive us eternally but judge us in the moment because of our attitudes that are not
pleasing to Him. This concept may be a bit confusing to us, but it is perfectly clear to the Lord. He loves us and hates sin. Both are true.

NOISE IN THE BASEMENT

Children are such powerful messengers of the relationship we have
with our Father in heaven. Often we can gain insight into how our
actions affect God by looking at the way children affect us. Now
imagine for a moment that you are a parent who is out for the evening

with your spouse. You arrive home quite late. Your oldest—imagine this—has been baby-sitting the younger two while you were out for dinner. As you enter the house, you expect to find them in bed, but they are not!

All the lights in the house are out, and the silence gets eerie as you begin to search for them frantically. You're looking around, checking rooms and calling out their names. Where are they? You walk through the kitchen, and, near the door that leads to the basement, you hear a noise. You stop! Someone is talking in the basement.

So you open the door slowly and step down the stairs. As you get closer, you recognize it's your children's voices, and by the time you reach the bottom of the stairs you've got their location. They are in the laundry room with a flashlight, sitting in a circle. They are obviously engrossed in their conversation because they haven't heard the commotion upstairs.

Of course, you're relieved that they seem fine, but you are also very curious to find out what they're talking about. So you listen in and you hear, "I wish Dad would get a better job. Is he lazy?"

Another child pipes in: "Why can't he take care of us like the Smiths at church or like the Joneses at school? Why can't we have . . . ?"

Another child speaks up: "I'm so sick of Mom's rules: 'Go to school,' and 'Clean up your room.' Who does she think she is!? I'm not gonna take her bossy ways anymore." And you listen as this complaining goes on.

Now as a parent, at first you are hurt. You think, "I have tried so hard. I've done so much. How could it not be enough?" But if I understand parents, the hurt part lasts for about ten seconds. And then you're angry. And you're thinking things like, "The nerve of these kids!" and "It's never enough!" and "The things that I have done for them!" You may say, "These little runts," and "They have no idea the sacrifices that we have made. Maybe we haven't given them everything, but do you know what? We've done our best!"

Now take that out of the context of imperfect parents and think of your attitudes in the hearing of our perfect heavenly Father. Then remember that He always listens and hears everything you and I say— yikes, everything! Is it any wonder that God—yes, in our day—still has righteous indignation over the attitudes of His people? God hears our complaining and He hates it! It breaks His heart. It's a slap to His face. It insults His grace. And He is angry.

WATCH OUT! A HOLY JUDGMENT

In Numbers 11:1 we read that the people's complaints not only kindled God's anger, but that **"The fire of the Lord burned among them."** That phrase "the fire of the Lord" appears five times in Scripture. Along with the phrase "the fire of God," it describes the all-too-common biblical outpouring of God's wrath and judgment. His holiness creates a cleansing fire. The results are devastating to those who provoke His judgment. Remember Moses' shock in Exodus 3. God appeared to Moses the first time in a burning bush. There was a multimedia experience of God's judgment and holiness. In Numbers 11, that same holy fire began to crackle and kill on the edges of the camp. The people crossed the line of complaining and discovered hot flames on the other side. God has never lost His holiness or diminished in His righteousness.

Even in this day of grace, God's fire still consumes in judgment. He judges a complaining attitude as surely as He judged the people of Israel in the desert. But, for now, God's fire doesn't consume our existence; it scorches our happiness. God's fire consumes all that is fresh and healthy and life-giving in our lives. And life becomes a wilderness. Those who choose complaining as their lifestyle will spend their lifetimes in the wilderness. Is your life like that? Has life for you become like a wilderness? All dry and dead and cheerless, a wasteland where joy is wilted away because your pattern of thinking formed over a long period of time always sees the negative?

LIKE WANDERERS IN THE DESERT

Not so long ago, my wife and I were at a wedding. We get to go to weddings often and usually enjoy ourselves a lot. At this particular wedding reception, we were seated with a couple that I had heard about previously and whom I was looking forward to meeting. But the enjoyment lasted for about sixty seconds because I suddenly found myself thinking, "Have you ever met such cheerless, joyless believers in your whole life?"

It was sad. And so I sort of took it on as a challenge to cheer them up. (I admit my wife doesn't really like this about me.) I was telling them a few jokes at the table and trying to lighten things up a little bit. My best stuff fell flat. They didn't even offer a courtesy chuckle. Wanting to do a little CPR on their sense of humor, I kept at it but made very little progress. They were barely tolerating me, sort of grunting and groaning, like mournful Eeyore the donkey in Winnie the Pooh: "Oh, Booootheeeerrrr!"

At one point, someone came around and said, "We're going to take a picture of your table now," like they do at most weddings. So we stood up with the bride and groom and formed a circle around the "stone family." They certainly weren't gonna move, so Kathy and I stood behind them and I thought, "Well, maybe this will break the ice." So I made these peace signs behind their heads during the photograph.

I could tell right away that they weren't digging that at all. So I leaned down and said to them, "Boy, I bet it's been a long time since someone has done that to you."

The wife looked up and said (in a voice somewhere between Gladys Cravitz on *Bewitched* and Mrs. Howell on *Gilligan's Island*): "Well, normally we don't spend so much time with immature people."

I just thought, "You poor soul! Back into the wilderness you go!"

Do you know something? These are not bad people; these are good people. These are people like you and me who, without realizing it, choose attitudes moment by moment and day after day that eventually become their lifestyle. Humor was not allowed in their lifestyle. No fun, no kidding or teasing, no relaxing banter between acquaintances, just a dry, joyless, wilderness existence. They had become desert wanderers. I'm getting thirsty just thinking about the life they are living and the attitudes they have chosen.

The stone family didn't want to laugh about wrong things but eventually got to the place where they couldn't laugh at all! Especially not at themselves. That is a sure sign of wilderness living—the inability to laugh at oneself.

Can You Laugh At Yourself?

I've always told my kids: If you can't laugh at yourself, the whole world stinks. That's true. Like the man who fell asleep on the couch in his home, and his playful children put a piece of Limburger cheese on his moustache. When he woke up, he smelled something terribly wrong and ran through the house yelling, "Something in this room stinks! No, something in this house stinks!"

Unable to locate the trouble, he went out on the front porch and yelled at the top of his lungs, *"This whole world stinks!"*

LET'S TALK SOLUTION

Remember that this chapter title is "Replace a Complaining Attitude . . ." Our concern has been to identify the telltale signs of complaining in our lives. Before I hint at the solution, I want to encourage you to continue immediately to the next chapter when you've finished reading this one. There we will put into practice an important spiritual principle: Once you empty something, you must fill it with something else. Jesus gave a chilling warning about the fate of someone who had a demon expelled but didn't fill the house with God's Spirit (Matthew 12:43–45). The demon returned with friends and made the man's life worse than before! When we set out to replace a bad attitude, we need to pray and then put a good attitude in its place. You can't simply put off bad habits and live in a vacuum; you have to put on good ones in their place.

Now let's look for a moment at solution steps. To do so, we need to ask ourselves some soul-searching questions. Ask yourself:

1. *Am I a complainer?* I challenge you to begin to pray from your heart, "God, am I a complainer?" Complaining is so hard to see in ourselves, especially when it's reached the habit stage. It's easy to see in others. When we complain, we say, "I'm just getting things off my chest." But when other people complain, we're quick to advise, "You're not helping anything." Let me ask you these clarifying questions: What two or three things about your life would you most like to change? Are you complaining about those things verbally or nonverbally? Are you accepting and thankful or resisting and complaining?

2. *Am I reaping the consequences of complaining in my relationship with God? Is that the problem?* Imagine that God whispered into your heart right now, "I'm listening. I'm listening. I hear everything you say. I hear every thought you think—all of it." Would that shed a new light on the landscape of your life? If your life lacks joy and a sense of God's favor and presence . . . if your heart is like a wilderness, it's your attitudes.

3. *Am I willing to repent?* Am I willing to turn from that attitude of complaining, acknowledge its wrongness, and ask God to change my attitude? We've been in the Old Testament for this lesson, but let's highlight the good news with these closing thoughts. That good news we celebrate is the message of Jesus Christ. His death provided a way for us to be forgiven and cleansed and have a fresh start in life and in our attitudes. We need only repent—agree with God that our complaints are sin— and choose to turn from complaining and ask His forgiveness.

I realize the above questions may have made you uncomfortable, but we will need to get over that. If you and I are serious about putting the wilderness behind us, we must get serious about why we're there, and that means answering probing questions at the end of every chapter. Questions like these help us accept responsibility for our attitudes. If you blew off the questions above, please look at them again. And if God reveals complaining as a problem in your life . . . acknowledge it! And then turn from it. Otherwise, expect more wilderness ahead.

In the next chapter I will be talking about the wonderful, positive, life-giving attitude that replaces complaining, but let me take a moment and share a bit of my own struggle in this area.

UP CLOSE AND PERSONAL

On a personal level, complaining has definitely been an issue for me. I'm really thankful to God for a wife who many times has taken me aside and said, "Do you know what? You're not helping anything. Your complaints are not making anything better." Then she'll often say, "We need to stop and pray about this." I complain about incompetence, I complain about traffic and pressure, and weather and moral decline, and . . . I can feel the sinful pattern welling up in me even now as I write to you (better stop, ha, ha).

Countless times in years gone by, Kathy and I have sat together while I pray, "God, I'm sorry for my attitude. It's wrong. I know it's not pleasing to You. Please forgive my complaining attitude and cleanse my heart." The Lord has been so faithful to do that. In fact, I encourage you to take a moment and pray right now.

Look Up

Lord, I thank You for Your Word. I thank You that You have revealed Yourself to me as You truly are. Thank You for directing Your holy, righteous anger at my complaining and how that keeps me from You. Thank You, Lord, that You not only love me, but You hate my complaining and the way that it makes my life like a desert.

In this moment, I ask that You would make me very aware of what I say and what I think. Keep the connection strong between how I deal with my circumstances and the joy that I experience. Forgive me for complaining, not just because of how it affects our relationship, but how it affects my relationships with those I love. Give me grace and faith to embrace the trials You allow, knowing what is best for me is always upon Your heart. Please teach me not to complain, and even as I look to this next chapter, teach me to put on the life-giving, joy-producing attitude that goes in its place. I pray this in Jesus' name. Amen.

2

... WITH A THANKFUL ATTITUDE

LUKE 17:11–19

SAY IT IN A SENTENCE:

Thankfulness is the attitude that perfectly displaces my sinful tendency to complain and thereby release joy and blessing into my life.

The hardest part about writing a book on our attitudes is keeping a good one while you're helping others work on theirs. Be encouraged, though; you're doing great! You're through the introduction and the first chapter and ready for more. Great things are ahead if you will press on with a humble, teachable attitude.

In the last chapter, we saw God rain down fire from heaven. And lest we dismiss that action from God as "that was then, this is now," we also learned from 1 Corinthians 10:11 that what happened to them was recorded as an example to us. So the partial statement that summarized the last chapter was "Replace a Complaining Attitude . . ."

We are concluding that statement in this chapter by adding, ". . . With a Thankful Attitude." We're going to put off the old attitude of complaining, and put on the new one of thankfulness. In fact, as you will see, thankfulness is the perfect replacement for complaining.

Do you know the story of Christ and the ten lepers—the time that Christ miraculously healed these ten dudes and only one even said thanks? If you ever thought thankfulness was not important to Christ, you were wrong. In fact, He got pretty steamed at the ungrateful ones. Let's look at the story more closely.

THANKLESSNESS IS NOTHING NEW

"As He entered a village, ten leprous men who stood at a distance met Him; and they raised their voices, saying, 'Jesus, Master, have mercy on us!'" (Luke 17:12–13).

This is nothing new. Since the beginning of time, humanity has called forth in an unbroken, mighty chorus: "God, do this for me! God, do that for me! God, I need this! God, I need that!" No time for God when things are going well; but in their moment of need, everyone is on their knees. Isn't it amazing that God in His infinite grace never tires of our fickle, thankless ways? "When He saw them," verse 14 continues, "He said to them, 'Go and show yourselves to the priests.' And as they were going, they were cleansed."

In the New Testament, leprosy is a broad term that covers a variety of skin diseases which brought pain and suffering and rendered the victim a virtual outcast from society. In order to get back to their families, they had to get approval from the priests, and this is what Jesus commanded them to do. In fact, it wasn't until they moved in that direction that they were actually healed. It wasn't until they had walked a fair distance from Christ that they began to say, "Hey! Check *me* out! I'm completely healed!" "Me too! Look at this; I'm totally cleansed and whole!" All at once, all ten of them were healed; each had received an incredible gift from the Lord.

When they saw they had been healed, nine kept going. Verse 15 begins: **"Now *one* of them"** (italics added). Only one turned and walked back to Jesus in order to express his thankfulness. **"When he saw that he had been healed, [he] turned back, glorifying God with a loud voice"** (verse 15). He was fired up with gratitude!

Notice the humility. **"He fell on his face at [Jesus'] feet, giving thanks to Him. And he was a Samaritan"** (verse 16). He not only fell down, but he did so as a Samaritan. That is very significant. The Samaritans were hated by the Jews as part of a complex and ancient racial prejudice. Though he was really outside the household of faith and had, on a human level, the fewest reasons to thank a Jewish man, this Samaritan returned gratefully. The point is, no one has an acceptable excuse for ungratefulness. Everyone can make the choice to give thanks and acknowledge the goodness and the grace of God.

Sadly, however, only a small fraction of the human population ever personally thanks God for His grace. Again, notice the contrast: a thankless nine and a thankful one. Ten actions received; ten attitudes chosen, but only one person thankful. Attitude is everything! And Christ notices too. Indeed,

Christ notices those who are ungrateful.

There is no doubt but that Christ Himself was aware and disturbed by such a flagrant instance of ungratefulness. **"'Were there not ten cleansed?'"** Jesus asked (verse 17). It was a rhetorical question. He wasn't trying to figure it out; He was simply pointing out their outrageous, thankless attitude. **"'Were there not ten cleansed? But the nine—where are they? Was no one found who returned to give glory to God, except this foreigner?'"** (verses 17–18). Just this one, who, based on the social injustices he had received, had many excuses for not coming and saying, "Thanks." If he could overcome all of that to express sincere gratitude, how could the others walk away?

Then Jesus turned to the thankful man, saying, **"Stand up and go;**

your faith has made you well" (verse 19). Circle the word *well*. Jesus was not talking about being physically well. All ten of the lepers were made well. To say that his "faith had made him well" would be incredibly redundant, because the ones who didn't have any faith, those ones who didn't show any thankfulness, were also made well physically. Christ was saying in effect: "Because of your gratefulness—because of your thankfulness—you have been made well in a much deeper way than those who refused to be thankful."

GOD, OUR GRACIOUS PROVIDER

Only when we acknowledge God as the gracious provider of general blessings, like life and breath, food and shelter, do we begin to comprehend our need for God in a personal way and begin to express faith in Him.

Let me say it again: Only when we recognize God as our gracious provider do we comprehend our need for God and begin to express faith in Him. That is a very significant point. Faith grows in the soil of thankfulness. Only when a person outside of Christ is willing to acknowledge—"Yes, there is a God. I have received much from His hand and probably owe Him something more than passive acknowledgment. Perhaps I should turn and consider whether I ought to be reconciled to this God who made me and gives me life and strength"—only then will he be ready for faith. Faith to believe in God as the One to whom we must all be reconciled sprouts in the soil of gratefulness.

Paul made this same point on a cosmic scale in Romans 1, when he wrote that:

- God created the universe.

- Within the heart of every human being is an awareness of the reality of God.

Apart from thankfulness, our awareness of God will always be suppressed.

As Romans 1:19–20 declares, **"Because that which is known about God is evident within them; for God made it evident to them. For since the creation of the world, His invisible attributes, His eternal power and divine nature, have been clearly seen."** Only the most resolutely unbelieving person would ever stand and look at the universe and say, "There is no God." **"The fool has said in his heart, 'There is no God'"** (Psalm 14:1). Any person with basic objectivity knows that all of this didn't come from a mindless and purposeless explosion. Random creativity doesn't make any more sense than taking a stick of dynamite, throwing it into a printing factory, and expecting the explosion to produce the Declaration of Independence. You don't get order from chaos, and there is no way that all we see around us could possibly exist without a God of some sort who brought it into existence.

OBJECTION! OBJECTION!

You may object: "But I don't understand God." Yet still you must make a choice about His existence—the alternative being that our entire universe evolved from nothing. I don't think so! Design shouts Designer.

Now amazingly your capacity to make the right choice about the existence of God hinges on the level of thankfulness in your heart. As Paul argued, **"For even though they knew God"**—even though there was something deep within them that said, "There is a God; there is a God"—**"they did not honor Him as God or give thanks"** (Romans 1:21). At the root of mankind's rejection of God is a resolute unwillingness to be thankful. **"But they became futile in their speculations and their foolish heart was darkened."** After that, things got really ugly.

My point to you is that all of the good things that God wants to bring into your life sprout in the soil of thankfulness, and I don't mean mere words.

Thankfulness is far more than saying the right words.

Genuine gratitude must be distinguished from the kind of thanks we are programmed to spout as children. Maybe your mom was the same as mine. No sooner had someone given me half a cookie, than I felt her elbow and heard the whisper, "Say thanks. Say thanks!" By the time we were three years old, the MacDonald children had said "thanks" about a million times. Then, before we knew it, we were poking our own kids: "Say thanks. Say thanks."

But does it really mean anything? I'm sure you find yourself in public situations where politeness requires a steady stream of duty-thanks, "Thanks. Thanks. Thanks."

"Here's your table, sir."

"Thank you."

"Here's your menu, sir."

"Thanks."

"Here's your coffee, sir."

"Thanks."

"More coffee, sir?"

"Thanks."

But as any waitress will tell you, the number of thanks and the amount of the tip do not necessarily go together. The kind of life-changing heart attitude that God desires is much deeper than surface verbal gratitude.

THE POWER OF THANKFULNESS

Even in the often-godless corporate world, people are waking up to the power of gratitude and discovering that it takes a lot more than free trips and Christmas bonuses for employees to feel appreciated. Recent studies have shown repeatedly that if employees don't feel genuine gratitude from the people that they work for, bonuses are useless. Insincere gratitude doesn't upgrade employee loyalty or productivity. If we are unmoved by perfunctory expressions of gratitude, just imagine how unmoved God is.

One magazine, *Mind and Body,* recently published an article entitled, "Twenty Ways to Feel Calmer, Happier, and Healthier" and the number one answer given was "to be thankful for all the good in your life." Researchers are recognizing that an attitude of gratitude directed toward God is a powerful source of health and personal well-being.[1] Check out these studies that show the benefits of being thankful to God and acknowledging Him:

- Regarding stress. In a northern California study on stress, nearly seven thousand Californians showed that "West-Coast worshipers who participate in church-sponsored activities are markedly less stressed over finances, health, and other daily concerns than non-spiritual types."[2]

- Regarding blood pressure. Elderly folks in a Duke University study on those who attend church, pray, and read the Bible regularly had lower blood pressure than their nonpracticing peers.

- Regarding recovery from surgery. A second Duke University study looked at patients of faith recovering from surgery. People who have faith and trust and thankfulness toward God spend an average of eleven days in the hospital after surgery. Meanwhile, patients who have no faith-based life at all spend an average of twenty-five days in the hospital recovering from surgery.[3]

- Regarding personal lifestyle. A recent review of several studies suggests that spirituality is linked with low suicide rates, less alcohol and drug abuse, less criminal behavior, fewer divorces, and higher marital satisfaction when life is filled with regular thankfulness to God.

▓ Regarding depression. I find this very interesting. Women with believing mothers are 60 percent less likely to be depressed ten years after they leave the home, according to a Columbia University study. Daughters belonging to the same religious faith as their mothers are 71 percent less likely to suffer the blues. Sons are 84 percent less likely to have life crises if they belong to the same faith group as their mothers.

▓ Regarding mortality. Research on more than 1,900 older adults indicated that those who attend religious services regularly have a lower mortality rate than who do not.[4]

Aren't those studies incredible? Even people who don't believe in God are recognizing that a God-centered, faith-oriented, thankful life is a healthier, happier life. Further proof of our overall thesis: *Those who choose complaining as their lifestyle will spend their lifetimes in the wilderness.* By far, the better attitude is gratitude.

Test yourself. I dare you!

The word *gratitude* is defined in the Oxford Dictionary this way: "to show that a kindness received is valued." Genuine gratitude requires that we get past obligation and somehow show that we deeply appreciate what we've received. Here's a test that will help you analyze whether your thankfulness is genuine or obligatory. Think back to the last time you were in church. What was going through your mind as you parked your car, got out, strolled into the building, passed through the lobby, picked up a bulletin, and sat down? Truthfully, what was at the center of your heart? Did any of these thoughts enter your mind?

▓ What am I going to get today?

- Am I going to be encouraged?

- Will I like the pastor's message?

- Will he keep my attention and make me smile?

- I wonder who's singing today. Oh, I hope it's not _____ again; she is just awful!

- Will I be glad I came?

If that kind of thinking was present as you "prepared" for worship, it reveals a self-centered, thankless theology that promotes complaining and stifles gratitude. The truth is, if we never received another thing from God for the rest of our lives, we could still fill each day with genuine gratitude:

- "Thank You, God, for this new day."

- "Thank You for life that I can use to serve You."

- "Thank You for breath that I can use to praise You."

- "Thank You for health."

- "Thank You, Lord, for strength."

But somehow we make the choice to turn from all that we've received and focus on what we still want to have. That's where complaining comes in. We minimize the blessings of life and magnify every negative circumstance we encounter.

"I can't believe the nursery workers are late again today," says an upset parent. "I am sick and tired of this lousy weather," a college student grouses. The litany of complaints continues: "Why can't the kids remember to pick up after themselves?" "Nobody appreciates me." We focus on the negative around us, and life becomes a wilderness.

LEVELS OF GRATITUDE

Instead, we need to develop our level of gratitude. There are three levels of thankfulness: elementary school gratitude, high school gratitude, and graduate school gratitude. Let's visit these schools of gratitude.

The elementary level teaches us to be thankful in the most basic sense. It instructs us to **"continually offer up a sacrifice of praise to God, that is, the fruit of lips that give thanks to His name"** (Hebrews 13:15). *Elementary school* is the sacrifice of thankfulness. "Thanks, God. There, I've said it, God, so You should be happy." In effect, we say to God, "Fine! You helped me, and now I said thanks. My obligation has been met; I recognize Your involvement." Now that's something, but it's not much. As long as thankfulness is just a sacrifice, like, "Well, I'll do it if I have to, I guess," you might get to the edge of the Promised Land, but you won't find much joy, and you'll still feel the heat of the wilderness at your back.

Level two is a better place. I call it high school thankfulness. **"In every thing give thanks: for this is the will of God in Christ Jesus concerning you"** (1 Thessalonians 5:18 KJV). In every situation, you and I can always find something to be thankful for—always. We can make that decision. We can look away from what's wrong and focus on what's right and give thanks. "In *every thing* give thanks." That's kind of a high school version of thankfulness, and it does produce joy as long as you're not going through anything too difficult.

But if you want the real joy—if you want to be done with the poverty, cheerless, joyless wilderness thing forever, then go on to level three—graduate school thankfulness. Be thankful for *all* things. This is beyond the high school thankfulness that searches to find a good aspect in a challenging circumstance. This is the thankfulness that trusts God and thus is grateful for the bad things, even the things you wouldn't choose. **"Be filled with the Spirit, . . . giving thanks always for all things to God"** (Ephesians 5:18, 20 NKJV).

This is the Mt. Everest of thankfulness, and it promises victory over every circumstance. Maybe you're reading this with a health crisis or a great sorrow that won't go away. Maybe you've got a financial need. You (and I) need to get to the place by faith where we can say, "Thank You, God. This is the thing that You're using in my life. You've allowed it because You love me, and I trust You. Thank You, God, even for this!" When we allow the Lord to bring us into that kind of thankfulness, we will experience a depth of joy we never thought possible.

POINTS OF VICTORY

One afternoon, I was running late to pick up my three kids from the Christian school they attend. A lot of things had been going wrong, and I was shuffling down the hallway mumbling under my breath about my top five complaints at that moment. I knew my attitude was wrong, but the negative emotion was very powerful, and I felt a complete inability to shut it off. Of course, I knew that victory was far more than putting a piece of duct tape over my mouth; I knew that something powerful had to replace my stinking thinking.

Just then I looked up and spotted on the wall in front of me a beautifully framed calligraphy of Psalm 107:8. The verse actually is repeated five times in that psalm as God pleads with us to put off complaining and put on genuine thankfulness. The New King James Version says it really well: **"Oh, that men would give thanks to the Lord . . . for His wonderful works to the children of men!"** (Psalm 107:8, 15, 21, 31).

The verse was like a knife in my heart. And my subsequent reflection on its truth yielded three specific points of victory.

POINT ONE: THANKFULNESS IS A DECISION

Thankfulness is a choice that we make. It's just as real as any other decision. The psalmist wrote, **"Oh, that men would give thanks to**

the Lord." By men, of course, he meant men and women—mankind. Notice the verse says *would* because if it said *could*—"Oh, that men *could* give thanks to the Lord"—well, then the ball would be in God's court, wouldn't it? And we would be free to say things like, "It's Your fault, God; if I *could* give thanks, then I *would*. If You hadn't made me so negative; if You hadn't made me so selfish; but I am, so I can't, but I would if I could, but You didn't, so I can't, so . . . whatever." But it doesn't say *could*, it says *would*, so the choice is ours.

"Oh, that men would . . ." This means "we have the technology"— God has made us with the capacity to express gratitude. It's a choice that we make. What a critical, happiness-inducing choice it really is! You can choose your attitude of gratitude as much as you can choose your diet or your underwear.

Recently, I spoke to the students, faculty, and staff at Cedarville College (Ohio). In the evenings, I spoke about Jonah. The call to Jonah—and the students—was to stop running from God and submit to His relentless pursuit.[5]

It turned out to be an amazing week. God was working as powerfully as I have ever seen. By Wednesday night, I could hardly wait to get into the worship center. The place was packed with almost 3,000 eager students, their Bibles open. We sang some songs, and began moving into an attitude of worship and attentiveness to God's Spirit.

All of a sudden, the doors flew open, and police officers came running down the aisle. They were dripping wet and in a hurry. Up on the platform they came, with their blaring walkie-talkies and all-business demeanor. They approached the school president who was sitting beside me, so I heard the urgent news. The officer in charge said, "A tornado is coming this way. You must get the students out of this room as quickly as possible."

It is heartwarming to watch a great leader in action. The college president walked to the center of the stage and in a calm and clear voice said, "Students, listen carefully to these instructions. We just received a report that we may be in the path of a tornado. We need to exit the worship center as quietly and as quickly as possible and take shelter."

Some kids were screaming and yelling a bit, but a general sense of order prevailed as we were directed into rooms with no exterior walls or windows and told to get down low. We couldn't see what was going on outside, and so we didn't have a sense of how immediate the danger really was. Word eventually came that we could go back upstairs. At that point, I didn't know if they were going to go forward with the service and my message from Jonah 3 on how to experience personal revival.

When we got back into the worship center, there was a new atmosphere of seriousness among the students. We sang a couple more songs and then I got up to preach.

Five minutes into the message, the entire worship center went black. You couldn't see your hand in front of your face. The generators had failed and every emergency light was out. We couldn't see anything! Immediately, the students started murmuring, but I clearly sensed that God wasn't finished with us yet.

Since the microphone died with the lights, I whistled for attention and then yelled into the darkness, "There is no way in the *world* that we're going to let an electrical problem get in the way of what God wants to do in our lives here tonight!" The students cheered and then got very quiet; somebody put a flashlight in my hand, and for the next forty-five minutes I preached my heart out, even though I could barely see my notes and not a single face in the massive auditorium.

When I was done, I closed in prayer, and then the students began to sing spontaneously. First quietly, but then incredibly, they chorused the great hymns of the faith at the top of their lungs for well over an hour. No instruments, no song leader, no lights, no words—just powerful, heartfelt expressions of praise and thanksgiving to God. It was one of the most moving things I have ever experienced in my life.

We later learned that the tornado came right over the school. Cars were damaged; tree limbs and debris were everywhere. Just ten minutes later, the tornado touched down in another spot. Several people were killed and many more evacuated as houses, large retail outlets, and at least two churches were demolished. More than forty people had to be airlifted to emergency rooms all over that part of Ohio.

Meanwhile, God had the full and undivided attention of that campus as we recognized in a fresh, new way how we take the simple things of life for granted, but God sends a little wind, and, apart from His grace, we can all be gone in a moment. Talk about an immediate reduction in complaining and a marvelous amplification of genuine thankfulness!

We really have *so* much to be thankful for. Did the sun come up again this morning? Do you have another day to live for the glory of God? Then there is plenty to focus on for thanksgiving. You say, "Yeah, but there's plenty to focus on and complain about, too." My point exactly. We have a decision to make.

POINT TWO: THANKFULNESS IS A DECISION BASED IN REALITY

That's a second lesson from that verse in Psalm 107. I'm not suggesting some mind-over-matter, power-of-positive-thinking nonsense here. I'm asking you to use your mind and ask, "Do I really have a lot to be thankful for?" The answer clearly is "Yes!"

The classic book (written in 1719) by Daniel Defoe, *Robinson Crusoe,* described a man who was shipwrecked. He spent twenty-seven years on a tropical island. His story illustrates perfectly that thankfulness is a decision based in reality. We find our hero, cast on this island all by himself. Here is his journal entry:

I now began to consider seriously my condition and the circumstance I was reduced to. I drew up the state of my affairs in writing to deliver my thoughts from daily poring upon them and afflicting my mind. As my reasoning began now to master my despondency, I began to comfort myself as well as I could and to set the good against the evil that I might have something to distinguish my case from one that is much worse. So I stated it very impartially, like a debitor and creditor, the comforts I enjoyed and the miseries I suffered.[6]

We'll call the list that he wrote, "The Complaining List and the Thankful List."[7] Notice the deliberate choices of thankfulness based in the reality he was facing.

Robinson Crusoe's Complaining and Thankful List

Complaint
"I am cast upon a horrible desert island void of all hope of recovery."

Thanks
"That I am alive and not drowned as all of my ship's company was."

Complaint
"I am singled out and separate as it were from all the world to be miserable."

Thanks
"But I am singled out, too, from all of the ship's crew to be spared from death. God, who miraculously saved me from death, can deliver me from this condition also."

"I have not clothes to cover me."

"But I am in a hot climate where, if I had clothes, I could not wear them."

"I am without any defense or means to resist any violence of man or beast."

"But I am cast on an island where I see no wild beasts to hurt me as I saw on the coast of Africa. What if I had been shipwrecked there?"

"I have no soul to speak to or relieve me."

"But God wonderfully sent the ship in near enough to the shore that I have gotten out so many necessary things as will either supply my wants or enable me to supply myself even as long as I live."

That is so powerful! Will you catch hold of this truth for yourself? We are asking God to change our attitude before we find ourselves card-carrying members of the wilderness club. We are also learning from His Word that our attitudes are decisions we make about how we are going to think. And that those decisions are based in reality. It's not Disney World thinking to choose to focus on the good things in our lives. It's wisdom!

Point Three: Thankfulness is a Life-Changing Decision

Here's a final thought from Psalm 107: *Thankfulness is a life-changing decision.* My favorite word in verse 8 is the first one, "Oh." It's the best part of the verse. **"Oh, that men would give thanks to the Lord . . . for His wonderful works to the children of men!"** That word *oh* tells us that something radical and life changing is coming. The psalmist is not being overly dramatic; he's fired up because he's recognizing that we are very close to getting hold of something powerful. And so he spontaneously says, "Oh, *Oh, Ooooohhhh!!* that you would get this! Oh, that men would give thanks to the Lord!" There is *passion* here because the message is important.

The message is important because to get it wrong is to fly low and miss the joy of altitude living. To put it simply:

Gratitude is the attitude that sets the altitude for living!

Unfortunately, there is a kind of low-altitude life that too many people live. It's a particular approach that grovels and slums and tries to get by under the radar of hope. It's a down-and-dirty, cloudy, damp, depressing, ungrateful, unthankful, complaining, negative, ugh! sort of living. We've all spent some days there. It's definitely a wilderness!

But there is another kind of living. It's a high-altitude attitude—up where the air is clean and the sun is shining and the future is as bright as the promises of God. This life soars above and refuses to focus on the negative. If you have ever flown up there, then you know *that's* where we want to live our lives.

How High Are You Flying?

You say, "I want to live up there; I hate living down in the depressing low-lands of this world." So do I, and I say again that it's gratitude that sets the altitude for the kind of living you're looking for.

I'm still learning that. After the dramatic week of ministry at Cedarville College, I boarded a plane to return home in a hurry. With a Sunday message on my mind, I couldn't wait to find my seat and settle in for some focused message prep. Unfortunately, I was wearing my new Cedarville College shirt, and the woman next to me began talking about her own daughter in college. "Beautiful!" I told myself as she began, not comprehending the blessing that God had in store for my complaining heart.

Once we covered the typical "get to know you" stuff, the conversation turned in a much more serious direction. She told me about the tragedy in her wonderful marriage. About three years before, her husband had noticed a little lump on the back of his neck. He went to the doctor and found out that it was a malignant melanoma. In six weeks, he was gone. One day, they were having conversations like, "Should we go to Disney World this summer?" and six weeks later she and her five children were alone.

"For six months, I did really good," she said. "People in the church loved us and cared for us. I was trusting in the goodness of God. But then," she added, "I remember very specifically making some choices. I began to complain and allow my thoughts to drift in a wrong direction. Before too long, I was very vulnerable."

She started to cry at this point and said, "A man came into my life who I had known before I knew the Lord. He began to say things to me." Through her tears she continued, "I just got so far off the track. I got so far away from God, and hurt my family and the Lord."

I waited for a moment and then asked, "What was it that turned your life around?"

She said, "I just woke up one day and I thought to myself, 'How did I get here? How did I get over to this place? This isn't what . . . I don't want to *be* here.'" She stopped and thought for a moment. "It was really just a decision. I came back to the Lord."

She smiled and said, "I was like the prodigal."

"God received you, didn't He?" I said.

"He did," she answered.

"He embraced you and forgave you, didn't He?" I said.

Her face filled up with joy and she said, "He *did!*" She added, "God has blessed me so much now. My thoughts are so centered on the goodness of God and all that I have to be thankful for."

Are you seeing the power of thankfulness?

She went on, "The Lord has brought another man into my life. When I was younger, I used to always watch that program on television, *Eight Is Enough*. I have five children and I always wanted eight. The Lord has brought a man into my life whose wife passed away, and he loves the Lord. He has three children."

Amen! What a story!

But listen. The power of thankfulness is not just for her, but for you and me! With my complaining heart, I almost missed the lesson God had for me on that flight. He had to confine me to an airplane seat so I would listen to that lady's great testimony. Let's listen, and hear His words to be thankful in *all* things.

UP CLOSE AND PERSONAL

I have learned over time that a commitment to teach the transforming truth of God's Word brings with it many opportunities to apply it in my own life. As I conclude this chapter, I am sitting in a tiny room and looking out my window at the mountains of Ecuador. My wife, Kathy, and I are here to minister to about thirty missionaries who serve the Lord in various parts of this poverty-stricken area. I agreed to this opportunity more than four years ago when my life was very different, and now I am feeling the pressure to complain. Of course, I am willing to go wherever the Lord wants me, but I can only speak away from my church so many times per year. For that reason, I wouldn't normally drive across town to address a group so small, let alone make a twelve-hour trip by plane, stay overnight in Quito, and then make a six-plus-hour, two-hundred-mile trip along a single-lane gravel road with a five-hundred-foot drop-off.

To make matters worse, it is blistering hot, and I found out when I got here that in addition to speaking twice per day and the counseling that will go with that, both my wife and I are on one of the work crews and must take our turns cleaning the toilets and scrubbing the dining hall floor.

OK, James! Time to apply the truth that thankfulness is a choice. Yes it is, and I am making it right now. Thankfulness is a choice rooted in reality. In spite of all that I see worthy of complaint, there is far more that I can choose to focus on that is worthy of thankfulness. And so I prayed: "Thank You, Lord, for the privilege of speaking Your Word. Thank You for these phenomenally committed servants who serve You in such a dark place. Thanks that we are not called here, though I know if we were, You would give the necessary strength. Thanks that we have three wonderful children and a loving church who allows us time away to minister to others. . . ." Oh, it *is* good to give thanks! My altitude is soaring at this very moment!

LET'S TALK SOLUTION

Now it's your turn to look inside—to see if the attitude of gratitude resides in you. That is where the solution comes, through a change in heart. Here are three questions to ask, each with an action step, to help you develop a thankful attitude:

1. *Am I a thankful person? Ask yourself that question.* Let's go to the school of thankfulness for a moment and learn from the graduate student Matthew Henry, the famous Bible scholar. More than 250 years ago, he wrote these words in his diary after he was robbed of all the money he had in the world. "Let me be thankful first, because I was never robbed before; second, because although they took my purse, they did not take my life; third, let me be thankful that although they took my all, it was not much; and fourth, because it was I who was robbed and not I who robbed." No doubt about it; thankfulness is a choice. Answer the question for yourself: "Am I a thankful person?"

2. *Am I seeing the blessings of thankfulness in my life?* "Do I know the joy that comes with gratitude? Or is my life like a wilderness? What percentage of my thought life is focused on good, positive, praiseworthy things? How often do I go out of my way to recognize with gratitude a person that God has used to bless me [a parent, neighbor, friend, or a small group leader]?" When thankfulness is part of the discipline of our lives, we will see increased joy and happiness.

3. *Am I choosing thankfulness over complaining moment by moment?* Gratitude is one moment at a time. It's like freeze-frame! Ask yourself, "Am I choosing thankfulness right now? Am I?" Remember, attitudes are patterns of thinking formed over a long period of time. But those long periods of time accumulate moment by moment and choice by choice. Choose to be thankful, moment by moment.

At the end of this chapter, there appears a small list, "Five Things to Be Thankful For." Don't write on that page. Instead, make 122 photocopies of it. I'm not kidding. (With the list shown three times, that will cover 366 days.) Then put the stack by your nightstand, and try filling one out every night before you go to bed—big things, little things, good things every day. Lay your head down with gratitude on your mind, and your dreams will soar. Get up in the morning and read what you wrote. You'll be flying high all day.

This exercise will absolutely change your life. Those sheets are your tickets to a new habit: thankfulness. Guaranteed!

Look Up

Lord, thank You for Your Word. Oh, that I would give thanks to You, Lord, for Your wonderful works in my life. I thank You today for the gift of life. I thank You for air to breathe. For health and for strength, I am grateful. And for loved ones around me—not perfect people, but people who support me and care for me—I am grateful. I thank You for my church family and the joy that I find in them.

God, thank You today for Your Word. And thank You for Your Holy Spirit, who pursues me so faithfully and brings Your truth to bear upon my behavior. Thank You for the life-changing experience of walking with Jesus Christ. Thank You for the assurance of sins forgiven and the promise of eternal life.

I choose today by an act of my will to turn away from those things that would frustrate and defeat me and to focus upon Your goodness. I pray even now that You would cause genuine gratitude to continuously come forth from my lips, for You are worthy. In Jesus' name. Amen.

Five Things to Be Thankful For

"In everything give thanks; for this is God's will for you in Christ Jesus." *(1 Thessalonians 5:18)*

1. _____
2. _____
3. _____
4. _____
5. _____

Five Things to Be Thankful For

1. _____
2. _____
3. _____
4. _____
5. _____

Five Things to Be Thankful For

1. _____
2. _____
3. _____
4. _____
5. _____

NOTES

1. The National Institute of Health Care Research has awarded federal grants to support university studies exploring spirituality. Harvard University is one pioneer in the academic research showing the relationship of spirituality and health, according to David N. Elkins, "Spirituality: It's What's Missing in Mental Health, *Psychology Today*, September/October 1999, 48.

2. Elkins, "Spirituality," *Psychology Today*, September/October 1999, 48, citing a study in the *Journal of Gerontology: Psychological Sciences*, 1998.

3. The two studies by Duke University researchers are reported in the *International Journal of Psychiatry in Medicine*, 1998, and the *Southern Medical Journal*, 1998, respectively; as cited in Elkins, "Spirituality," *Psychology Today*, September/October 1999, 48.

4. The findings on lifestyle, depression, and mortality are reported in the *Religion and American Practice* journal, 1996; the *Journal of the American Academy of Child and Adolescent Psychiatry*, 1997; and the *American Journal of Public Health*, 1998, respectively; as cited in Elkins, "Spirituality," *Psychology Today*, September/October 1999, 48.

5. If you know someone struggling with rebellion, and those tapes could help them, you can call 888-581-WORD for ordering information. For additional resource information, read about Walk in the Word at the back of this book.

6. Daniel Defoe, *Robinson Crusoe* (Philadelphia: Running Press, 1990), 85.

7. Adapted from Daniel Defoe, *Robinson Crusoe*, 85–86.

3

REPLACE A COVETOUS ATTITUDE . . .

NUMBERS 11:4–5

SAY IT IN A SENTENCE:

Covetousness, rampant in the Western world and in the evangelical church, blocks the flow of God's fullness in our lives.

Imagine the scene as a great cruise ship is sinking into the ocean. Picture yourself among more than a thousand others, including this pastor. The ship's bow falls beneath the surface, and heads are bobbing on the water everywhere. Most passengers did not have time to don life jackets. Some are hanging on to a little piece of wreckage; others are treading water as best they can.

Tragically, before long, people all around us are giving their last gasps and going under for the last time. You hear screams of anguish rising from every direction. You're wondering to yourself, "Will I be next?" and "How long do I have?" and "Help is hundreds of miles away, and it's all so hopeless."

Now suppose that I keep my head just far enough above water to preach a final sermon and begin with this statement: "I'd like to give a little talk on the problem of water."

You and others stare at me in anger. "What?!" you'd say. "Talk about understating the problem! We are all *drowning* here! And you want to talk about water?"

Now I know that's a bizarre picture, but if you understand it, then you understand how I feel describing wilderness attitude two, which is *covetousness*. I am certainly not overstating things to say that our nation is drowning in a sea of covetousness. We are far more infected with materialism than we realize, and some of the worst victims are the ones who think they're living in victory.

AWASH IN COVETOUSNESS

Materialism and covetousness are battering the shores of our great nation. What follows is just a sample of the statistics that describe our condition.

There have always been Americans who wanted to earn a lot of money. But the *percentage* of Americans willing to admit it grew from 38 percent to 63 percent in the twenty years ending 1994.[1] I would have guessed that faulty notion to have peaked sometime in the 1980s. Instead, the perception that happiness is found in money is at an all-time high.

In fact, when the Higher Education Research Institute at UCLA conducted a massive survey of college freshmen, they found that the number of college freshmen who link prosperity and happiness grew from 41 percent in the late 1960s to 74 percent by the mid 1990s. These are kids whose parents got divorced because they gave themselves to careers, finances, second homes, and third cars. You would think that college kids with a background like that would be saying, "Who needs money? Look what it got my parents." In fact, it's the opposite. Now, more than ever before, college freshmen are setting their sights on money and income as the source of happiness.

The UCLA survey also found that the percentage of college fresh-men who said developing a meaningful philosophy of life was a top priority fell from 83 percent to 41 percent. Today half as many college freshmen value a meaningful philosophy of life as did freshmen thirty years ago.[2]

Notice the evidences of coveting attitudes and spreading wealth in society:

- Stealing on the job is more than $400 billion per year.

- In 1999 40 percent of boys and 30 percent of girls stole some-thing from a store.

- Since 1970 America has generated for its people each year an average $700 billion of new wealth.

- The number of millionaires soared from 120,000 in 1970 to al-most 2 million in 2000.[3]

WATER, WATER, EVERYWHERE . . .

I could go on and on with statistics until we are all feeling seasick. But here's the bottom line: You don't have to tell a man drowning in the ocean that he has a water problem, and you don't have to tell a group of people who are drowning in a sea of covetousness that we have a materialism problem. The ironic thing is that it doesn't feel like a "water problem." Covetousness makes you feel dry and thirsty, like a desert. And no wonder; God will not tolerate murmuring, and cov-etousness is one of the five wilderness attitudes that constitutes *mur-muring.*

Constant covetousness was one of the attitudes that caused God to send a whole generation of His children into the wilderness to die. His stern words to Moses in Numbers 14 ring with judgment for those who grumble, or murmur.

How long shall I bear with this evil congregation who are grumbling against Me? . . . Say to them, "As I live," says the Lord, "just as you have spoken in My hearing, so I will surely do to you; your corpses will fall in this wilderness, even all your numbered men, according to your complete number from twenty years old and upward, who have grumbled against Me." (verses 27–29)

WHAT COVETOUSNESS IS

Here's a four-part definition of covetousness. First, *covetousness is wanting wrong things*. Wanting power without a reason. Wanting control so I can be at the center. Wanting wealth for myself. Wanting glory and praise from others. In other words, *wanting wrong things*.

Second, covetousness is also *wanting right things for wrong reasons*. Take, for example, the role of spiritual leadership. The Bible says that if a man desires the office of an elder, he desires a good thing (1 Timothy 3:1–7). Wanting to be a spiritual leader and make an impact on the lives of others—that's a great thing to want. But you have to not just want it; you have to want it for the right reasons. To want it for the wrong reasons, like personal recognition or power over others, or for a personal agenda—that is covetousness.

There is a third aspect to covetousness. Covetousness is not just wanting wrong things or wanting right things for the wrong reasons. Covetousness is also *wanting right things at the wrong time*. A young couple comes in and sits down for premarital counseling. They say, "We love Christ and we love each other. We've committed ourselves to a lifetime together. We're going to get married in three months, but we want to start sleeping together now!" They want right things. They want them for the right reasons. But they want them at the wrong time. That's also covetousness.

The final aspect of covetousness is *wanting right things but wanting them in the wrong amount*. Take, for example, money. Money is not a wrong thing; it's a necessary part of life. Paul told Timothy that if a person doesn't provide for his own—that means anyone in one's extended family who has need—if a husband, for example, doesn't do everything he can to provide for his own, **he has denied the faith and is worse than an unbeliever**" (1 Timothy 5:8). Providing for others requires that we make money, and yet it puts us in danger of not knowing when to stop. When I want more money than I need to adequately provide for my family, that is covetousness. I may think that more money will make me happy, but I will soon learn it does not. More of anything other than God will never fill that longing for fulfillment He has placed within you and me. So, to summarize: *Covetousness is wanting wrong things, or wanting right things for the wrong reasons, or at the wrong time, or in the wrong amount.*

THE BARRIER . . .

I have learned over many years of teaching the Lord's people, especially in North America, that covetousness has a powerful stronghold in people's lives. In fact, we are not only in bondage to covetousness, but we are in serious denial about it. Therefore, I challenge you to open your heart as wide as you know how. Be willing to submit yourself to God's Word as we move deep into this biblical study of covetousness. Is it possible that the desire for greater joy and blessing in your life which has kept you reading this far, has been frustrated because of this matter of covetousness? Let's open God's Word together, and allow Him to deal with us as He wills.

. . . AND THREE SHORT ACTS

The events recorded in Numbers 11:4–35 break down into three short acts, much like a play. In between those acts, there are brief changes in subject, like intermissions. Then the action returns to the main story line again.

ACT I:
Yielding to Covetousness and Why God Hates It
(Numbers 11:4–10)

I call Act I, "Yielding To Covetousness and Why God Hates It." Three realities from the text amplify that heading. Here's the first: *Covetousness becomes sin when we yield.*

Look at Numbers 11:4: **"Now the mixed multitude who were among them yielded to intense craving; so the children of Israel also wept again and said: 'Who will give us meat to eat?'"** (NKJV).

The *New International Version* and the *New American Standard Bible* translate "mixed multitude" as "rabble." The term refers to Egyptian people and Israelite people who had intermarried. Please note that interracial marriage is *not* forbidden in the Bible anywhere. Intermarriage of different races in the Bible is *never* condemned. What is condemned in the Bible is inter*faith* marriages. So the "mixed multitude" of Numbers 11:4 refers to worshippers of false gods married to worshippers of the one, true God. Over and over, Scripture says those two things do not go together.

This *mixed multitude* (circle the next words if you have your Bible open) "yielded to intense craving." The NASB says, "had greedy desires." What the phrase means literally is that they "craved a craving." They started looking for something else to make them happy. They wanted to want something other that what they had. Sometimes I go to the fridge like that. Not really hungry but not really satisfied. Sort of looking and waiting for something to grab me. As bad as that can be for our diets, it can be even more devastating if we are doing that in life. Sort of surveying the landscape of our behavior options, looking for something that might make us happier than we are at a particular moment.

We all have desires come into our minds. I could command you: "Don't let any desires for anything come into your mind at all." Now that would be a cruel trick! You'd immediately start thinking of things that you would like to have or like to experience. It is practically *impossible* not to desire things, experiences, and situations. So people are always asking the question, "When is it sin? When does a covetous thought or desire become a sin?"

Men will frequently say, "I see a woman and a lustful thought occurs to me; when does that *looking* become sin?" Or, "I'm in a state-of-the-art shopping mall, and I just entered my favorite store. In my billfold is at least one credit card that isn't 'maxed out.' I'm thinking about buying something for which I know I don't have the money. Actually, I don't even need that item. But I'm thinking about buying it, anyway. When does covetousness become sin? Is it a sin to *think* about it? When is it a sin?" Here's the answer:

Covetousness becomes active sin when we yield.

It's a sin when we yield. By sin, I mean a sin of action. Of course, wrong attitudes are also sinful. That is the theme of our book.

The Bible teaches that even as believers we still have two natures. (Check out Romans 7.) There is the old part of us that wants to sin and satisfy itself, and there is a new nature that we receive when we are born again (2 Corinthians 5:17), which wants to live righteously and please God. Like two cars approaching the same intersection at the same time, our two natures are often on a collision course with each other. Galatians 5:17 says that our two natures actually battle one another, but eventually one yields. Our new nature calls for us to do what is right, and our old nature calls for us to do what is wrong. When we obey the covetous demands of our old nature and yield, we have gone from attitude sin to action sin.

Back to Numbers 11:4: **"The mixed multitude who were among them *yielded* to intense craving"** (italics added). They gave in to those desires. Romans 8:5 says, **"For those who live according to the flesh set their minds on the things of the flesh, but those who live according to the Spirit, the things of the Spirit"** (NKJV). You're standing in front of a refrigerator. You know the last thing you need is that piece of chocolate cake. Then you see it, look at it, and want it, but it's not sin yet. You take out the cake and put it on the counter. Now you're on the edge. You get out a knife with very specific intent, cut a bigger piece than you need, and begin to stuff it in your mouth—you're done. The struggle is over. You've yielded. I'm belaboring this distinction because there is so much false guilt people feel for sensing wrong desires. Intense awareness of the attractiveness of sin is not sin. When we yield, we've ignored the warning signs. *Yielding* to covetousness is what God hates. Covetousness becomes overtly sinful when we yield.

You say, "Why do people yield? I don't want to yield." If you really mean that, this next principle will help you greatly.

When we dwell on desire, yielding is only a matter of time.

When you dwell on the desire, when you focus on the thing that you're wanting, you're hanging on the edge by your fingernails.

Notice that the Israelites were yielding to intense craving. First, they asked the question in verse 4, **"Who will give us meat to eat?"** Then they started dwelling on their desire. **"We remember the fish which we used to eat free in Egypt, the cucumbers and the melons"** (verse 5). "Oh, the fish; we remember the fish." Here they were in the middle of the wilderness, and God had been feeding them manna. "Oh, the fish! And the cucumbers! You never saw cucumbers like this! Big and juicy and piles of them—incredible! And the melons! Thousands of melons, more than we could ever eat! And the leeks and the onions and the garlic"—well, I guess that's a little harder to relate to.

Notice how covetousness inflates the pleasure. When you covet something, you begin to make it more attractive and accessible than it really is, because you want it. You convince yourself you can pay for it. Eating too much? You promise yourself you'll diet tomorrow. Smoking? "I know lots of people who have smoked for fifty years and they're still healthy." You create rationalizations in order to get the thing you want. Covetousness inflates the desire while it ignores the danger.

It is very unlikely that the children of Israel, as slaves in Egypt, had melons and cucumbers and all these things to eat. They remembered selectively! The fish, cucumbers, melons and the leeks, onions, and garlic were back in Egypt all right, but not for the children of Israel. If they saw a cucumber or something fresh and wonderful, it wasn't for them to eat. They were slaves and were very harshly treated. They were not eating at a buffet every night; that's for sure. They had a sparse diet. But as they dwelt upon the past, their memories became radically selective.

In that sense, we are just like the children of Israel. It is impossible for us to dwell on desire for any length of time without rationalizing a way to get it by making the particular sin more attractive and accessible than it really is. When we dwell on desire, yielding is only a matter of time. Dwelling on a sinful desire is like starting the countdown for the space shuttle—it's just a matter of time until liftoff. So if you're dwelling on a desire, you can set the clock; yielding is only a matter of time for you. Yes, your wilderness experience is just around the corner.

Now watch that principle work itself out with the children of Israel. **"But now our appetite is gone. There is nothing at all to look at except this manna"** (verse 6). Can you hear the disgust in their voices as they look at what God had provided them to eat? As if to say, "This is lame, God, You call this meeting our needs? The same thing every day, every week, every month; we are getting so sick and tired of this ___" (expletive deleted).

Was the manna really that bad? Verse 7 describes the manna, the bread that God rained down from heaven. **"The manna was like coriander seed"**—OK, sort of a sesame seed deal—**"and its appearance like that of bdellium"** (verse 7). *Bdellium?* Actually, the word *bdellium* is a common Hebrew word that meant the manna was pearl-like in appearance. Exodus 16:4 indicates that God had given the manna as a test. He wanted to know if they would walk in obedience and be thankful for His provision or if they would covet something more, or better, or different. Every day they went out to gather the manna, and every day God was inspecting their attitudes. He was not very impressed.

In fact, they began crying over their "plight," even though the manna tasted like **"cakes baked with oil"** and fell nightly: **"When the dew fell on the camp at night, the manna would fall with it. Now Moses heard the people weeping throughout their families, each man at the doorway of his tent"** (verses 9–10a).

Can you imagine that? They were so bent about the gap between what the Lord was giving them and what they wanted that they were actually lying in their tents and crying about it. Can you get like that? Can you get so worked up about wanting something that God isn't giving you that you weep?

That's what happened: "Weeping throughout their families, each man at the doorway of his tent." What a sick picture! Talk about losing perspective. If you had walked with Moses through the tents at that time, you would have heard the moans and groans, the sobs and the sniffles. "Wa waaaa wa waaaaaaa," like little babies. Every flag at half-mast as if the nation was in mourning. Here is God's heart in the matter: **"The anger of the Lord was kindled greatly, and Moses was displeased"** (verse 10b).

At the root of covetousness is a rejection of God's sufficiency.

That's really the bottom line, and it's the reason God hates covetousness. In effect, they were slapping God's face by saying; "It's not enough, God. Nice try, but it's not enough. I have needs, and You're not taking care of them. You promised to be all I need, but You're just not meeting my expectations."

Remember that 1 Corinthians 10:11 says that what happened to them was as an example for us. God has also provided for our basic needs. The question is, Will we be grateful and satisfied with God and

His provision for us? Or will we covet more and better and different?

Our problem is not that we don't want God; it's that we covet God *and* . . . For instance, we covet:

- God *and* the perfect spouse.

- God *and* an impressive career.

- God *and* the house by the lake.

- God *and* the exotic vacation and the big bonus and whatever catches our fancy next.

- God *and* _____ (you fill in the blank).

What will it take for us to come to that settled place where the central passion of our lives is, "God, I just want You. All Your joy and peace and fullness and friendship, and that's enough for me."

The hard truth is that at the root of my covetous attitude I am rejecting the sufficiency of God in my life. I'm saying in effect, "God, You're not enough for me. You're fine where You fit, but my life had better be a lot more than just You. I need experiences and relationships and opportunities, lots of them in increasing measure. My life had better not be boring, God. I've gotta have lots of grins and lots of fun all the time. It's fine if worship is one of them, but I want way more than that." As common as that kind of thinking may be, it is definitely a wilderness attitude, and in case you're wondering about the consequences, they are right here in Numbers 11.

ACT II:
A Gift from God You Don't Want
(Numbers 11:16–20)

After a few verses of intermission, the curtain rises on Act II with God speaking to Moses: **"Say to the people, 'Consecrate yourselves**

for tomorrow, and you shall eat meat; for you have wept in the ears of the Lord [think of that], **saying, "Oh that someone would give us meat to eat! For we were well-off in Egypt." Therefore the Lord will give you meat and you shall eat'"** (verse 18). God's response came in ominous tones. To paraphrase: "Do you want meat? Do you think that's such a big deal? You think that's better than Me? Do you think that's going to meet your needs? Do you think that's going to make you happy? That's what you've been begging and crying and whining and complaining about? You think that's better than Me? Really? Then you're going to have it!" And God gave it to them: **"Therefore the Lord will give you meat and you shall eat. You shall eat, not one day, nor two days, nor five days, nor ten days, nor twenty days, but a whole month"** (verses 18–20a).

Now if you really understand what was happening here, it should make you shudder. God was giving them something that was not really good for them. He was giving them something bad to teach them a good lesson. They thought what they were demanding was good, but it was going to ruin them. So significant was this action by God that several hundred years later it was still the talk of the Lord's people. In Psalm 106:15, God's action is mentioned, as well as the consequence that came after. **"He gave them their request, but sent leanness into their soul"** (NKJV). In giving them what they "had" to have, God withdrew Himself and thrust them into the wilderness.

With God, we can be satisfied and fulfilled with very little, but without Him, all that we have will always be dry and deeply disappointing. They had all the meat they could eat. They could get physically fat if they wanted. But spiritually, they were starving. I wonder what thing in your life might parallel the meat the children of Israel had to have. Something you're coveting or craving, something you're putting your life on hold for, something for which you're continually begging God.

Nothing is essential but God. Things were never designed to take God's place. When we covet something and make it essential—and then beg God to give it to us—we are asking God to replace Himself with something we consider more important. When we do this, God will often allow us to experience firsthand the consequences of substituting anything for Him. Maybe as you read this book you are hurting over the poor health of your own soul. Maybe God is bringing to mind even now something that you have substituted for Him—a relationship or a financial goal, or a specific material dream about your future for which you have been suspending your happiness. Covetousness is such a cruel enemy. It promises prosperity and brings only painful poverty of spirit. Indeed:

In time we may hate what we had to have.

Beware of begging God for nonessentials, because *in time you may come to the place where you hate the very thing that you had to have.* **"'Therefore the Lord will give you meat and you shall eat. You shall eat, not *one* day, . . . but a whole month, until it comes out of your nostrils and becomes loathsome to you'"** (Numbers 11:18–20, italics added). No doubt about it; God was pretty ticked off at their arrogant rejection of His adequate provision and goodness. Because they thought meat could satisfy them in a way that God could not, He gave them so much meat that they choked on it.

I have had the privilege of traveling to many places in the so-called Third World. Every time that I have seen staggering poverty, I have also seen stunning joyfulness and peace in the simple things of life. I get so tired of hearing people refer to material wealth as a "blessing." As in, "I got a raise—what a blessing." Or, "God has really blessed me this year; my investments are performing far beyond what we anticipated." The United States of America is the most prosperous nation in the world financially, but when will we wake up to the fact that money is not synonymous with blessing? In fact, I often wonder if it is not a curse. Maybe our financial prosperity is the "meat" that we have begged God for and now we are choking on what we had to have.

By world standards, the church of Jesus Christ in North America is incredibly wealthy in financial things but weak and malnourished in the "joy of the Lord." (See James 1:2 for a contrast.) More than 80 percent of Bible-believing, gospel-preaching churches in North America are either in a plateau mode or in steady decline. Multiplied thousands of church leaders are laying down their Bibles in the name of evangelism and "healed the hurt of My people slightly, saying, 'Peace, peace!' when there is no peace" (Jeremiah 6:14 NKJV). Where the Word of God is preached, it is far too often a cut-and-paste approach that targets "itching ears" (2 Timothy 4:3 NKJV) and fails to declare "the whole counsel of God" (Acts 20:27 NKJV) in a way that arrests the sinful condition of the hearers. Everywhere people are lamenting the spiritual poverty of the church but failing to make the connection: **"He gave them their request, but sent leanness into their soul"** (Psalm 106:15 NKJV).

THIS CONSUMING COVETOUSNESS

I've seen this consuming covetousness in the careers of men and women climbing the corporate ladder. "I've got to be successful. Other things can wait. I have to make money. I have to be like my dad. I have to be on the top." How heartbreaking as a pastor to sit with the same people, now in their late forties and fifties, having spent their lives coveting various components of the American dream, with God at the edge and family in the background. They've built their piles of gold, but looking back they realize their folly, and through tearful cries of regret they tell amazingly similar stories of shattered marriages and prodigal children. And so the psalmist declares, **"He gave them their request, but sent leanness into their soul."**

I've seen this covetousness in the single adult who *had* to get married. "I *have* to get married! I *have* to find that person! I have to!" Specific young women come to mind even as I write. Single adults who loved the Lord and waited many years for God to bring along "Mr.

Right." Those women made choices, without asking God.

"I have to have a husband," a woman pleads with God. "I can't be happy until You meet this need." But then she goes out on her own. How sad it has been to flip the calendar forward a few pages and see that same person in my office weeping, "I made the worst mistake of my life. How could I have ever made this choice? I'm so miserable now." How heartbreaking to see a wonderful young lady with so much potential reaping so soon the consequences of her compromising, covetous choice. The psalmist rightly wrote: **"He gave them their request, but sent leanness into their soul."**

I've seen this principle at work in the unhappy husband or wife consumed with their spouse's shortcomings. I've seen it in parents struggling with the burden of infertility, wanting children and begging God for children to the point of demanding. Having children is a great blessing, but it is not life. Kathy and I love our three kids, but they are not all of our life. It is very scary to see people who begged and pleaded with God to give them children actually receive them. When they finally conceive and later give birth, I become so afraid for that child, being born into a home where children are more important than God. That's a dangerous home to be born into.

God doesn't want anything substituted for Him in our lives. Children who have to take God's place in their parents' lives have a hard time. **"He gave them their request, but sent leanness into their soul."**

If your life resembles the covetousness found in these stories, be warned! Covetousness will take you to the place in life where you hate the very thing that you had to have. God says, "Do you think that's better than Me? You go ahead and have that." *Beware of begging God for nonessentials. In time you may hate what you had to have.*

Numbers 11:21–30 records another intermission where Moses deals with his own attitude. But in verse 31, we come back to the issue of the meat and the people. God brought them the meat that they were convinced they had to have. Now watch the consequences.

ACT III:
The Consequences of Covetousness
(Numbers 11:31–35)

"Now there went forth a wind from the Lord and it brought quail from the sea, and let them fall beside the camp, about a day's journey on this side and a day's journey on the other side, all around the camp and about two cubits deep on the surface of the ground" (verse 31). A couple of definitions: *Quail* are tasty and tender little birds, sort of like a pheasant in our day in terms of the amount of meat. *Two cubits* are equivalent to about three feet. There is a little bit of confusion in the text at this point. It's hard to tell from the Hebrew expression whether the birds were flying three feet above the ground or were stacked three feet deep. Either way, this wasn't much of a hunt.

God said, "You want them? You can have them! I'm going to make it very easy for you." They could journey a day outside camp and collect birds everywhere.

"The people spent all day and all night and all the next day, and gathered the quail" (verse 32). They were going nuts! Thirty-six hours spent gathering birds three feet deep! How many birds could you get? Well, notice what it says: **"He who gathered least gathered ten homers"** (verse 32). That's sixty bushels of birds. The guy who gathered the *least*—the vegetarian or the lazy guy—still ended up with sixty bushels! So you have to believe that some people had much more than that!

But imagine the chaos. Samuel comes home and says to his wife, "Sarah, could you come into the kitchen for a moment? There's a little cooking for us to do."

She looks around and says, "Twenty bushels of birds to clean and cook? You gotta be kidding!"

Then he says, "Well, not exactly, honey; the other forty bushels are out on the porch."

Now imagine the complications in those days when there was no refrigeration of any kind. What would you do with sixty bushels of birds? Have you ever cleaned a bird? I've cleaned a pheasant. I'm telling you, by the time you get all the feathers off, there is not a lot there. They faced a lot of work for a little bit of meat. Sixty bushels! Imagine the smells on the second day of processing! No . . . don't!

One of the consequences of covetousness is that it destroys the capacity to discern sufficiency. It distorts our thinking to the point where:

Enough is never enough.

When your life is a covetous life and you're living for something else—more, better, or different; or perhaps a relationship, a possession—when desires for something are controlling you, you lose your capacity to discern sufficiency. And enough is never enough.

ABC News correspondent John Stossel once interviewed CNN and Time Warner executive Ted Turner about all his money. Turner has billions of dollars. Stossel, noting that the media mogul is near the top of *Forbes* magazine's list of richest Americans, asked Turner if the magazine's rankings motivated him to try to get richer.

"You're on this list, you see, and you want to move up the list. You want to be number one. Nobody will ever catch Bill Gates. Warren Buffet isn't going to catch Bill Gates." But, Turner suggests, it's fun thinking about how you can get higher on the list.

Stossel then asked, "Everybody wants more. . . . And that's OK?"

"I think it's OK," Turner replied. "It's your money. . . . You can do whatever you want to. You want to buy a big yacht? You can buy a big yacht."

Earlier the interviewer asked about the presence of greed in America. Turner's reply? "Oh, greedy, greedy, greedy. Everybody's greedy."[4]

The last ten years of unprecedented wealth in our country have created some astonishing results. One of the features of this economic prosperity is that CEOs are taking up to six times the amount in salaries that they used to take. But although there is fabulous wealth, most leaders are not sharing the prosperity with the others who worked to bring it about. CEOs are consuming more and more for themselves, so that leaders in Fortune 1000 companies have become like athletes and people in Hollywood. These people, who have extreme giftedness and ability, expect the lion's share of any profit to go to them. The motto seems to be: Less to others; more to me. Why? Because covetousness destroys the capacity to discern sufficiency. Enough is never enough. The more you get, the more you want.

Now I'm not saying that money or possessions equal sin. I am not saying that the most covetous person is the wealthiest person. There is no direct correlation between wealth and covetousness. The most covetous person you know may also be the one with the least. There is no direct connection between what you have and what you desire. It has everything to do with your attitude. Do I love people or do I love things? Am I looking to the future regarding people I can impact for Christ or regarding things I can acquire for myself? Am I a covetous person?

You may say, "I'm going to beat the odds." No, you're not! Millions have tried and failed before you. "I'm going to be the one person—money is going to make me happy." No, it isn't. One of the consequences of covetousness is enough is never enough.

GET READY FOR CACTUS COUNTRY

Notice what it says in verses 33 and 34: **"While the meat was still between their teeth"**—what a picture!—**"before it was chewed, the anger of the Lord was kindled against the people, and the Lord struck the people with a very severe plague. So the name of that place was called Kibroth-hattaavah, because there they buried the people who had been greedy."** Those who choose covetousness as their lifestyle will spend their lifetimes in the wilderness. Life in the

wilderness: a dry, dead, dusty, cheerless, grief-filled, unhappy existence. It's not really worth going there, and it's a real tragedy to die
there.

I expect readers to put up resistance to these truths. You may well
be reading this but not buying it. After all, covetousness has deep roots
in our lives. Your thoughts may sound something like, *Whatever . . . but
I'm going to beat the odds. I'm gonna have God and* ____ *(fill in the
blank)*.

It's your choice, of course. But I'm telling you, life in the wilderness is where you're headed if you want God *and* . . . ; if there's something else you have to have.

Recently I read about a pastor who decided to visit some people in
his church. He just showed up at their home one day and said, "Hi, I'd
like to have a little visit with you guys." They invited him in and he sat
down. The mother, of course, wanting to put her best foot forward,
said to her little daughter, "Honey, please run and get the Good Book
that we all love so much, and bring it here." The little daughter ran off
and came back with the book under her arm, and right there in front of
the pastor she handed her Mom the Sears catalog.

UP CLOSE AND PERSONAL

During my twenties and most of my thirties, covetousness was
never a big issue. While my brothers were earning lots of money, I was
content to follow God's leading and be a pastor. Now for most pastors,
ministry and money are an oxymoron—they don't go together. It's
just not an issue, and I was content with that. But more recently, as our
church has grown, my radio ministry has expanded nationally, now my
second book, and speaking engagements . . . Well, we are far from
wealthy, but for the first time the MacDonald family has more income
than we have necessity. I have been experiencing the very things that I
talked about at the end of this chapter. Covetousness was never an issue in my life until I had enough income to think about it.

Kathy and I have had to make some pretty radical choices with our giving. We chose to give over and above the tithe to the church and other ministries, so that this matter of finances could not become an issue for us. I have seen it ruin many ministers, and we are putting safeguards into place so that by God's grace we will not fall into that same snare. Psalm 62:10b says: "If riches increase, do not set your heart upon them." I'll say more about the choices we are making in the next chapter. Now, what about your life?

LET'S TALK SOLUTION

Time again to look inside our hearts. As we look at these soul-searching questions, we can begin to put in place some solution steps.

1. *Am I a covetous person?* Ask yourself honestly before the Lord. Make that question a prayer, "God, am I a covetous person?" Here are some better ways to determine your heart's genuine desire. Ask yourself: (a) Do I spend more time thinking about people to impact or things to accumulate? (b) As I think about the future and my happiness, am I thinking, "Boy, when we finally get that deck built out back," or "If we could just get our family relational conflict settled," that's when I'm going to be really happy? (c) As I think about a happy future for myself and my family, do I imagine us with more things or more impact in the lives of people? As people grow older, many times they convert to a more people/ministry-oriented outlook, and report that they wish they had converted sooner.

2. *Am I reaping the consequences of covetousness in my relationship with God?* Perhaps the idea of reading God's Word or studying God's truth is all kind of tiresome to you. Maybe the last time you gathered with others for worship you found yourself thinking, "What are they going on about?" It's all very tedious to

you. Do you know why? Because your life is a wilderness. Do you know why? Those who choose murmuring as their lifestyle will spend their lifetimes in the wilderness, and covetousness is part of murmuring. God puts people in a wilderness existence when they want things other than Him. So if you're reaping the consequences of covetousness in your relationship with God, the third question will help give you direction.

3. *Am I willing to repent?* If that word "repent" is outside your vocabulary, here are two different questions on the same concept: (a) Am I willing to change my mind and attitude about covetousness in my life? (b) Am I willing to say, "I have been living for things and for relationships and for stuff other than God?" You need honest acknowledgment before God. Maybe you could begin praying, "God, I need to have my mind changed about this area of covetousness. It hasn't been pleasing to You. I want to get my priorities in order. I don't want to live in the wilderness."

Repentance is the key action step. To repent may seem hard. It will be humbling. But there is blessing there. To help you, a suggested prayer follows. I'm including one at the end of each chapter as an encouragement for you to bring the matters we have been thinking about to God while they are fresh on your heart and mind.

Look Up

Lord, in this moment, I want to say thank You for dealing with my heart about covetousness! Lord, my life is racing by so fast; please forgive me for wanting things other than You. Forgive me for longing for stuff that is not Your heart for me and for believing that I can be satisfied in this life apart from You. I repent of covetous attitudes this day, and pray that You would cleanse my heart.

Teach me what it means to love You above all else.
Help me recognize the futility of begging You for
things that are not essential. Continue to remind me
that things will never fill the longing in my heart that's
made for loving You. Might You become all to me,
and other things be in their rightful place always.

I look forward with joy to Your continued work in me, and
I delight to move on to replacing a covetous attitude with
what Your Word will supply. In Jesus' name. Amen.

NOTES

1. Harrison Rainie, "The State of Greed," *Newsweek*, 17 June 1996, 67.

2. Ibid.

3. The $400 billion amount comes from "Report to the Nation," a publication by the Association of Certified Fraud Examiners (ACFE), 2000, as shown at the ACFE web site: www.acfenet.com/newsandfacts/fraudstatistics; the percentages of boys and girls engaged in stealing come from "New Survey Reveals Moral Illiteracy that Needs to Be Addressed in Educational Reforms," a press release of the Josephson Institute of Ethics (Marina Del Rey, Calif.), 16 October, 2000; accessed at the web site, www.josephson institute.org, on 7 December 2000. The final two bulleted facts are from Rainie, "The State of Greed," *Newsweek*, 62.

4. "Greed with John Stossel," an ABC News special, 3 February 1998; transcript from www.abcnews.go.com/onair/specials/html_files/spe0203a.html.

4

... WITH AN ATTITUDE OF CONTENTMENT

1 TIMOTHY 6:6-10

SAY IT IN A SENTENCE:

A consistent attitude of contentment can bring lasting joy and lead you out of the wilderness of covetousness.

Stop for a moment and picture a place with me. Lean your head back and close your eyes —after you read this part, of course—and imagine a place that is more peaceful than any you've ever known. Life is not perfect in this place, but it is peaceful. You are not in a hurry to do anything, and you are not submerged in the demands of others. There are houses near yours, but not on top of where you live, and there are no pressures to buy or do or experience anything. You don't hear horns, mess with traffic hassles, rush to appointments, or hate the phone when it rings. Just time, lots of time to do the things you need to do and time left over to do what you like. There is room to breathe, walk, and think. You live in a modest home, and your kids may wear hand-me-downs, but your family is happy and your needs are met. No wonder your life verses are Proverbs 30:8–9: "Give me neither poverty nor riches; feed me with the food that is my portion, that I not be full and deny You and say, 'Who is the Lord?' Or that I not be in want and steal, and profane the name of my God."

So, Where Are You?

Your life is not perfect but you are OK with that, since you are resting in the Lord and taking each day as it comes. If hardships arise, they won't sink your ship because you've left room for the inevitable. Sounds so good, doesn't it?

To say it in a word, the place I am describing is *contentment*. Contentment is the atmosphere in the Promised Land where God embraces and prospers all who choose the attitudes that please Him. Contentment is a pattern of thinking that replaces wilderness attitude number two. And every move you make in replacing the covetous thinking that plagues all of us, with true, biblical contentment is a step out of dry and dead, and into happy and whole. Let's see what God's Word has to say about contentment.

The Biblical Path to Contentment

Our starting point is 1 Timothy 6:6–10. I'm including these verses in the *New American Standard Bible,* but you can also check them out in your own text:

But godliness actually is a means of great gain when accompanied by contentment. For we have brought nothing into the world, so we cannot take anything out of it either. If we have food and covering, with these we shall be content. But those who want to get rich fall into temptation and a snare and many foolish and harmful desires which plunge men into ruin and destruction. For the love of money is a root of all sorts of evil, and some by longing for it have wandered away from the faith and pierced themselves with many griefs.

DEFINING CONTENTMENT

Contentment—kind of a nice word, isn't it? Take a deep breath and absorb the crisp, clean air atop Mount Contentment. But what does it mean, and how do we get there? Here's a definition: *Contentment is a satisfaction with God's sufficient provision.* Satisfied. You don't need anything else. You're satisfied with what God has entrusted to you. Talk about going against the grain of the culture! Contentment means *to rest in what one already has and seek nothing more.* To say without fear of the future or resentment of others, "I have enough." That's contentment. I really like this line: *Contentment is a settled sense of adequacy.*

It's like: "Hey, dude, what do you need?"

"Ummm, nothing!"

"Wouldn't you like some more—"

"No."

"What do you have?"

"Enough. I have enough."

Contentment. It's like a breath of fresh air to a person suffocating. Like a cup of cold water to a man in a desert. Get it? Desert means thirst. Coveting means wilderness. Contentment? It means the Promised Land!

CONTENTMENT HAS A PARTNER

Now notice that contentment has a partner. Do you see it in verse 6? Contentment has a partner, like salt and pepper, like Dallas and Fort Worth, like my wife and me—meant to be together. Contentment's partner is *godliness.* "Godliness with contentment is great gain," as the *New King James Version* puts it. We must never be content with *who* we are, only with what we *have.* That is why these two words are such powerful partners. Godliness deals with *who* I am; contentment deals with *what* I have. Godliness is being unsatisfied with my character formation in God, and contentment is being satisfied with what I possess in God. Together, they add up to great gain.

Please notice that Paul is not condemning the desire for gain. Deep within each of us is a hunger for improvement. Did you know that? Down in the secret places of who you are, Almighty God has given you a desire to make your life better. Isn't that good news? My life can be better. It doesn't have to be the way it is right now, and it doesn't have to be perfect, but it can definitely improve a lot! That desire for your life to improve, that passion to "gain," is not only not wrong, it is God-given!

But often that desire for gain causes many people to desire wrongly. We exercise desire in the wrong ways because our minds are depraved. Face it, we're bent! We're rarely satisfied with what we have. Abraham Lincoln was walking with his boys one day as they argued and cried and generally made a scene in public. A curious man approached Lincoln and asked, "What is wrong with your boys, to make them carry on like this?"

Lincoln replied, "Well, just what is wrong with the whole world. I have only three walnuts and both lads want two." The desire for gain is not wrong, but because of our sinful hearts, it often causes us to desire wrongly.

Yes, godliness plus contentment is great gain. That is an equation as absolute and unalterable as 2+2=4. It's a winning formula:

Godliness + contentment = great gain.

Yet in a world that increasingly rejects absolute truth, that formula is not only rejected, it is ridiculed.

I love sarcasm as a form of humor and enjoy many of the funny lines that come from Jack Handy, a sort of verbal "Far Side" type comedian. When he's poking fun at our society's rejection of absolute truth, he says, "Instead of giving answers on math tests, I think we should just give impressions. That way, if I have a different impression than you have . . . well, can't we all be brothers?" That really cracks me up because, of course, the idea is ludicrous. No one would ever agree to the idea of different emotional responses to math questions all being valid. But in the realm of God and life, our culture insists on just that kind of foolishness. Sad but true—people don't believe there is absolute truth anymore. But let me tell you something—there is. And there are equations that absolutely work because they come from the Creator and Designer of the universe.

Let me ask you this: How many gases are absolutely essential for human life? Just one: oxygen. If I pick up any object, and then drop it, what happens? Obviously, it falls. How many laws of physics make that a reality? Just one: gravity. You say, "No, I think it's falling because—"; or "It seems to me that—"; or "I feel—." Forget about that! There is only *one* reason why an object falls: It's called the law of gravity.

How many roads lead to God? Just one. "But I'm going to try this other way." Don't do that. That's a very bad plan. A road isn't right because you choose it; it's right if it's God's road. There is only one way that leads to eternal life. Jesus said, "I am the way" (John 14:6). Just one. No more.

Now let me ask you this: How many books has God written to tell us about Himself? Just one. How many formulas lead to human happiness? There aren't five or six or eight or ten. There is just one. You're reading about it right now! If you want to be happy and fulfilled in this life, you'd better do the math on the only equation that leads to human happiness. Godliness + contentment = great gain.

WRONG ANSWERS

It's not all that surprising that people who don't believe in absolutes have a hard time believing in a God who gives absolute answers. What's a lot sadder than that is to see those of us who claim to believe that God wrote a Book called the Bible, and ought to know better, trying to mess with God's equation. Their lives are messed up because of a lot of "fuzzy spiritual math." Here are a few equations Christians are trying that definitely don't add up:

Godliness + prosperity = great gain. Not.

Buzz. You failed the test. But how many people are pursuing that? In fact, since the mid-1970s, the doctrine of "godliness plus prosperity" has been getting a lot of airtime in North America. Practically every Christian television station airs the messages by men who teach this false prosperity gospel. It's the idea that Jesus died not only so that we can be eternally forgiven, but also so that we can be healthy and wealthy.

If you think that only a few fringe followers embrace this false formula, you are fooling yourself. One well-known health-and-wealth preacher sold more books during the early 1990s than all of those sold by Charles Swindoll and James Dobson combined.[1] People are eating it up because they want it to be true. But it is not. It's a false equation.

Here's an opposite equation:

Godliness + poverty = great gain. Not.

Some people overreact. "Oh! I get the picture now. It has nothing to do with having money; it has to do with *not* having money. I don't have any. I've renounced all of that. I've taken a vow of poverty. I'm as poor as a church mouse, and now I'll be happy for sure." Buzz. Wrong answer. You've failed the test. Remember what we pointed out in the last chapter? Those in poverty have no immunity to covetousness! Godliness plus poverty is not the equation that leads to human happiness.

Godliness + power or influence = great gain. Not.

Some people say, "Well, I know it's not money—it's influence. It's

P-O-W-E-R! I have to have control of everything and everybody all around me!" That kind of thinking is what has produced a generation of control freaks. Maybe you're trying to control your own home and your own income and your own yard and your own—. Everything has to be perfect! You demand everything be in order. "I'm going to be a godly person, and I'm going to control my own little kingdom here and make everything perfect. I'll be perfect; my world will be perfect. I'll have great gain."

First of all, you will never be able to control all that is around you; God will see to that. Second, even if you could, it would not make you happy. Sorry again . . . another wrong answer.

Godliness + family harmony = great gain. Not.

Could it be? But, no. Buzz. (Sorry; I don't want the buzzer to become annoying.) While I have great respect for ministries like Focus on the Family and others that promote biblical principles of godly, family living—you will never have a perfect family. At least one of your kids will make sure of that, or you will mess it up in some way yourself. Please don't put all your happiness eggs in the perfect family basket. Yes! Let's obey God's Word. Yes! Let's do all we can to help our families mature in the things of God. But let's not set ourselves up for a lot of hurt and heartache in the future by thinking, "If I could just have the perfect Christian home, then that would be all I would ever need."

No. No. No. Godliness plus family harmony does not equal great gain.

Godliness + ministry success = great gain. Not.

Here's an emphatic *buzz*. Been there, done that. The above equation definitely does not lead to happiness. That's one the Lord had to teach me many years ago. I remember early on when Harvest Bible Chapel included maybe two hundred people. I thought, *Well if we could just get to five hundred people*, I would be satisfied with what I had accomplished. Then I thought a thousand or two thousand or three thousand. As the church has continued to grow and start other churches and with all that the Lord is doing, I have discovered for sure that no amount of ministry fruitfulness will satisfy my heart.

There's only one equation for great gain. It's an unalterable formula, and nothing else comes close to working: Godliness + contentment=great gain.

Godliness plus contentment is great gain. Notice the word *great*. It's *great* gain. We're not playing for small stakes here. We're playing for all the marbles. The positive results of embracing this truth are massive. Have you been trying one or more of these false equations, and then judging God harshly because it doesn't work? Please don't do that. God loves you and wants very much for you to be happy in this life. You just have to commit to the new math—God's math. Godliness plus contentment is great gain. Say it out loud. Begin to embrace it with your whole heart.

Good! Now let's get to the "how." 1 Timothy 6 includes three steps that break the pattern of covetous thinking and lead to contentment.

CONTENTMENT STEP ONE: LOOK TO ETERNITY

Thoughts about eternity promote earthly contentment. Paul wrote, **"For we have brought nothing into the world, so we cannot take anything out of it either"** (verse 7). I love simple things like that; it's so clear. You brought nothing into the world. Right. And you're taking nothing out. When a person dies, his/her friends will often ask, "How much did he leave?" The answer is always the same, "Everything!" How clear is that?

There's something amazing about seeing a baby born. What a privilege! When each of my three kids was born, I was so happy. Nine months of waiting and waiting and waiting. Then it's time to go to the hospital. Kathy and I went through all of that pain of delivery (slightly harder for Kathy than for me). Finally, the baby came! But, funny thing about each of my kids—they arrived empty-handed! They came naked. They came with nothing! Now get that picture clearly in your head, because you're leaving with just as much in your hands. Nothing!

Think about a person who is going to leave a lot behind. I thought about Bill Gates. "Bill, you're leaving the world with nothing! You're not taking your reputation. You're not taking your software. You're not taking billions of dollars. You came in with nothing, and that's what you're leaving with. No special treatment and no limo ride to the throne room of God. Nothing!" In fact, Hebrews 4:13 says that we will be "naked and open to the eyes of Him to whom we must give account" (NKJV).

You may have heard of the seminary student who didn't have two dimes to rub together. I remember those days! This seminary student had to do his very first funeral. He was so nervous, and he didn't have any formal clothes. So he went down to the Goodwill store to buy a cheap suit, something dark and conservative, for his very first funeral. When he got to the store, he found rows of black suits: double-breasted, single-breasted, in every size. He asked the clerk, "Where did you get all of these black suits?"

She answered, "The funeral home down the street went out of business, so we got all these extra suits they use to bury people in."

Ugh! he thought, a little grossed out at the thought of wearing a suit made for dead people. But then he remembered how little money he had, and this seemed like his best option, so he bought one.

As he stood before the whole congregation, in his brand-new suit, he began to talk about the brevity of life and the nearness of eternity. He put his hand in his pocket—and was shocked to find there were no pockets!

"Of course," he thought. "It's a suit made for some dead guy! What would he need pockets for?" No one needs pockets for eternity because we are not taking anything with us when we go.

Contentment Step Two:
Let Enough Be Enough

Paul puts it so simply in 1 Timothy 6:8, **"If we have food and covering, with these we shall be content."** There you have it: Bare bones. . . . Bottom line. . . . The absolute minimum. The things you have to have? Only two: food and covering. According to verse 8,

All you need for contentment is *room* and *board*.

Let's start with our board. Notice the simple word *food*. There's no caviar or champagne guarantee. There is no "Three square meals a day with dessert. More Jell-O, please." God never promised the people with Moses a good balance of the four food groups: just manna and water. That's what they had to have. Now there aren't many people who believe that they could be happy on a bare-bones diet like that. So let's let the Word of God renew our minds. We don't have to have a fancy diet and wonderful delicacies—the food we wolf down! We don't have to have a buffet. It's not part of the happiness equation. When we expect to be satisfied with the basics, God will often surprise us with treats. If we demand 31 flavors, we forfeit contentment, and our heart becomes like a wilderness.

Now let's consider our "room." The word in verse 8 is "covering." Just covering—that's all we need for great gain. Not multiple outfits with matching shoes. Not a three-thousand-square-foot home with central air and plans for a summer home. Just shelter to protect our heads, and clothes to help warm our bodies.

I'm not saying a larger home or a second home is wrong. I'm just saying you don't have to have it, and the pursuit of it often leads to misery! You just need food and covering. That's enough. There's a Roman proverb, "Money is like seawater; the more you drink, the thirstier you get." Well, contentment is breaking that cycle of thirst and being able to say, "I don't need anymore." **"If we have food and**

covering, with these we shall be content" (1 Timothy 6:8). Content. That's saying: "I have enough."

CONTENTMENT STEP THREE:
LEARN BY EXAMPLE

Beyond thinking about eternity and letting enough be enough, here's the third step for contentment: Learn by example. The craziest thing about the human race is that we think we have to learn everything on our own. How dumb is that? Why can't we learn from other people? We're not the first people to talk about contentment, right? And we're not the first ones to struggle with covetousness or experience its fallout and devastation.

Indeed, thousands and thousands of people before us have already figured this lesson out. Most of them found out too late. (That's what this book is all about: *Lord, Change My Attitude [Before It's Too Late.]*) John D. Rockefeller said, "I have made millions, but they have brought me no happiness." Cornelius Vanderbilt said, "The care of millions is too great a load. There is no pleasure in it." John Jacob Astor, who acquired immense wealth in his lifetime, said, "I am the most miserable man on earth." Though he owned a luxurious estate, Henry Ford said at the end of his life, "I was happier as a boy working in a mechanic's shop, though we had nothing." Why not take these examples seriously and avoid their mistake?

DANGER, DANGER, DANGER

I wonder if any of those men ever read 1 Timothy 6:9: **"But those who want to get rich fall into temptation and a snare"**? That word *want* is from a Greek word that means, not a momentary emotional desire, but a "settled desire born of reason." Does this sound familiar? "I've thought it through, and this is what my life will be about—money. I'm going to make as much as I can. I'm going to get some things. I'm going to build something. I'm going to stand on top of it and say,

'Look what I did.'" That's a very bad plan. We've got God's Word on it, which warns, "Those who want to get rich" are easily ensnared.

Note the word *temptation*. Money allows you to go places and do things and experience pressures to sin that someone in poverty will never know. With money comes amplified temptation. "Those who want to get rich fall into temptation and a snare." The word *snare* there can also be translated *trap*. Money traps people. How often I have heard people say:

"I want to serve God, but I would have to sell this big house of mine." Trapped!

"I want to spend more time with my family and pursue eternal priorities, but I'm working at this company where everyone at my level works sixty hours a week. If I don't keep working the way everybody else is working, I'm going to lose my career." Trapped!

"I don't want to spend so much money on clothing and on cars, but everybody on our street does the same thing." Trapped!

"I don't want my kids to feel foolish going to school in discount clothes or hand-me-downs." Trapped!

That's the thinking of those who want to get rich as their objective in life. They fall into temptation and a snare.

You say, "I don't want to miss church as much as we have, but we have this membership at the club and we have to be there. I hate to miss church, but we bought a boat. I don't want to waste the money, so since we bought the boat, we have to be on the boat." Are you having fun yet? "Well, I'm trying to . . ." It gets worse: "and many foolish and harmful desires . . ." A fool is a person who has no discernment. "I think that will make us happy. Maybe if we get that we'll be happy." Not all our desires are innocent. Some are very harmful. Some wants bring devastation to our lives long before we acquire the thing itself. They have already done their damage at the desire stage.

And then, the ultimate consequences: " . . . ruin and destruction." Living for my desires over a lifetime brings far more than damage; it brings devastation. The eternal results of a lifetime of living for my own desires is destruction. That's why Jesus said, **"It is easier for a camel to go through the eye of a needle than for a rich man to enter the kingdom of God"** (Mark 10:25). He explained: **"Where your treasure is, there your heart will be also"** (Matthew 6:21). If you live for things and for self and for your own satisfaction, then you ought not to be surprised when you hear the Lord say at the very end, **"I never knew you; depart from Me"** (Matthew 7:23). You might be able to fool others, but God knows the truth.

First Timothy 6:10 brings Paul to his conclusion, **"For the love of money is a root of all sorts of evil."** How many times have you heard that misquoted? People always say, "Money is the root of evil." But that's not what it says. There isn't anything inherently evil or un-righteous about money. Money is just a currency, a commodity. Money is no more evil than chocolate chip cookies. The problem is the *love* of money. Loving it! Wanting it! Living for it! Believing that "Money will make me happy."

Notice also that loving money is not *the* root of evil but *a* root of evil. All evil is not rooted in money. What Paul is saying is that loving money is just one of many roots that feed the tree of evil in this world.

Two Ugly Pictures

Paul added two ugly pictures to conclude the warning in verse 10. First, **"Some by longing for it have wandered away from the faith."** Do you know anybody like that who used to seek and worship the Lord? They used to love Him with their whole hearts, but now they just love money. They adore the "almighty dollar." They have to have more, because they love it! Do you know anybody like that who has wandered away from the faith?

Here's the second, even sadder, picture. Those who have longed for it have **"pierced themselves through with many sorrows"** (NKJV). Pierced themselves. How ugly is the picture of a person stab-bing themselves? Imagine the dialogue:

"What are you doing?"

"I'm stabbing myself."

"Why do you keep doing that?"

"Well, because I love money."

That's so stupid it would be funny, if it wasn't totally sad! Loving money is piercing yourself through with many sorrows.

No matter what it looks like on the outside, loving money does damage on the inside—soul damage. If it persists, it's taking you to a place where there is no contentment. But there's a better way: Godliness plus contentment is great gain.

UP CLOSE AND PERSONAL

The phone rang recently. A new buddy of mine from Michigan was on the line. He knows I love to golf, and that's my favorite thing. He asked, "What are you doing December 4?" "I don't know."

"I've just made a donation, and I'm going to be playing in the Second Annual Payne Stewart Memorial Tournament in Orlando. Would you like to come and play with me?" I'm like, "Yeeahhh. That would be great. I'd love to do that."

"Well, excellent." Then he adds, like a sly afterthought, "The thing that's amazing is I've made the second highest donation. So I get to pick who I want to play with."

I asked, "Who will we be playing with?"

He says in an offhanded way, "It will be me and you, another guy named Frank, and Tiger Woods. So check your calendar."

"I'll check right now." I eagerly flipped open my calendar. "Stink!" I almost shouted. "I'm going to be in Israel."

I have to tell you, my attitude took a little dip! For a couple of hours I was like, "Stupid Israel trip. I cannot believe it!" In fact, my attitude got so bad that by the time I got home and was watching the nightly news about all the violence in Israel, I was thinking, "Maybe it'll get worse and I won't have to go!" That's bad! Now just to encourage your heart about this buddy, no sooner had I thought that than the Lord rebuked me and said, "You've got a rotten attitude."

I had to choose a different attitude. And ever since then I've been, "That's right. I'm going to Israel. I'm going to go where Jesus walked. I'm going to see things that people long to see. It's going to be a spiritual highlight of my whole life! Stinking golf tournament. Forget that!" (As it turned out, the trip to Israel was canceled due to the Middle East conflict, and Tiger Woods backed out of the tournament. I realized that being content is best of all, no matter what.)

That experience reinforced in my mind this truth: We have so many options in life. Contentment is choosing to be satisfied in what I do have and not expending my best energies pressing for more.

LET'S TALK SOLUTION

You say, "You convinced me! I want that sense of contentment." Then make a note of these three choices that will help you make progress in replacing covetousness with contentment— genuine, biblical, lasting contentment.

1. *Seek it.* Seek contentment as a lifestyle, as a choice. Make it your aim to come to the place where you really believe that more does not equal happier. Acknowledge that you would not be happier with more. You wouldn't be. As we saw in the warnings from God's Word, often you'd be more miserable.

2. *Say it.* Cultivate the capacity to say, "I have enough." Let the words "I have enough" ring from your home. Push yourself back from the table early and say, "I have had enough." After work, stand with the surprise bonus in your hand considering what you might buy, and resist by saying, "I have enough" or by even praying, "Lord, how can I use this for You?"

In fact, why not begin right now and say by faith out loud,

"I have enough." I know we don't say that very often, and it's so contrary to the culture. But there is victory here. So even if you don't believe it yet—even if you haven't seen it yet—decide to trust God's provision and say, "I have enough." The trust of contentment is just like the trust we exercise at conversion: "I don't know if this will change my life, but my thing is not working. Lord, if You're real, come into my life and forgive my sins." That's a salvation breakthrough. Have a sanctification breakthrough and say by faith, "I have enough." Say it. "God, I have enough." Let those words ring from our cars and our churches and our times at the mall.

3. *Settle it.* Psalm 62:10 says, **"If riches increase, do not set your heart upon them."** I would challenge you to choose a lifestyle. Don't let your income dictate your lifestyle. Choose a comfortable level of living that you need, and do not compromise that with more spending when more income arrives. If you don't choose a lifestyle, this culture will choose one for you, and it will be the lifestyle of living beyond your means. Be countercultural and radical! Let your lifestyle be biblically based. Eternally focused. Others-oriented. Let enough be enough. Learn from the example of others. If you do, you will save yourself a world of hurt and know the joy of a truly contented attitude.

S T A R T   H E R E

Don't miss the chance to have God speak to your heart about the following questions.

Am I a contented person?

I know some will say, "Look to eternity? Yeah, I guess I think about death once in a while, but what does it mean to think eternal thoughts? What's that?" Well, here's an example: If all the grains of sand on all the beaches in all the world represent eternity, then you could say that one grain of sand represents life on this earth. And all the rest of the grains of sand on all the beaches in all the world represent that same amount of time in eternity. We're over here grinding this one grain of sand, our time on earth, to get everything out of it (and failing miserably)! But too often we ignore all the rest God has in store for us. To be content, focus on eternity. Let enough be enough. Learn by example. Get to the place where you can say yes to the question, "Am I a contented person?"

Am I seeing the blessings of contentment in my life?

Contentment brings blessings. Blessings such as joy in the present, and health and satisfaction in the simple things of life. Contentment brings a settled sense of sufficiency and a peaceful pace that proves "more" is not the focus of your thinking. You have life. What a privilege to be alive in this world! Contentment brings joy in the present.

Contentment also builds our capacity to enjoy ordinary pleasures. If you're content, simple stuff makes you happy. Like a nice walk. Go for a walk today with a member of your family, and hold his or her hand. Talk about important things. Enjoy a simple pleasure; for example, a loving conversation or a good meal without racing to your next appointment. Simple things: a nice piece of music savored. Cultivate your capacity to enjoy ordinary pleasures.

Contentment also promotes true joy in eternal things. You know, the angels have a party when one sinner is saved (see Luke 15:10). How phenomenal is that? They know how to have a good time!

If you anticipate picking up your Bible and can't wait to hear God speak, that's contentment. If you can sit quietly rejoicing in a simple pleasure and not need to think of what you will do next, that's contentment.

Am I choosing contentment over covetousness moment by moment?

Contentment is a choice. When you choose contentment repeatedly, you create a lifestyle. Don't expect to replace covetousness with contentment in a moment. You don't wake up in the morning and say, "Wow, I think I got contentment last night. It just happened. This is so cool—." No; contentment begins with a choice. And then another choice. And then another. It happens moment by moment.

Put off covetousness; put on contentment. It's a choice. Thus, a desire for something comes into my mind. "Not necessary," I respond. "I have enough." That's contentment.

Paul said in Philippians 4:11, **"I have learned to be content in whatever circumstances I am."** Contentment is something you learn. You can practice it. God wants us to improve at this every day we live. Contentment is what replaces wilderness attitude number two. Take a moment to pray about that.

Look Up

Father, thank You again today for the truth of Your Word. Lord, I've learned by experience that hearing Your Word is not enough. I know I need to act upon Your Word. It's doing what it says that brings results! Lord, don't let me deceive myself today into thinking that I am changed because of what I have read. Let me be changed because of what I do in response to what I have read. Let my home and my place of work and my life this week be filled with contentment.

Lord, I do have enough—I have You. I have Your promises. I have Your faithfulness. I have Your strength and wisdom to pursue change in the hurtful areas of my life. I know I can trust You with my burdens. Forgive me for thinking that my happiness is in anything external. Help me to embrace the truth that godliness with contentment is great gain. All that I pray, I pray in the name of Jesus, who is my ultimate example of true contentment. Amen.

NOTE

1. Randy Frame, "Same Old Benny Hinn, Critics Say," *Christianity Today*, 5 October 1992, 52.

5

REPLACE A CRITICAL ATTITUDE . . .

NUMBERS 12:1–12

SAY IT IN A SENTENCE:

A continuously critical attitude toward those around me will consume all that is healthy and joy-producing in my life.

A farmer stood by the road one day and observed a large wagon filled with household goods moving toward him. Dust flew as the wagon pulled to a stop and the driver shouted, "We're moving from Brownsville to Jonestown. How much farther is it?"

"About thirty miles," said the farmer.

"And what kind of people shall we expect to find there?" asked the traveler.

"Well, what kind of people did you leave behind in Brownsville?"

"Oh, they were so negative and so cheerless, so deceptive and so ungrateful, just a godless bunch, all of them. That's the main reason we are moving. What kind of people will we find in Jonestown?"

"The very same kind, I'm sorry to say," said the farmer.

And he was right. He knew the traveler would find in the next town the same kind of people he perceived lived in Brownsville. Far more often than we care to admit, outlook determines outcome. The way that we look at a matter, the attitude that we choose, has direct bearing on how we experience reality. Two people can look at the very same circumstance and experience it entirely differently based upon the attitude they choose—the patterns of thinking that they have formed over a long period of time.

THE SPECK AND LOG SYNDROME

Are you familiar with the words of Christ regarding a critical attitude? He asked His followers during the Sermon on the Mount: **"Why do you look at the speck that is in your brother's eye, but do not notice the log that is in your own eye?"** (Matthew 7:3).

I have made a pretty big deal thus far focusing on the truth that we choose our attitudes. I have focused upon that because it is true and because until we accept responsibility for our attitudes, we will never be able to change. However, that concept of personal responsibility is in no way intended to ignore the role of background on our attitude. Some of us struggle more with certain attitudes because of the cultures we are from, the kind of homes we grew up in, or the kind of churches we attended during our formative years. Those factors have certainly influenced my tendency toward certain attitudes.

Maybe you grew up in a home that was forever picking at the imperfections of others and finding fault with anyone and everyone. Maybe you sat through countless Sunday dinners of "roast preacher." Maybe you were endlessly criticized yourself and now hear that same attitude in the way you talk to your children. Possibly you struggle in many public settings to simply relax and enjoy what is going on, because all you have known how to do is inspect and examine and form opinions about what you see and experience. If you grew up learning to criticize the speck in others' eyes while a logjam formed in your own, keep reading. If any of this rings true, you could be in for a breakthrough chapter. We're looking at "Replacing a Critical Attitude," so let's get God's heart in the matter by opening His Word.

Back to the desert . . .
And Wilderness Attitude Three

Open your Bible to Numbers 12. We've been going back and forth between the Old Testament and the New Testament, between failure and victory, between wrong attitudes and right ones, between the wilderness and the Promised Land. Here we go again. Numbers 12 records one of the five events that led up to God's decision to thrust the children of Israel into the wilderness because of their *murmuring,* a summary term we are using for five wrong attitudes.

Verse 1 begins, **"Then Miriam and Aaron spoke against Moses because of the Cushite woman whom he had married."** The words *spoke against* are translated in the *New Living Translation* as *criticized.* No doubt as he faced the heavy burden of leading the Lord's people, Moses needed leaders he could rely upon to help him shoulder the load. Miriam and Aaron were Moses' sister and brother, the people closest to Moses and the ones he trusted most. For a while it seemed like everything was going great. Then, all of a sudden, Miriam and Aaron made some choices. They got sideways on the tracks. Very quickly and without warning, the leader they were supporting—their own brother—became a target for their criticism.

A CRITICAL ATTITUDE DEFINED

We made a distinction in chapter 3 when we noted that complaining relates to situations, whereas criticism relates to people. Our negative thinking that relates to people is called criticism. Miriam and Aaron had definitely fallen into it big-time in regard to Moses.

Here's a definition of *destructive* criticism, so we will be clear as we discuss this painful subject. Criticism is *dwelling upon the perceived faults of another with no view to their good.* That's what we're actually doing when we engage in criticism. We're dwelling upon the perceived faults of another with no view to their good.

Let's break down the definition. First, note the word *perceived.* The reason why I say "perceived faults" is because my perception of what is wrong with you is not necessarily accurate. There may be circumstances that I don't understand, or maybe the problem is actually with me, not you at all. In reality, we can become very critical of others, yet be entirely wrong in our opinion. Now let's move away from the issue of whether the faults are real or perceived, because either way the attitude is destructive to us. So that's the first thing—*the perceived faults.*

Now consider the words *dwelling upon* the perceived faults of another. That's the key issue, isn't it? Some people are very positive, upbeat, and encouraging.

But others are often critical of people and their actions. Are you a person who walks through life saying to yourself; "That's not right!" and "Who thought that looks good?" and "Someone should have taken care of that"? If you think that way, then you're dealing more directly with the dangers of a critical spirit than a person who is more positive and upbeat. Whether it's one fault in one person we lock into, or we get ourselves to the place where we can't see anything right, we are in danger of the wilderness attitude called criticism.

Does this ever happen to you? You sit through a worship service with your church, and you make mental notes. *That's not the way that I would do that* or *Why would they do that?* or *Why is he moving around that way?* You think, *I would never do it like that.*

If you're an analytical person, there is a lot of data surfing on those brain waves. You can't necessarily stop that general way of thinking. It's the way God made you. The problems come when you choose to dwell upon your observations—when you can't set them aside.

You might ask, "But how can I help a person if I don't dwell upon what they are doing?" Great question. That's why I added that last part to the definition: *with no view to their good*. It's not criticism to dwell upon a fault you observe in someone, provided: 1) you're gonna pray about it, and/or, 2) you're gonna pursue a solution. You have to dwell on the problem to pray about it, don't you? If you observe a brother or sister who is struggling in a certain area, it's not a negative, critical attitude if you begin to pray for them and ask God to help them. Also, if you know them personally, it's not a critical attitude to focus long enough to decide, "You know, I'm going to try to help her. I'm going to go to her and I'm going to talk to her."

SHOULD YOU TALK WITH SOMEONE ABOUT SOMEONE ELSE?

When teaching about criticism, someone will inevitably ask, "What about talking to a third party about a person's fault? If I see something that's wrong in my friend's life, would it be wrong for me to talk to another friend about what I observed? Is that a critical conversation?" Not necessarily. *It's only wrong if my intention is not to help the friend in whom I observe the fault.* It's not a critical conversation when the goal is trying to help.

Has this ever happened to you? You want to help somebody, but you wonder, "Am I crazy? Am I just imagining something wrong here?" You feel like you want to go to someone else for some counsel. That's not wrong, provided the reason you're talking to the third party is to do a *better* job of going to the person you want to help. You say, "That's kind of sticky." Yes it is! Here's how you keep from getting stuck. When you go to Sue about Sally, if you can't stop at the end of your conversation about Sue and say, "Now let's just stop for a moment and pray about this situation, because I really want to help Sally," you've got a problem. If you are not clear about your motives in sharing the situation with a third party, then you're probably practicing gossip and not a genuine, helpful spirit.

By pulling all of those factors together, we should have a clear picture of the difference between constructive criticism and a destructive attitude. A critical attitude is a choice to dwell upon the perceived faults of another with no view to their good.

MEANWHILE, BACK IN THE WILDERNESS . . .

Now, back to Numbers 12. "Then Miriam and Aaron spoke against . . ." Let's just stop there again for a second. Remember, these are Moses' sister and brother. Now, right off the bat, that's pretty tough, isn't it? How do you take unexpected and unfair criticism from those closest to you? The verb in Hebrew that means "spoke against" is in the feminine. That means that the primary critic in this case was Miriam. I guess Aaron sort of got dragged into it. That happens sometimes. One person gets a critical attitude and drags other people into it. One person's bitterness can defile many people. That's what happened here.

Now, before we get too hard on Miriam, or for that matter ourselves, let's remember that Miriam was no slouch; in fact, she was a very godly woman. Big sister Miriam was the one who took Moses and put him into the bulrushes in the basket (Exodus 2:1–10). She also arranged for Moses to be nursed by his own mother even though Pharaoh's daughter adopted him as her own. Miriam *loved* Moses. Beyond that, during the Exodus, when the nation miraculously crossed the Red Sea, it was Miriam who wrote the song of worship to celebrate that great victory (Exodus 15).

Miriam really was a godly, righteous woman, which tells us, among other things, that we don't want to think that we're so far along spiritually that we couldn't be guilty of a critical attitude. We're just as vulnerable as Miriam. None of us can say, "Well, that's behind me," and "Criticism is just not an issue for me," and "I never—." Wrong! Everyone can struggle in this area.

"Then Miriam and Aaron spoke against Moses because of the Cushite woman whom he had married." Some translations say, **"the**

Ethiopian woman whom he had married" (NKJV). Now that's strange, because we know that Moses' wife was Zipporah, and she was a Midianite. The text doesn't say here, but that phrase "for he had married" seems to indicate that maybe Zipporah had died and that Moses had chosen another woman as his wife. And guess what? Big sister didn't like the new choice.

Do you think that's the issue? It may have been the surface issue, but reading a little further we find the root of the problem. **"And they said, 'Has the Lord indeed spoken only through Moses? Has He not spoken through us as well?' And the Lord heard it"** (verse 2). Moses' wife was the surface issue, but the real issue was Moses' prominence. Their real beef was, "How come Moses gets all the attention? We're leading too! Why does he get all the perks and petunias? 'Moses this' and 'Moses that.' We're so sick of hearing Moses' name. What about us? What about our place? What about our role?" They said, **"Has [God] not spoken through us as well?"**

CRITICIZING A HUMBLE MAN

Now look at verse 3. **"Now the man Moses was very humble, more than any man who was on the face of the earth."** That's an amazing verse if indeed Moses wrote the whole Pentateuch (the first five books of the Bible) including Numbers. I believe he did; most Bible scholars believe he did; most important, Jesus believed he did. When Jesus referred to the Pentateuch, He often said, "Have you not read in the book of Moses . . . ?" (Mark 12:26; see also Luke 24:44). So, if Moses is the author of the Pentateuch, how can a guy who is the most humble man that ever lived write, "Now the man Moses was very humble, more than any man who was on the . . ."?

It's a fair question. We believe that the inspiration of Scripture extends both to the writing and to the gathering of the books of the Bible. If you think that Moses sat down one day and wrote the Pentateuch, that's not how it happened. He wrote on many fragments and in different places at different times; he probably kept journals—all under the inspiration of the Holy Spirit. After Moses' death, the fragments that Moses had written were gathered together into the Pentateuch. In several places in the Pentateuch, comments are added. For example, Deuteronomy describes Moses' death. Could he have written about his own death? Of course not. Moses died, and the people who gathered it all together wrote about his death.

So, that phrase about humility? Someone later on added the explanation, wanting us to understand how harsh it was to criticize Moses and how it would have wounded him. So here was the most humble man alive, and even he can't escape the pain of some self-appointed critics attacking the work he is doing for God.

Confrontation? No . . . God-frontation

There were consequences for this unjust attack. God commanded Aaron and Miriam to join Moses at "the tent of meeting." **"In a pillar of cloud [God] stood at the doorway of the tent and called forward Aaron and Miriam"** (see verse 5). God confronted Aaron and Miriam as Moses stood right there. God said this in verses 6–8: **"'Hear now My words: If there is a prophet among you, I, the Lord, shall make Myself known to him in a vision. I shall speak with him in a dream. Not so, with My servant Moses, he is faithful in all My household; with him I speak mouth to mouth, even openly, and not in dark sayings, and he beholds the form of the Lord.'"**

In other words, God was saying, "Do you have any idea who you are talking about? I don't have another servant like Moses in all the world. I speak to him directly. Who do you think you are to be raising your voice in criticism against him?" **"'Why then were you not afraid to speak against My servant, against Moses?' So the anger of the Lord burned against them and He departed"** (verse 8).

Notice God's deep feelings. Miriam and Aaron must have been scared to death. They didn't have time to think, "Well, we weren't being *that* critical! We just pointed out a few flaws. I mean—wait a minute, nobody's perfect." God didn't wait for explanations, and they didn't wait long for the consequences. Verse 10: **"But when the cloud had withdrawn from over the tent, behold, Miriam was leprous, as white as snow. As Aaron turned toward Miriam, behold, she was leprous."** Just like that . . .

Miriam was suddenly as good as dead.

Aaron pleaded to Moses for their sister. He realized that Moses was their only hope. **"I beg you, do not account this sin to us, in which we have acted foolishly and in which we have sinned. Oh, do not let her be like one dead, whose flesh is half eaten away when he comes from his mother's womb!"** (verses 11–12). Then Moses, always humble, always compassionate, turned to the Lord. **"Moses cried out to the Lord, saying, 'O God, heal her, I pray!'"** (verse 13). The Lord had her quarantined for seven days, and the rest of the people waited, no doubt aware of the judgment. Finally Miriam was restored and they moved on (see verses 13–16). Unfortunately, that seven-day time-out didn't have much of a lasting effect on the rest of the people.

PRINCIPLE ONE:
CRITICISM IS WRONG

This story about God's judgment on one critical person gives us insight into how God feels about critical attitudes. Miriam was not the only critical person. Remember that just two chapters later, in Numbers 14, we can read of how God sent a whole bunch of them to die in the wilderness because of incessant murmuring, which certainly included critical attitudes. Miriam's experience illustrates a number of principles about criticism that were typical of God's people (and us).

The main one should be obvious:

Criticism is wrong.

You don't have to be a Bible scholar to pull that one from the text: Criticism is a sin, and the passage says so. Aaron said, **"Do not account this sin to us, in which we have acted foolishly and in which we have sinned."** Criticism is a sin. Obviously, we want to soften the judgment on criticism; we want to believe that it's a weakness. We would rather call it a bad habit. Criticism *is* those things, but beyond those characteristics, from God's perspective, criticism is a sin. God is totally not into it when we dwell on the perceived faults of another with no view to their good. The point of this whole passage is that God hears the criticism and judges it as sin.

Effects of a Critical Attitude

Principle number one—criticism is wrong—also means consequences for this sin (as there are for any sin). Indeed, when we develop a critical attitude, we experience some of the same consequences that came to Aaron and Miriam. First,

Criticism ruins our fellowship with God.

It doesn't destroy our relationship with God, but criticism changes our capacity to sense His love and presence.

If you have come to the place in your life where you turned from your sin and embraced Christ by faith as the only basis for your forgiveness, all of God's judgment for your sin was placed upon Christ at the cross. Your relationship with Him is established. Yet there are judgments for sin that are not related to that—not vertical, eternal judgments, but horizontal, temporal judgments related to ongoing sin. The horizontal judgments upon sin that everyone has to deal with are often called *consequences.* The primary consequence of a critical attitude is seen in our fellowship with God. Sin hinders our fellowship with God.

We see this principle at work in human relationships. Having a critical attitude toward your wife doesn't mean she stops being your wife, but it definitely affects your fellowship with her! Miriam and Aaron started out criticizing their brother, but ended up feeling the consequences most in their relationship with God. God pays attention to the way we treat each other.

If you have a critical attitude, it is hindering your fellowship with God. If your spiritual life is like a wilderness—dry, dead, cheerless, and joyless—maybe it's because you've allowed a critical attitude toward a person or group of people in your life. It's a choice that not only injures your relationship with that person, but also with God

If my fellowship with God is broken, what do I do? God gives us the answer. First John 1:9 says, **"If we confess our sins, He is faithful and righteous to forgive us our sins and to cleanse us from all unrighteousness."** The Greek term *homologeo* translated by the word *confess* is insightful. It's made up of two words: *homo*, meaning *the same;* and *logeo*, meaning *to say.* To confess is *to say the same thing.* Now my fellowship with God is hindered when I'm saying something different about my critical attitude than God is saying. What is God saying about my critical attitude? God is saying, "That's sin! That's wrong!"

"Oh, but you don't know my situation. You don't know how hard it is for me, and she's driving me crazy. Somebody has to point out the truth in her life, or their situation . . ." We all have rationalizations to justify our critical attitudes. But our fellowship with God can only be restored when each of us "says the same thing God says" and acknowledges that criticism is sin. You and I have to agree with God, "Yes, Lord, that critical attitude is not acceptable. I am sorry; it's sin and I choose to stop."

A second kind of fallout from criticism being wrong is this:

Our critical attitude hurts us.

Criticism deeply affects us personally in a negative way. It takes a costly toll from us as spiritual beings.

Though I teach my church from many different places in God's Word, we return to some principles again and again. Here's one: *Choose to sin; choose to suffer*. God is not some arbitrary being up in heaven who says on a whim, "Well, that is right and this is wrong." Everything God calls sin is injurious to us as human beings—everything. When God says, "Don't!" what He really means is, "Don't hurt yourself!"

When God says, "Don't criticize," it's not because He is trying to deprive us of some satisfactory experience. He is actually saying, "That goes against the nature of who I have made you to be." Fish were made to swim. Birds were made to fly. People were made to live in fellowship with God. When we sin, we break our fellowship with God. We hinder our human happiness, and life becomes like a wilderness.

Now even people who don't claim to know the Lord are observing the negative effects of sin, of criticism, upon human beings. Dr. David Fink, the author of *Release from Nervous Tension*, worked with thousands of people who were mentally and emotionally disturbed or troubled. Most of them asked Dr. Fink for some kind of a short-term quick-fix; they asked, What is the secret to emotional health? So many people, all with the same questions. In his search for answers, he studied two groups: The first group was made up of thousands of people who were suffering in some way—tension, emotional turmoil, significant stress; the second group contained only those—thousands of them—who were free from such internal struggles.

Gradually one fact began to stand out: Those who suffered from extreme tension had a single trait in common—they were habitual faultfinders, constant critics of people and things around them. Meanwhile, the men and women who were free of all tensions were the least critical of others. No doubt about it then: The habit of criticizing is a very personally destructive pattern of thinking.

That's why we have listed a critical attitude among the habits God wants to replace. It puts you in the wilderness. Look out if you're always, "Why didn't she?" and "Why can't he?" and "When will he ever learn?" and always negative all the time. Criticism can destroy you! It carries you into the wilderness.

If criticism is wrong for our fellowship with God and for us personally, then, just as surely, it's wrong for our relationship with others.

A critical attitude destroys our fellowship with others.

As a pastor, I frequently hear people say, "I just don't seem to be able to find any friends" or "Every time I try to find friends . . . " And before they're three sentences into their sad story, you just want to say, "Do you know what? It's your attitude! It's your critical, negative, faultfinding attitude. Do you know why you're alone? They're not into your attitude."

Who wants to spend Friday night with someone who they know from experience will consume most of the conversation updating everyone on their top-ten-people-to-hate list? You can go out with them if you want—I'm staying home; *Wheel of Fortune* reruns are more appealing than that dinner party. Are you getting this? There is fallout in our relationships with others when we become known as critical people. Criticism is wrong.

The complaints of Aaron and Moses clearly point to principle number one: Criticism is wrong. Let's look at five other principles from Numbers 12.

PRINCIPLE TWO:
CRITICISM IS PETTY

The second principle is *criticism is petty.* That principle was at work when Aaron and Miriam *criticized* Moses for marrying the Cushite woman. "I don't like the woman he married. I don't know why he married her. Why didn't he check with us first? Why didn't he talk to me? I would never have—" The real issue was not Moses' wife. Moses' wife was the petty-criticism cover-up for the real issue of their own jealous hearts. Someone needed to stop them and yell, "Hey! What's really bothering you?" What's behind this petty criticism? There was a lot behind it, and very little of it had to do with Moses.

I see this often in my role as a marriage counselor. I sit down with couples and try to help them with their marriage. Out come the petty complaints. "I don't like his job; he travels too much." But that's not the problem; that's what the person's criticizing. There is something behind that. Could it be she's insecure? Maybe he hasn't been the nurturing husband he should be. So every time he is out of town, you're not sure; you're insecure. The criticism is a petty covering for the real issue. The concern may be justified, but your criticism won't get you to the truth.

Or take another frequent criticism, "He (or she) doesn't like my parents." Why doesn't he? What's behind that? Get past the criticism to the deeper issue. "She loses my socks." Yeah, as if your marriage is cracking because of that. Or she says, "He never picks things up." The critical, petty things are covering up the real problems. If you want to go forward in that relationship, get to the real issue. I know this first-hand. Together, couples and I solve the problem they raise, and before they can get to the car, guess what? They find something else wrong. The reason they're on to something else is because the petty criticism is a covering for the real heart issue.

Did you hear the cool story in Aesop's fables about a man and his grandson traveling to town? The old man walked while his grandson rode the donkey. But some people said, "Would you look at that old man suffering on his feet while that strong young boy who is totally capable of walking sits on that donkey?" So the old man, hearing this, switched places and began to ride the donkey while the boy walked. Now he heard people saying, "Would you look at that? A grown man taking advantage of that little boy. Can you believe it?" And so the man and the boy both rode the donkey. Then they heard people saying, "Would you look at those heavy brutes making that poor donkey suffer?" So they both got off and walked until they heard some people say, "How pitiful, a perfectly good donkey not being used!" The final scene

REPLACE A CRITICAL ATTITUDE . . .

of the story showed the boy and the old man staggering along as they carry the donkey. The point is this: If a person's heart is to criticize—if their heart is to find fault—there is absolutely nothing that can satisfy them. Behind the petty issue is a real heart issue. Let's talk about those "real issues" next. At least three significant issues hide under the covers of criticism. One of them is *a blend of unforgiveness.* Unforgiveness and the bitterness that goes with it fuel criticism. I was traveling out of state recently, and I met a family who love the Lord with all of their hearts. At one point, I was talking to the mother of the home, whom I respect as a godly woman. That's why I was amazed by what happened when the subject of a family member came up. This sweet-spirited lady, who just a moment ago had been discussing the Scriptures and the things of God, suddenly burst out—

"He's a jerk! I hate him!"

Whoa! I couldn't believe it. All this bitter stuff poured out of her about her feelings toward this family member who had caused so much injury. I could certainly see there had been a lot of hurt, but unforgiveness and bitterness were causing those wounds to fester rather than heal. The criticism was not the real issue; it only covered the deeper issue of unforgiveness and bitterness. When unforgiveness is in the heart, criticism will be on the lips.

Second, criticism masks *envy, jealousy,* or *resentment.* People are often critical because they are envious of the success of another. So they try to pull the person down. As they dwell on the other person's good fortune, they begin to be overcome by resentment and start to find fault with what that person is doing. Again, the real issue is not the critical attitude; that's just a petty covering for the problem of jealousy.

A third heart problem that lies under the covers of criticism is *personal failure.* People can become critical of others because they're living in defeat themselves. Maybe you're discouraged about the direction of your life, or what you have been able to accomplish so far. Maybe you're struggling with a personal sin that has you defeated most of the time. How easy it is to become critical of others to sort of level the playing field. "Well, they don't have it together, either" and "Yeah, maybe I'm struggling, but he's not perfect. She's doesn't have it all together, either."

Criticism is petty. And it covers serious issues that lead to wilderness living.

PRINCIPLE THREE:
CRITICISM IS SELF-EXALTING

Here's a third principle about criticism that we find illustrated in the attack by Aaron and Miriam: *Criticism is self-exalting.* Ultimately, criticism inflates the self. Oswald Chambers, the great devotional writer, wrote, "Beware of anything that puts you in the place of the superior person." Anything that makes you feel superior is not conducive to your spiritual life. That's what criticism does: It takes the focus off me and my faults and highlights me as the one who knows. "I know; I see." Criticism elevates me as the highest and best. Criticism reduces the pain of being in the spotlight and gives me the fleshly satisfaction of running the spotlight. And in a sick sort of way it can feel good to put that kind of pressure on others. People find it much harder to see my life if I am shining the glaring light of criticism on others!

Be careful you don't find yourself saying subconsciously, "If I can't make my mark in this world by what I do, maybe I'll make it for knowing what others could do better." Criticism is self-exalting, and God will not honor that.

PRINCIPLE FOUR:
CRITICISM IS PAINFUL

Here is a fourth, unexpected principle of criticism in our biblical story: *Criticism is painful.* Let's look at criticism's impact on the other person. You are probably well aware of the pain of someone criticizing you. Imagine Moses: His brother and sister, the ones he thought he could count on, suddenly turned on him. The betrayal must have cut deeply. Sometimes the ones who injure us the most are the ones closest to us. Our immediate families at home and at church know our faults and where we are vulnerable to injury.

A person who is constantly or continually criticized can become good-for-nothing. The effect of criticism can knock all of the confidence and power out of a person's life. The pain from the "coldwater bucket brigade" can be devastating.

If your ideas are ignored and your efforts ridiculed, if you have been mocked by those from whom you most need support and encouragement, my heart goes out to you. Parents often leave their kids' lives in shambles by creating a household filled with criticism. Maybe you have been thinking about your parents or some other significant person this whole chapter—hardly able to focus on your own life because you have been seeing the face of your harshest critic. You remember someone who has left deep scars upon your life by constantly criticizing you. "That's not good enough!" Or, "You'll never get it right!" Maybe those words ring in your ears.

How do you respond to such criticism? The key is to remember we are not here to win people's approval but God's. The apostle Paul wrote, **"Am I now seeking the favor of men, or of God? Or am I striving to please men? If I were still trying to please men, I would not be a bond-servant of Christ"** (Galatians 1:10).

Theodore Roosevelt said, "It's not the critic who counts, not the one who points out how the strong man stumbles or how the doer of deeds might have done it better. The credit belongs to the man who is actually in the arena, whose face is marred with sweat and dust and blood, who strives valiantly, who errs and comes short again and again, who knows great enthusiasms, the great devotions, and spends himself in a worthy cause, who, if he fails, at least fails while daring greatly; his place shall never be with those cold and timid souls who know neither victory nor defeat."[1]

I encourage you to turn down the volume on the critics in your life. Center your attention on what God thinks of you, and life will be better. Otherwise, it's so easy to get sucked into the wilderness by someone who seems to love it there.

PRINCIPLE FIVE:
CRITICISM IS OFTEN INADVERTENT

A fifth principle of criticism that we learn through Aaron and Miriam is that *criticism is often inadvertent.* This is a very important point. Not every person who criticizes has a wicked, awful heart. A healthy portion of the critical things that people say are words they wouldn't say if they thought twice.

People, including you and me, often utter careless, thoughtless words that strike others like a slap in the face. Our verbal missiles are not targeted for intentional injury, but loose lips often do damage we don't anticipate. On a better day, filled with the Spirit and focused on what's right, we would never choose to say those things. Criticism is often inadvertent. Notice in the text how quickly Aaron said, **"We have acted foolishly"** (Numbers 12:11). He didn't try to defend his position. He doesn't stick up for what they said with, "Yes! Moses did marry the wrong person!" And, "We should have more prominence!" He realized his position, and as soon as he did, notice how quickly he and Miriam retreated.

His example makes this point: Inadvertent criticism does damage to people we really do care about.

PRINCIPLE SIX:
CRITICISM PLUGS THE FLOW OF GOD'S BLESSING

A sixth principle about criticism can also be found in our passage: *Criticism plugs the flow of God's blessing.* Oswald Chambers made a brilliant observation: "Whenever you are in a critical temper, it is impossible to enter into communion with God." That's a scary thought! Criticism makes us hard and vindictive and cruel. It leaves us with the flattering notion that we are superior persons. It is impossible to develop the characteristics of a saint and at the same time maintain a critical attitude. Criticism harms our relationship with God and others, and that will block the flow of God's blessing.

I have observed a pattern over the past five years as a number of people have come to Harvest Bible Chapel from other churches. They have arrived wounded, tired, and sometimes angry. My primary concern has not been about their critical attitude as new members. What I'm concerned about is the critical attitude they might have toward the churches that they left. Perhaps things were said during their departure that caused injuries. If they have brought hurts, frustrations, and unresolved conflicts with them from their past experiences, these may come out in continual criticism that will poison them and their new relationships. There is a solution: The offense must be addressed. Thus, I regularly challenge new people, in Jesus' name, to write a letter or make a phone call in order to settle past offenses. I would challenge you also: If criticism from past emotional injuries has leaked into your family, you must find a way to apply healing. If your kids know your frustration and have heard your negative attitude toward others, you are injuring them spiritually. Please remember that our children get a lot of their early attitudes from us.

I challenge you to have a righteous, gracious attitude toward the church of Christ and toward the servants of Christ. The momentary relief you may get from criticizing other Christians is not worth the damage you will pass on to your family. And the critical attitude festering in your heart is not worth the damage you will do to your relationship with God. To restore God's blessing, we need to confess and forsake this wilderness attitude, and replace it with a Promised Land attitude. That brings us to the solution . . . but first, some personal words about my response to criticism.

UP CLOSE AND PERSONAL

It's probably not surprising that I get a significant amount of criticism. It seems to go with the pastoral territory. I know a lot of it is deserved. Some of it is even helpful. But whether deserved or not, negative comments are hard to deal with. My greatest struggle, however, is not to deal with the pain of being criticized but to make sure that I don't catch the disease. Too often I have heard myself speaking words of criticism that, upon further reflection, were rooted in the pain I felt from being harshly treated. This is not an acceptable excuse.

Some of the pain that fuels criticism must be quickly dismissed as not worthy of our attention. In this respect, I value the example of Abraham Lincoln. He received an amazing cascade of harsh criticism during his lifetime. Mr. Lincoln himself once commented:

> If I tried to read, much less answer, all the criticisms made of me and all the attacks leveled against me, this office would have to be closed for all other business. I do the best I know how—the very best I can—and I mean to keep on doing this down to the very end. If the end brings me out all wrong, ten angels swearing I had been right would make no difference. If the end brings me out all right, then what is said against me now will not amount to anything.[2]

But all of the criticism we receive cannot be dismissed. What remains must be taken to the Lord.

God wants to help us bear the pain when others sin against us. I had to learn that when the pain of criticism shows up in wrong attitudes to those around me, I have not really taken my burden to the Lord. First Peter 5 speaks of the pain of false accusation and unjust treatment, telling us to cast our cares upon Him, because He cares for us (see verse 7). That's what breaks the chains of criticism from others and keeps a critical spirit from growing in us.

LET'S TALK SOLUTION

I trust that you have sensed God connecting these words about criticism to your life. We need to have a clear idea of what we're asking God to replace when it comes to our critical attitude. I invite you to seriously consider the following personal questions.

1. Am I a critical person? Is that too general a question? Try this: Am I negative and harsh in my opinions of others? Am I quick to find fault? Am I an analytical person who gets carried away into criticism? I am particularly sensitive to this because that's who I am. I know the frustration of defeat in this area myself. Those who are analytical—who have all kinds of thoughts and ideas constantly coming through their minds—need to respond to this challenge: Am I a critical person?

2. Am I reaping the consequences in my relationship with God? As is true of each of these negative attitudes, we may be able to spot the results in our lives more clearly than we can see the causes themselves. A critical spirit creates all the effects we have mentioned in this chapter. So ask yourself: Is my life like a wilderness? Is my heart like a wasteland? Am I reaping the consequences in my relationship with God? Am I ready to agree that my critical attitude is one reason I'm in the desert?

3. Am I willing to repent? Am I willing to turn from the rationalizations that allowed me to form that pattern of thinking? Am I willing to turn from the habit of a critical attitude and repent? If so, I encourage you to review the prayer below, and then make it your own as you ask God to help you deal with your critical attitude.

Look Up

Lord, thank You for the priceless privilege to worship and live alongside my brothers and sisters in Christ. Thank You that each one is known and loved by You and has his and her own story of Your grace and goodness in their lives. Lord, I am like them in that You found me in my sin also. And You have shone the light of Christ into my life. Now I am in the process of growing and becoming more like You. Help me along the way to discern the difference between loving, constructive criticism and the kind of criticism that destroys. Help me to think highly and graciously about others. Help me to pray for others.

Thank You that Your Word has shone into my heart. Thank You for using it to reveal the price that I pay for my critical opinions. Forgive me for thinking so highly of myself. Forgive me for thinking that my perspective is always the right perspective. God, I recognize the arrogance in that. Give me graciousness, love, and forbearance with others. Thank You, God, that You have made us all different. Help me to celebrate our differences and not demand that all the world see things exactly as I do. Give me victory over a critical spirit. Make me quick to turn from that pattern of thinking so that I might know Your fullness in my life. I pray this in Jesus' precious name. Amen.

NOTES

1. Michael P. Green, ed. , 2nd ed. *Illustrations for Biblical Preaching* (Grand Rapids: Baker, 1989), 87.

2. Paul Lee Tan, *Encyclopedia of 7,700 Illustrations: Signs of the Times* (Rockville, Md.: Assurance, 1979), 294.

6

. . . WITH AN ATTITUDE OF LOVE

1 Corinthians 13:1—8a

SAY IT IN A SENTENCE:

The only attitude big enough to replace a critical attitude is an attitude of love.

A business traveler I'll call Chris was waiting in a "Red Carpet Club"; you know, one of those frequent-flyer-perk places in airports where you can hang out during flight delays. Chris was just chilling on the phone and noticed that just across the aisle was Bill Gates, that guy from Microsoft. Not having enough class to just leave him alone, he walked over and asked, "Are you Bill Gates?"

Bill looked up from behind his newspaper and said, "Yes."

"I'm so excited to meet you. I can't believe I'm finally meeting a famous person. This has never happened to me before!" By then, he was babbling. Bill's response was an unspoken smile that said, *It's happening now.*

So then the irritating guy says, "This is like such a big deal. I just can't believe that I finally get to meet you. Here's the thing. In a few minutes I've got a really big meeting here with some very important clients. I don't know if I should ask you this or not, but I really want to impress these people. So, is there any way while I'm meeting with them—my name's Chris, by the way—that you could come over and tap me on the shoulder and say, 'Hey, Chris. How's it going?' or something like that? Because they would really be impressed if they thought that I knew you. And I'll just play along or whatever."

Surprisingly, Bill Gates said, "OK."

So, a few minutes later, Chris was in this meeting with the clients he was trying to impress. Sure enough, he felt a tapping on his shoulder. He looked up as Bill Gates said, "Hey, Chris. How's it going?"

And he said, "Take a hike, Gates. Can't you see I'm in a meeting?"

A friend sent me that story by E-mail. (You can judge for yourself whether it is true.) When I heard the story, I thought, *I know what that feels like.* I know what it feels like to really try to help somebody or go out of your way for somebody, and all of a sudden they give you that "fingernails on a chalkboard feeling," or worse! Most of our difficulties in life are the result of difficult people. And, more often than not, our reaction is negative and becomes the larger issue as it relates to our own attitudes and our desire to stay out of the wilderness.

We're talking in this chapter about replacing a critical attitude. Sometimes, that's really hard to do because people can be so irritating. Criticism, I think, more than any other wilderness attitude, is the one that can really trap us. When we allow the inevitable frustrations that come from others to make us critical, negative, and faultfinding, then we are headed for the wilderness for sure.

WHAT TO DO

Here's how to get out. The attitude that replaces a critical one is love. Now if you have some people in your life you're just dying to criticize, you're probably like, "Beautiful. That's it? I have to *love* everybody—even . . . ? Do you know who you're talking about—do you have any idea—you're asking me to love them?" Yes, you can love that person—husband, boss, neighbor, or whoever—and the Bible tells you and me how.

Open your Bible to 1 Corinthians 13. People call it "the Love Chapter." Normally you don't go there except if you're at a wedding or wedding anniversary. First Corinthians 13 is like a flower that loses its beauty if you start dissecting it and pulling all the petals off. I want to make sure we don't do that to 1 Corinthians 13. If you have only heard it in church and never studied it for yourself, then you may have missed the powerful transforming truth that is found there.

The church in Corinth had many powerful traits going for it. The members did have real problems, but 1 Corinthians 1:7 says that they had spiritual gifts; and 11:2 points out that they had good solid doctrine. What was missing, however, was love; and Paul, under the inspiration of the Holy Spirit, did not hesitate to tell them how much they were really missing.

Let's begin with this thought from 1 Corinthians 13:1–2: *All truth and no love is brutality.* Speaking only the raw truth and not loving others is a very brutal thing. First Corinthians 13:1 says, **"If I speak with the tongues of men and of angels, but do not have love, I have become a noisy gong or a clanging cymbal."**

The concept of love in the world is terribly distorted. Those distortions affect the way we hear God's Word.

LOVE *IS* A MANY-SPLENDORED THING

As you may know, there are three Greek words in Scripture for the word *love.* I want to focus on the word *agape,* because that's the word Paul used in this chapter. At the time the Scripture was written, almost two thousand years ago now, this *agape* love was very rare and seldom used in society. People used the more common terms *eros,* which refers to sensual love, or *phileo*, which describes a brotherly relationship. But the term they hardly ever used in New Testament times is the one we see most frequently in Scripture. *Agape* means a selfless love, giving love, you-before-me love. It describes love as an act of the will; a choice I make.

However, what we often mean when we say "I love you" is not, "I've made a commitment to place your needs above my own." Instead, we often mean, "I love what you do for me. You make me feel good. What you are doing right now is working for the person that I truly love most, which is *me*." What we're really saying is, *"I feel something."* Aren't we saying, "You're making me feel something that I really enjoy feeling"?

Now that is not love. That is self-centeredness. If you build a relationship upon that, some very difficult days are ahead.

ANGEL TALK

In this specific passage of Scripture, we are challenged to make love complete. It says, **"If I speak with the tongues of men and of angels."** Now there is no such thing in Scripture as an angelic language. The angels don't speak a different language. Anytime an angel appears in Scripture, the angel always speaks in a human language. Angels are messengers; they speak in the language of those to whom they are sent. What Paul is saying here is, "If I could be the most eloquent man . . . no, no, wait—if I could be the most eloquent being . . . if I could be like one of those angelic messengers and speak so clearly and plainly for God that it made a difference in people's lives, but I didn't love the people whom I was talking to," people wouldn't hear the message over the ringing in their ears.

That's what verse 1 means. No matter how clearly you understand God's truth or how capable you are of bringing truth to bear upon a person's life, if you don't love the people you're talking to, if you don't have a broken heart for the people that you're trying to share truth with, you are wasting your time. Your words are just like a clanging in their ears. We find that our effort creates destruction in their lives instead of good things. When we present the truth aggressively or with a critical attitude, they are irritated by what we say rather than blessed and uplifted. We're like clanging cymbals.

ANOTHER BARRIER

We could even have a great knowledge of God and a great faith in God and fail to communicate if we don't have a loving attitude. Paul continued, **"If I have the gift of prophecy, and know all mysteries and all knowledge; and if I have all faith, so as to remove mountains, but do not have love . . ."** (verse 2). What if you understood every deep theological issue? What if you had your Ph.D. in *God and the Bible?* Doesn't matter. And if you had "all faith" —such confidence in God that you could do what Jesus talked about and move mountains (see Matthew 17:20; 21:21); this phenomenal vertical thing with God—then could God use you? Not if you didn't love people.

If you don't love the person that you are trying to reach, you could have A+ faith and still fail the test. No, it's worse than failure. When you try to make a difference in someone's life by bringing them truth, what does it say in the text? It's, like, don't even bother marking the test; just throw it in the trash. Give the guy zero, because he doesn't love. All truth without love just causes damage. It's brutal.

Whether we exhibit great communication skills, knowledge, or faith, if it is not accompanied by a loving attitude, the message will fall flat. People care how we say it as much as what we say. If we have a critical attitude—toward the lost or even Christian brothers and sisters—those watching us will be unable to fully accept the message. That's why a loving attitude toward others is the only antidote to a critical attitude.

What do people say about the followers of Jesus Christ? Do you know what they call us? I was talking to a guy the other day who said,

"You're not one of those Bible-beaters, are you? You won't shove the Bible in my face, saying, 'Wise up or go to hell'?" I didn't know what to say. "Well, uh yes, but, er . . . no, not like that. I mean, I hope I'm not. . . er, well, never mind." It's so sad that those who have the greatest message of love in the universe can be so unloving with it. It's brutal; it's harsh. And we're hurting people—not helping. We're not making the difference that we want to make, because the love isn't there.

WILL GREAT SACRIFICES HELP?

Paul takes an interesting turn in verse 3. His thought goes in the complete opposite direction. **"If I give all my possessions . . . "** OK, so then if love is putting others' needs ahead of my own, then I'm going to be just crazy. I'm going to give, give, and give. Get some food and some clothing and some money, and I'm going to meet needs. You all can stand around and study the Bible all you want to; I'm going to make a difference in this world. I'm going to pour myself into people.

We've got our "What Would Jesus Do?" bracelets, key chains, and shirts. And we're out here meeting needs. You all are over there studying the Bible; we're out here meeting needs. But wait a minute, **"If I give all my possessions to feed the poor . . ."** All of them? That's love, right? But Paul goes on, **"If I surrender my body to be burned, but do not have love, it profits me nothing."**

Did you get that?

If I make the ultimate sacrifice but have no love, it's worthless!

Now that's not what you expect God's Word to say. You think to yourself, "Well how could you possibly give everything you have to people in need and give yourself for them and not love them?" The point that Paul is making is that love is a balance between affection and truth. We tend to think of love as affection. Love is far more than affection. Biblical love is both truth and affection put together and kept together.

Time for Some Balance!

An imbalance of biblical love has often infected the church. On one hand is radical fundamentalism that emphasizes all truth and is legalistic and screaming, "This is what the Word says, boy!" That's not what Jesus did. On the other hand, we have a liberal Christianity that says, "Bag the Bible; we have Jesus! We have His heart for the hurting, and we're going out to make a difference in this world." Jesus didn't do that either. Neither one of those is what Christ intended. It appears we need a balance between these two: truth and acts of mercy; acts of mercy and truth. Anything less is not biblical love. For instance, Jerry isn't sure how to show love yet speak truth. He described his dilemma: "My friend has a drinking problem. I can tell it by his breath. I can see it in his eyes. I know it by his actions. I know that he is hurting himself and his family. So what do I do? If I go and speak truth to him, he might reject me. So I'm just going to love him and care for him. But that's not really right either, because if I just leave him and I know that he is hurting himself, something inside me tells me that's not loving."

A lot of times we feel caught in between these two choices: God's truth, given in His Scriptures, and the command to love, which Jesus said is how "all men will know that you are My disciples" (John 13:35). And so we get into this balancing act of love and truth, truth and love. Most of us fail on one side or the other.

Stop the Presses—New Headline!

I'm going to tell you: *It's not about balancing truth and love.* We can't replace criticism with a tightrope walk between truth and love. We need a paradigm shift. Do you know what a paradigm shift is?

A paradigm shift occurs when you have been looking at something one way for such a long time that you think that's the only way it is. All of a sudden, you walk around the other side of the issue, and you're like, "Agh! It's *totally* not like what I thought it was! It's completely different."

We need to make that complete shift in how we look at truth and love. We're not supposed to be balancing love and truth as though they are separate things. What 1 Corinthians 13 is teaching—and you won't hear this very often at a wedding—is that truth is *part* of love and that you're not really loving if speaking truth is not part of the equation. All truth and no love is brutality. The rest of 1 Corinthians 13 can be summarized in the following statements:

On the majors—action.
On the minors—acceptance.
In all things—love.

Let's look at verses 4 and 5 in a moment. First Corinthians 13:6 says love **"does not rejoice in unrighteousness, but rejoices with the truth."** Notice, it's not truth versus love; truth is part of the biblical definition of love. Without truth, any expression of love is crippled. Love cannot rejoice in sin, or iniquity, or unrighteousness. Love can only be fired up about what is true and what is right.

ON THE MAJORS—ACTION

There come times in every relationship when the issues are serious. Failure to take action will produce big fallout. In those instances, love does not sit passively by. "I love him, so I won't upset him." Wrong! Love takes action on things that are major. You say, "What's major?" We'll start with this: If the behavior involves sin, Paul made it clear: **"[Love] does not rejoice in unrighteousness."** It just can't. Love cannot be happy about iniquity; it can't sit passively by.

You say, "Well, wait for a minute. If I'm going to have a confrontation with every single person who has sin in his life, I'm going to have a lot of confrontations going on," because Romans 3:10 says, **"There is none righteous; not even one,"** and 1 John 1:8 reminds us, **"If we say that we have no sin, we are deceiving ourselves."** We're all sinners, no doubt about it, and if love means to confront sin all the time and in every place, then life will become one big free-for-all. No, we don't take action on every single sin. I would recommend strongly that you not say, "Hey, Bill, I noticed you're a little lazy. I was reading in Proverbs that's a sin." That's a very bad plan.

WHAT ARE THE MAJOR THINGS?

Here are three guidelines we can use to determine what are major things where love means taking action:

1. *Is this a critical path?* If failure to take action will produce major fallout, biblical love is on the move. If it's a major doctrinal error, a case of marital unfaithfulness, a criminal act, or an abusive behavior, please don't collect stories for ten years and sit passively by. Step up! Get involved! Say something! Love takes action. If the person you love is involved in sin that could destroy him or someone else, it's a critical path—it's major—and therefore love will get involved.

2. *Is the problem chronic?* If you see the same thing happening over and over, it doesn't have to be big to get your love into gear. The Song of Solomon says it's the **"little foxes that spoil the vines"** (2:15 NKJV). "Smaller things" call for action, too, if they're part of a chronic pattern. If you have observed a behavior repeated many times, it invites a loving response. A gentle word of correction can bear great fruit in the loved one's life. To say to someone, "Is it possible that you have a problem with

gossip?" that is loving a person. So if you're close enough to observe chronic patterns, you have to get involved. You have to step up. On the majors, love takes action.

3. *Does your proximity imply responsibility?* The third guideline after critical path and chronic problem is the factor of close proximity. How close are you to the situation? There are some things that we can live with in our neighbors and our friends, but we can't live with in our spouse and our kids. Right? Your closeness to the situation may involve responsibility. For example, if I saw a friend making a purchase that I thought was unwise and wondered if he could afford it, I probably wouldn't say anything, because that's not really my business. But if I saw my wife doing that—or more likely, if my wife saw me doing that—it would be very appropriate for her to say, "We're not buying that! We can't afford that! That's just going to give us problems down the road."

HOW LOVE LOVES IS VERY IMPORTANT

Now we're ready to look at verse 5, because that's where the *how* is. Here's *how* love takes action.

Notice, "**[Love] does not act unbecomingly.**" It's not rude. Love is gracious. There is no place for an aggressive, boisterous, obnoxious, open-wide-while-I-jam-this-down-your-throat kind of approach. That is not true love. Love "**does not seek its own,**" Paul continued. That's the essence of love. In the context of this discussion, as I come to speak truth to someone—if I have to confront someone and say something that they don't want to hear—I'm not concerned about my needs.

Suppose, friend, that I had to confront you about something. What would be *my* needs? I would probably want to make sure that you're not going to reject me. I would want to make sure that you're not going to blow up in my face. So my tendency might be to soften and water down what I am saying, because my real bottom line is that I don't want us to have an explosion. That is not really loving you. In order to confront in love, I must forget about my needs to be loved and accepted, and make sure that what you hear is filtered only by kindness. Genuine love reminds me not to act unbecomingly. But at the same time, I'm not going to walk away having only said half of the truth. It's going to get said, because love makes sure that it all gets said. "Love does not seek its own."

What happens when we love this way?

When you love someone this way, be prepared, because the person may not appreciate you at first. She may respond angrily. And my response, if it's with love—will not be provoked. So, after I have graciously spoken the whole truth, if you fly off the handle and say, "Who are you to tell me this? What about *your* life!?" I'm not going to get into that with you. I will go to my knees and get my heart to a good place, so that no matter how angry you get, I'm not going to be provoked.

Paul's list is tracking how genuine love gets treated sometimes. So he adds, love **"does not take into account a wrong suffered."** As I go to speak truth to a person—before I go to take action—I must remember that I may have been injured by the person's sin. The text indicates I'm not going to unload on the person because he has hurt me. I will deal with all that before I ever get to the person; I will really exercise forgiveness. Wives who have something difficult to tell to their husbands need to get it said, but first they must get their hearts to a good place so that as they confront, they're not just venting a wrong suffered. That won't produce anything good, and certainly not biblical love.

Get those hurt feelings dealt with in prayer and good counsel from a trusted friend. Get your own pain behind you, so that you're really coming only for the good of the person that you're going to. That's love in action. And it's powerful. If you would become that person, God could use your life greatly, because there are precious few people in this world who really love people enough to take compassionate action.

How much of this should I expect to do?

You might think as you read the above that there are a lot of those confrontations in life. Not so. If you were to list a hundred things that could possibly require confronting your boss, your spouse, or your neighbor, maybe three things on that list could fit the category we just called major. The other ninety-seven things come under category two: They are minors. They only irritate you and me because of our own sinfulness and our own pride. We are so prone to take minor molehills and make them into major mountains, and it's in that soil that a critical spirit can flourish and grow.

ABOUT THE MINOR ISSUES

Here's the major principle for dealing with minor issues: *On the minors—acceptance.* By minors we mean personal preference, personality differences, even sin issues that are not critical or chronic. It's essential that followers of Christ be the most accepting, nonprejudiced, nonfaultfinding, noncritical people on the face of the earth. Again, 97 percent of life's issues are minor: little irritations; the differences between me and you; and she-thinks-like-this-but-I-don't-see-it-that-way, and he's-a-little-different-kind-of-a-person-than-me, and no-way-did-he-handle-that-totally-properly. Each of these is not an issue of right and wrong. We are different people, and we handle things differently. Most of the things that are breaking down marriages, that are breaking down friendships, and that are causing you problems with the person that you work for are not major—they're minor things! In those contexts, love learns to accept the person with his failures. Love doesn't deny the irritation; it simply recognizes that the one I love is far more important than my own desire to live an irritant-free life. On the majors—action. But on the minors—most things—acceptance.

SPOTTING THE MINORS

By minors, we mean matters of personal preference. "Well, I would do it *this* way"; "Well, I really prefer this." We need to spot the minors and leave them alone. Here are some minors that masquerade as majors:

- *Musical taste.* Churches all over the country are splitting over musical preference. "I don't like drums." "Hymns are too old-fashioned." Get a grip! It's just personal preference! It's a minor thing; it's not a major thing.

- *Personality differences.* We're all unique. Some of you are *really* unique. If you ever meet me, you'll probably think *I'm* pretty strange. That's OK! The sad thing is that we resent and criticize each others' weaknesses while God "will rejoice over [us] with shouts of joy" (Zephaniah 3:17).

- *Cultural differences.* One of the healthiest experiences we can have as Christians is to visit other cultures to worship and live with believers. In those contexts, we discover that what we think is superspirituality is a pretty superficial collection of "dos and don'ts" that add up to a lot of minors and don't really address essential issues of life and faith. Even sin issues—hear me—can be minor things we should accept in each other. Pray for others about the minor things. Turn them over to God. "God's at work in her life." "God's going to change him." If it's not a critical path, if it's not a chronic problem, if it's not in close proximity to you—maybe you just ought to accept and pray for the person, meanwhile praying for Holy Spirit conviction. As they say, "Let go and let God."

It's essential that the followers of Christ be the most accepting people on the face of the earth. The world desperately needs to see Jesus, and we're the only picture they get. We should be the most loving, accepting people in the world. Often we're not, but we should be. On the minors—you see it here in the text—acceptance. Just look at verse 4, **"Love is patient."** Let the wind of that beautiful breeze blow across your mind. Love is patient. It waits for people to change. Love is long-tempered; God help us! Love is persistently compassionate in the face of opposition.

ONE OF MY HEROES

By now you know I admire the life of President Abraham Lincoln. One of his earliest political enemies, Edwin M. Stanton, was extremely harsh and critical. In one speech, he called Lincoln a "low cunning clown." He also called Lincoln "the original gorilla." In fact, in another speech Stanton said, "It was ridiculous for people to go to Africa to see a gorilla when they could find one just as easily in Springfield, Illinois." How hurtful would that be if that was said publicly about you? Yet Lincoln never responded to that slander. He never spoke a word against him. He never retaliated. He never criticized him! Why? Because love is patient.

But that's not all; **"Love is kind,"** as well (verse 4). This means:

- Not just passive endurance, but active goodwill.

- Not just passively accepting people, but actively accepting people.

- Not just standing on the other side of the room and saying, "She drives me nuts, so I'm going to just steer clear of her," but actually going across the room and finding ways physically or in conversation to embrace that very person.

Love is kind. It looks for ways to express acceptance to people that we might otherwise choose to be targets of our criticism.

THE REST OF THE STORY

Lincoln never responded to Edwin M. Stanton, who attacked him repeatedly. He refused to reciprocate the slander. But when he was elected president and he needed a secretary of war, guess whom he chose? He chose Edwin M. Stanton, the man who heartlessly defamed and disgraced Lincoln. When his incredulous friends asked Lincoln why he had made this choice, he said, "Because he is the best man."

Years later, as the slain president's body lay in state, Edwin M. Stanton looked into the coffin and said through his tears, "There lies the greatest ruler of men the world has ever seen."[1] His animosity was finally broken by Lincoln's long-suffering, nonretaliatory spirit. Love is patient, kind, and a powerful antidote to a critical attitude.

WHAT ABOUT YOU?

Is someone injuring you? Has someone chosen a place of opposition in your life? How have you been responding? Have your attitude choices taken you to the dry and deserted wasteland that we call the wilderness? Do you want to get out of the wilderness? Do you want to get victory over that critical spirit? Displace a critical spirit with an attitude of love! Move toward those people who are hurting you and injuring you and, in the power of God's Spirit and in the fullness that only He can give, love those people!

Love them and watch God bring a powerful victory that heals and makes whole in a way that we never could. On the majors—action. On the minors—acceptance. Verse 4 also tells us that love **"is not jealous."** Often the greatest obstacle to putting off a critical spirit is when those around us seem to prosper more than we do. "I was fine with her until she got . . ." "I was fine with him until . . ." How do you handle the successes of the people whom you love? Love is not jealous. Love says:

- I accept you even when you are more successful than me.

- Even when you are more prominent than me.

- Even when you are more recognized and more rewarded than me.

- I am for you. I have always been for you.

- I rejoice in your success and will not let a jealous outlook sour my love.

- I accept your prosperity—no, I *revel* in your prosperity because I love you. I will not be caught up in a jealous spirit.

As hard as that is, the next phrase in the definition of love is even harder. What about when *you're* the successful person? Can you continue to love people, or do you leave them behind? **"Love does not brag and is not arrogant,"** Paul explained. "Well, we used to be close, but I have a little more in this world. He's not as important to me as he used to be." No! Instead, I say, "I accept you even when you are less successful than me, even when you are less prominent, less recognized, less rewarded. I will not make you uncomfortable by boasting in my success. I will not highlight my life in any way that embarrasses or belittles you."

LOVE ON THE BASKETBALL COURT

I got a great blessing recently from my son Landon and one of his closest friends, Michael Muller (who, with his family, attends Harvest Bible Chapel). The two were trying out for the seventh-grade basketball team. It's called the Feeder Program. All the interested junior high kids who were planning to go to a certain high school tried out for the team. Forty went. On Thursday night, the coach would cut the practice roster to twenty. On Friday, he'd cut it down to just twelve. So I just knew that there wasn't a strong possibility that Landon was going to make this team. But off went both of them to the tryouts.

The next day, the players were supposed to phone for the results. Each kid had a number—Michael's was 13, Landon's, 12— and the phone message listed the numbers of the kids who had made the first cut. So, during the Friday lunch hour at school, Michael and Landon were on the phone, together. They both wanted to make the team so much. The recorded voice announced that the following people should report to practice that evening: "Number 1, number 2, number 3, number 4, number 6, number 8, number 9, number 11, number 13. . . ." Michael made the first cut; Landon didn't.

When Landon came home, he shed some disappointment tears and we talked. He said, "You know, Dad, as soon as we hung up the phone, Michael turned to me and said, 'Landon, you're a better basketball player than I am. *You* should have made the cut. And if you don't want me to go to this practice tonight, I won't even go.'"

Landon turned to him and said, "Do you know what? I want you to go. I hope that you make the team."

Ding! That's love for sure, and I was amazed and thankful for the maturity of their responses. When you love the people in your life, there is no way in the world that you're going to let *your* success or *their* success get in the way.

HANDLE THE MINORS WITH ACCEPTANCE

Verse 7 is a good summary of acceptance: Love **"bears all things, believes all things."** Love bears the weight of misunderstanding, and it defends the heart. Love finds itself saying on a regular basis, "That's not what she meant." It believes the best about the other person. "You don't know what you're talking about. That's not why he did that."

When Jesus said, "Judge not lest you be judged," He was specifically dealing with motives. Of course, we have to judge actions. What we're not to judge are motives. We don't know why people do what they do.

Don't ever say, "I know why she's up there. I know why he does that." You probably do not. When you hear somebody criticizing someone you love, just say, "I don't believe that, and I won't believe it until I check with him myself."

Love always believes the best about people. Love bears all things, believes all things, and love **"hopes all things"** (verse 7). Love sees people not as they are, but as they will be by God's grace. Wouldn't it be great if God could just download that into your church? Then we would not see each other as we are today, but as God is making us. We're not the people that we were. God is changing all of us. What's the last item in the definition of love? Love **"endures all things"** (verse 7). *Endure* is actually a military term. It means that we drive a stake in the ground. Isn't that great? It's like, I will stand my ground loving you. You can retreat if you want, but I'm never going back from this place right here. I'm going to be there for you. In his book *Love, Acceptance, and Forgiveness,* Jerry Cook describes a church out in Washington State that grew in fourteen years to more than four thousand people. The book is a story of a commitment, and it includes the commitment people at that church made to each other. It moves me every time I read it:

> You will never knowingly suffer at my hands. I will never say anything or do anything knowingly to hurt you. I will always, in every circumstance, seek to help and support you. If you're down and I can lift you up—I'll do that. If you need something and I have it, I'll share it with you. If I need to, I'll give it to you. No matter what I find out about you, no matter what happens in the future—either good or bad—my commitment to you will never change. And there is nothing you can do about it.[2]

Wow! When believers are willing to make that kind of commitment to each other, they are going to be a powerful force for God.

KEEP THE MAJORS AND
THE MINORS IN PERSPECTIVE

This may seem obvious, but the overriding attitude that keeps the majors and the minors in their proper place is the third point in our 1 Corinthians 13 summary: In all things, love. Paul expresses the big picture in these words, **"Love never fails"** (verse 8). Not wishy-washy sentimentalism and not harsh brutality, but truth and love—perfectly combined—God's selfless love. That kind of love never fails. Never! A poem that I'm quite fond of says this:

Of the themes that men have known
One supremely stands alone.
Love is the theme, Love is supreme.
Sweeter it grows, glory bestows.
Bright as the sun, ever it glows.
Love is the theme,
The eternal theme.
AUTHOR UKNOWN

UP CLOSE AND PERSONAL

When Kathy and I started Harvest Bible Chapel, we'd been praying, "God, we'll go anywhere You want us to go, but we want to stay wherever You send us. We want to put our roots down deeply." God has answered that prayer with twelve wonderful years in the same church, with dreams for many more.

I don't normally do the baptisms in our services. We have others who can serve in that way. But I specifically did the baptisms in one service recently because there was a young boy who, nine years earlier,

I had dedicated as a little baby in a Sunday worship service. Now he was getting baptized. That's doing life together. That's walking with people through the passages of life. And by God's grace, I would *love* to stand at the front of the church someday when that young man makes a vow to spend his entire lifetime with one woman.

Making that kind of lifetime commitment to one church can be very difficult for a pastor and his wife. As for my own character formation, the leaders and most of the people at Harvest have no illusions about me. They know where I am strong and where God's still got a lot of work to do. There's no use trying to fake it, because people know who I really am.

Many times I have been tempted to pick up life's lessons, take my family, and start over somewhere else. You know, be on a new page where the weaknesses I have left behind could be just that—behind! But in my heart I know that is a compromise of the vision God has given our fellowship. Biblical community means learning to *really* love one another. When ministering here has brought messages to us that we didn't want to hear, we have chosen to remain under the pressure and love one another through the pain of personal change, because that is what the body of Christ is really all about.

How thankful I am for a fellowship of believers who have embraced that vision. It's also been heartbreaking at times to see others who signed up for the same vision and stuck with it until the truth had to do with them. Too often, they have walked away as they did from Jesus' ministry, saying, **"This is a hard saying; who can [accept] it?"** (John 6:60 NKJV). But I have come to embrace that pain as part of the price that must be paid to build a church seeking to experience all that 1 Corinthians 13 really teaches. It's the kind of love that unbelievers will wake up and watch because they have never seen it before. **"By this all men will know that you are My disciples, if you . . ."** What? Teach them? Help them? No, **" . . . if you have love for one another"** (John 13:35).

A FINAL THOUGHT

The promise is that love will never fail. Think about the implications of the promise that God is making in this verse. He is saying, "Love will never fail! If you will embrace with your whole heart what it means to love another person . . ." Ultimately, God's love will not fail.

You may say, "But my husband . . . or my wife . . . " But if you will love him or her, God will use that. Love will never fail. Love will never fail to accomplish God's highest and best purposes. If the thing goes south, it wasn't because of love. Love always takes things to a better place. If you will pursue it with your whole heart and embrace the people in your life as they are—warts and all—even when they hurt you, God will use that. Love will never fail—not at work, at home, nor in the church. Where can you take me in Scripture to a better promise than that? Love never fails. Never!

LET'S TALK SOLUTION

To find the solution to a critical attitude—that biblical, loving attitude—let's once more answer three questions. The first one is primary: *Am I a loving person?* That's the question that has to get answered. Am I a loving person? Years ago, evangelist D. L. Moody sensed that the Lord wanted him to grow in this matter of love. He wrote this more than one hundred years ago:

> I took up that word Love, and I do not know how many weeks I
> spent in studying the passages in which it occurs till at last I could
> not help loving people. I had been feeding on love so long that I was
> anxious to do everybody good I came into contact with. I got full of
> it. It ran out of my fingers. You take up the subject of love in the
> Bible! You will get so full of it that all you have to do is open your
> lips and a flood of the Love of God [will flow] out.[3]

Here are two additional questions to ask that lead to a loving attitude in your life:

▪ *Am I seeing the benefits of love in my life?* Do the relationships in my life evidence that love is pouring forth from me upon the people around me? And remember all that love is. Love that is shown on the major issues and the minor issues. Both. Is there evidence of love in my life? Am I seeing the benefits?

▪ *Am I choosing love over criticism moment by moment?* Attitudes are patterns of thinking formed over a long period of time. Am I choosing love moment by moment?

Remember, whether the issue is major or minor, whatever action or attitude we choose, it is all to be done in love. On the majors, take action; on the minors, show acceptance; in all things, display love.

Look Up

Lord, thank You for this meaty passage of Your Word. It's all there! It is as relevant today as the day it was written. And it speaks to my experience. It calls me to less criticism and more love, sometimes speaking truth, most often accepting and embracing people who, like me, are in the process of transformation.

God, forgive my negative, critical, faultfinding ways. Give me a heart to love people and bear with them, to speak truth when it's needed, whatever the cost. But most often, a heart to accept others. Bring to my mind a specific person or two with whom I could apply these truths. Help me to confront halfhearted attitudes. Remind me that two thousand years ago Jesus Christ came into this world. He is love. He died on a cross and rose from the dead for me. His love is stronger than death! I want to let Christ love others through me. He can give me a supernatural endless capacity to love the very people that exhaust me.

Lord, thank You for Your love that has been shed abroad in my heart. Thank You for the capacity to love others, given by You and sustained by You. I rejoice and delight in that. You are a good and faithful God. I celebrate Your love. Thank You that You love us perfectly, unconditionally. I accept Your love right now, right here. I am not worthy of it, but I worship You and thank You in Jesus' precious name. Amen.

NOTES

1. Michael P. Green, *Illustrations for Biblical Preaching* (Grand Rapids: Baker, 1989), 258–59.

2. Jerry Cook with Stanley C. Baldwin, *Love, Acceptance, and Forgiveness* (Ventura, Cal.: Regal, 1979), 13.

3. As quoted in George Sweeting, *Who Said That?* (Chicago: Moody, 1995), 309.

7

REPLACE A DOUBTING ATTITUDE . . .

NUMBERS 13:1—14:11

SAY IT IN A SENTENCE:

Those who make doubting their lifestyle will spend their lifetimes in the wilderness.

Keep going—we're making big-time progress on our attitudes. Now we're going to wilderness attitude number four: "Replace a Doubting Attitude . . ." "Wait a minute! Is doubt an attitude? Really?! I mean, I can see complaining and coveting—but doubting?"

Yes, the title of this chapter is "Replace a Doubting Attitude . . . " That's my conviction, and I'm sticking to it! Wilderness attitude number four is *doubt*. Here's a definition of doubt: Doubt is the *absence of faith*. I worked on that one for hours . . . OK, no, I didn't. Here's a fuller definition: Doubt is *a lack of confidence or assurance that God will keep His promises.*

Doubt is the mind-set that keeps saying, "Well, I just don't know if God will keep His promises . . ." Doubt involves a settled and persistent choice to live with uncertainty. It's not the stubborn "show me" of Thomas, that went looking for answers, but the steady unresolved attitude of Jonah that said, in effect, "I don't know and I don't care. I don't believe and nobody can change that."

Such doubt is dangerous. It's destructive and completely detrimental to any kind of relationship with God. I mean, if you don't have confidence that God will keep His promises, what do you have?

IRREVOCABLE PROMISES

Let's get on the table some sample promises God has made, so we can push our definition of doubt a little further.

■ God has promised to provide for us. Philippians 4:19 says, **"My God will supply all your needs according to His riches in glory in Christ Jesus."** "No, no—maybe God won't provide for all of my needs. Maybe I'll end up poor, and even destitute." That's doubt.

■ God has promised to protect us. Isaiah 54:17 says, **"No weapon that is formed against you will prosper. . . . This is the heritage of the servants of the Lord"** (NKJV). God promises to protect you—against anything or anyone intent on your harm. "But maybe He won't protect me," you think. "Maybe something awful is going to happen." That's doubt, for sure.

■ God has also promised to prosper us—though, as some are quick to add, that doesn't necessarily mean financially. But Psalm 84:11 says, **"No good thing does He withhold from those who walk uprightly."** Your life will not lack one single thing that could increase your happiness if you will walk uprightly with the Lord. Now either you believe that or you don't.

All three of the above promises, along with hundreds of others, are signed by God Himself. Doubt is a lack of confidence or a lack of assurance that God will keep those promises. When questions about God's willingness or ability to keep His promises persist, the attitude becomes a lifestyle—and we are on a bus to cactus country. An attitude of doubt can be traced back to our very walk with the Lord. But it may not be as easy to see in your own life as it is to see in the lives of those Israelites on the edge of the wilderness. What we find in their choices will help you see your own life more clearly.

Numbers 13 takes us back to the children of Israel, poised between the Promised Land and the wasteland. In their experience, we can find five specific principles that show us how God deals with doubt, and why He causes life to become parched to those who persist in this attitude. Take a moment to prayerfully read Numbers 13:1–14:11.

PRINCIPLE ONE:
GOD PLACES REGULAR
TESTS OF FAITH BEFORE HIS CHILDREN

Faith is so important and doubt is so detrimental that God places *regular* tests of faith in front of His children. These are not intended for our failure, but for our success. Similarly, when the children of Israel were at the halfway point of their journey, almost ready to enter the Promised Land, they faced a challenge that was meant for their success. The land wasn't vacant; there were other nations there. If they were going to take the land that God had promised, there was going to be some war. There was going to be some conflict and hardship. The questions create a choice: *Will they trust and conquer, or will they doubt and despair and be defeated?*

In Deuteronomy 1, Moses recalled what happened on the edge of the Promised Land that day, pointing out that God's number one plan was that they would just go up and take the land. Just keep on marching; go right in and take over. "I've already won this battle for you,"

God told them. In fact, God says in Deuteronomy 1:20–21, **"'I said to you, "You have come to the hill country of the Amorites which the Lord our God is about to give us. See, the Lord your God has placed the land before you; go up, take possession, as the Lord, the God of your fathers, has spoken to you. Do not fear or be dismayed."'"**

In other words, "Don't doubt. You will win the battles. You will have the victory. God will take this land for you. Now get after it!" But, of course, lack of faith had their feet paralyzed, and they stayed where they were. Later God added, **"Yet you were not willing to go up, but rebelled against the command of the Lord your God. . . . But for all this, you did not trust the Lord your God"** (verses 26, 32). There's the bottom line: The reason they didn't go up and take the land was because they couldn't trust God.

They failed the test because they wouldn't trust God.

Now what's God going to do?

Cast them off, right? Wrong! God loves them, and so He gives them another opportunity to trust Him. That's where we are in Numbers 13. Plan A was, "Go take it." Plan B was, "All right, all right. I know you're weak, but I love you. I'm a God of grace. We'll send in some spies. They'll bring back a good report and then you'll be fired up with faith and you'll go get this done."

So God sent them in: **"Then the Lord spoke to Moses saying, 'Send out for yourself men so that they may spy out the land of Canaan, which I am going to give to the sons of Israel; you shall send a man from each of their fathers' tribes, every one a leader among them'"** (13:1). Here were the Navy Seals, spiritually speaking, the cream of the crop. God instructed Moses to handpick a twelve-man reconnaissance team to go behind enemy lines and spy on the land.

"So Moses sent them from the wilderness of Paran at the command of the Lord, all of them men who were heads of the sons of

Israel" (13:3). Up they went for a sneak preview of the Promised Land. God was so faithful to provide that opportunity. They went to spy out the land, return with a scouting report, and then the people would have a choice. They could go up by faith and possess the land, or be filled with doubt and go back into the wilderness. God was saying, in effect,

"Are you going to trust Me—or doubt Me?"

Think about how often in life it really comes right down to that. Am I going to trust God? Or am I not going to trust God?

It was really a choice that they were making. But more than a choice, they were expressing an attitude. Doubt is an attitude; faith is an attitude. Remember that attitudes are patterns of thinking formed over a long period of time. Maybe your life has been about doubting for so long that it has hardened into an attitude. Even if you've trusted Christ for your conversion and forgiveness of sins, maybe you've continued to practice doubt. Maybe you don't really know how to lay hold of and embrace the promises of God as the fuel for your own victory. It's so important that each of us learns that lesson.

Faith is not just a part of the Christian life . . .

That's right! Faith is not a part of the Christian life . . . it's the whole thing! Faith isn't like love and joy and hope. Faith isn't something to add to your spiritual arsenal. Faith *is* the gun that fires the bullet! Faith is everything! If you can't trust God; if you can't lay hold of His promises, expect a lot of defeat in your life. We'll say a lot more about this in the next chapter, which will be entirely about faith!

The thing about faith is that you can't tell by looking at a person how much faith he or she really has. Faith in a person is like water in a bucket—you find out how much is inside when you bump it. When circumstances bump you, you spill what you're full of.

What are you full of? If you're filled with faith, then faith comes out. If you're filled with doubt, and circumstances bump you, *doubt* comes out. God places regular tests of faith in front of His children.

Splashes!

Maybe you've had a reversal at work with a bad quarter, and the sales are way off. Bump! It's a test. What spilled? Doubt or faith? Maybe you got some bad news from the doctor, and you're going for some special tests. It seems like dark clouds are gathering on the horizon. Bump! What splashed out of you? "Oh, this is the end! Oh, no! Oh, no!" Or was it: "God is good! God is faithful! I'm going to continue to trust Him no matter what."

Maybe you have a child who is resisting and rebelling and breaking your heart and pressing you constantly. Bump! When you're bumped, you spill what you're full of. If you're filled with faith, that's what comes out. If you're filled with doubt, that's what comes out.

It's one or the other: faith or doubt. Bumps are going to happen. You will be tested. The purpose of the test isn't just to reveal your faith; it's also to refine your faith. God doesn't test your faith so He can know how much is there—He already knows. He tests your faith so that you can know how much is there and see it grow. Every good thing God wants to give to us comes through the funnel of faith. He refines our faith because He loves us and wants to bless us more and more.

PRINCIPLE TWO:
THE CIRCUMSTANCES OF LIFE
WILL EITHER SHRINK OR STRETCH YOUR FAITH

Numbers 13:4–16 describes the twelve men who were chosen and sent out. Then in verses 17 and 18, Moses gave the men their marching orders: **"Go up there into the Negev; then go up into the hill country. See what the land is like."**

Twelve people, all going to see the same thing. But God wants to see *how* they will see it.

> "See what the land is like, and whether the people who live in it are strong or weak, whether they are few or many. How is the land in which they live, is it good or bad? And how are the cities in which they live, are they like open camps or with fortifications? How is the land, is it fat or lean? Are there trees in it or not? Make an effort then to get some of the fruit of the land." Now the time was the time of the first ripe grapes. (verses 18–20)

What happened to the spies? They saw a lot: strong cities, power-ful armies, and impressive giants. The also saw evidence of abundance. But *how* did they see it all? Did they see it through the eyes of faith? Did they rely on the confidence that God had built into their lives? Or did they see it through the eyes of doubt? Forty years later, when Moses reviewed these events in Deuteronomy 1, he pointed out what God said: **"Then I said to you, "Do not be shocked nor fear them** [that's the people in the land when you see them]. **The Lord your God who goes before you will Himself fight on your behalf, just as He did for you in Egypt before your eyes, and in the wilderness where you saw how the Lord your God carried you, just as a man carries his son""** (verses 29–31). How does a man carry his son? If your son were to fall and be hurt or to break his leg or to be deeply injured, how do you pick up your son and carry him? With great tenderness, love, and attention. Yet how did the spies respond? **"But for all this, you did not trust the Lord your God"** (verse 32).

So the things the spies saw would either shrink their faith or stretch their faith. I wonder, can you identify what might be going on in your life that's shrinking or stretching your faith? God places those regular tests in front of us, doesn't He? Either we get closer to Him and more filled with faith, or we get further away from Him and more filled with doubt.

In 1988, Kathy and I were living at Trinity International University, where I was a seminary student. On February 3 Kathy gave birth to our middle child, Landon. The delivery went on schedule without complications. Landon was born late that night in Highland Park Hospital. After all the excitement, I went home to catch some sleep. When I came back to the hospital the next morning, Kathy was standing there crying, with packed suitcase in her hand. Landon was not there.

"What's wrong?" I asked. She explained that in the middle of the night the medical staff discovered a problem they had missed at delivery. Landon was born with something called a diaphragmatic hernia, which means his diaphragm didn't close together while he was developing. At birth, his intestines were all up in the left side of his chest, and his heart was pushed over on his right side. One of his lungs was only 50 percent developed; the other was hardly formed at all. The doctor told us 88 percent of the babies born with that condition die within the first twenty-four hours. It's a rare and very serious birth challenge.

In the middle of the night, Landon had experienced breathing problems. He started to turn blue. The nurses, thank God, were paying attention. They rushed him by helicopter to Lutheran General Hospital immediately, where they did emergency surgery. They repositioned his intestines and closed up his diaphragm. But he was still struggling to breathe. There were many procedures ahead.

We rushed to Landon's side. Most of the babies that survive this complication spend three to four months in intensive care. Have you ever been in a newborn intensive care unit? It's a very sad place. I walked down rows and rows of babies in these small glass trays, lying helplessly under heat lamps. Then I saw Landon.

I saw my son lying there covered with bandages, wires, and tubes.

So much had changed in a few hours! God places regular tests of faith in front of His children.

I'll never forget the moments after we got in our van outside Lutheran General, just before we went home. I took Kathy's hand and said, "We need to pray about this." They had told us before we went to our car that Landon might not live through the night. Of course, we didn't know. I remember praying, "God, You are good. We trust You. 'The Lord [gives] and the Lord [takes] away. Blessed be the name of the Lord,'" recalling the words of Job 1:21.

Over the next few days, the doctors performed two additional surgeries. The last procedure required a tube in Landon's side. The doctors were trying to create a vacuum in his chest cavity in order to pull his heart back over a little bit in the right direction. They were planning more surgery.

Of course, I was right in the middle of everything and trying to figure out what was going on. I watched a "Dr. Jay" put Landon's X ray up on the screen; he looked at it intently. After a moment, he pulled it down, and checked the name. He then put it back up on the screen again. He turned to his intern and asked, "What is wrong with this baby?"

The intern looked and looked and said, "I don't know."

"Right! Nothing!" the doctor replied. Why he seemed aggravated I am not sure, but he slammed the light off with his fist, turned on his heel, and walked out. I knew he had seen us praying over Landon and committing him to the Lord.

The Lord had miraculously healed Landon. Even I could see on the X ray that his two tiny lungs were filled with air, and everything was back in place. I thought of all the wonderful people from the Arlington Heights Evangelical Free Church, where I was on staff, who had been praying along with people all over the country.

The Lord just flat out healed him! No doubt about it.

Of course, he's all boy now and thirteen years old, full of energy and vitality for the Lord. I know very well that the medical crisis could have gone in a lot of different directions. The stretching of our faith could have gone a different way. I could tell you other stories about when I trusted God just as much, but things didn't turn out the way I thought they should. All that to say this: God places regular tests of faith in front of us.

In those critical moments, you make a crucial choice: Either you let your faith grow and flourish, or you choose doubt. Choose the first, and you'll add another story to your file of the faithfulness and the goodness of God; choose the second, and your faith will shrivel up like a piece of leather in the wilderness sun. The circumstances of life either shrink or stretch your faith. Either you get better or you get bitter. The choice is yours. Think about the hardest thing that's going on in your life right now. Ask yourself the question, "Is this circumstance shrinking or stretching my faith?"

PRINCIPLE THREE:
DOUBT SEES THE OBSTACLES;
FAITH SEES THE OPPORTUNITIES

Two people can look at the same situation and see the exact opposite. One heart filled with doubt focuses only on the obstacles. Another person, looking at the same situation, not filled with doubt but filled with faith, can only see the opportunity. Notice Numbers 13:25–26. The spies came back. **"When they returned from spying out the land, at the end of forty days** [that must have been quite a wait], **they proceeded to come to Moses and Aaron and to all the congregation of the sons of Israel."** Imagine the anticipation as the people saw the spies approaching. They must have been so fired up—at least, the people who were filled with faith. They were like, "It's time to move!"

Unfortunately, everybody wasn't quite seeing it that way—not even the spies! The twelve **"brought back word to them and to all the congregation and showed them the fruit of the land. Thus they told him, and said, 'We went in to the land where you sent** us; and it certainly does flow with milk and honey, and this is its fruit'" (verses 26–27).

But then the majority spokesperson opened up his mouth and said this awful word, "Nevertheless" (verse 28). The word literally means *except that*. In other words, "We went into the land. It certainly does flow with milk and honey. Look at the size of these grapes. Nevertheless . . ."

And then, the picture suddenly changed. Their report got really negative. Doubt sees the obstacles; faith sees the opportunities. Notice verse 28. "**'Nevertheless, the people who live in the land are strong, and the cities are fortified and very large; and moreover, we saw the descendants of Anak there.'**" Agh! I guess that was a scary thing to them. "**Amalek is living in the land of the Negev and the Hittites and the Jebusites and the Amorites** [and probably the termites, too] **are living in the hill country, and the Canaanites are living by the sea and by the side of the Jordan'**" (verse 29).

The bottom line is that they listed all of these armies with reputations. But the problem never was the giants or the cities or the weapons; the problem was their attitude:

They had a lack of confidence that God would keep His promises.

But not everyone lacked confidence in God. Notice in verse 30, "**Then Caleb** [and Joshua, the two men filled with faith] **quieted the people.**" Why did he have to quiet the people down? They were *murmuring*. They were freaking out; they were saying, "What on earth!" So Caleb had to calm the people. "**Then Caleb quieted the people before Moses and said, 'We should by all means go up and take possession of it, for we shall surely overcome it.'**" Wow! Great faith! Then there was this doubting response: "**But the men who had gone up with him said, 'We are not able to go up against the people, for they are too strong for us.'**" Faith sees the opportunity;

doubt sees the obstacles. What you see is what you get!

I like this poem because it helps me think about the difference between faith and doubt.[1]

> *Doubt sees the obstacles.*
> *Faith sees the way.*
> *Doubt sees the darkest night.*
> *Faith sees the way.*
> *Doubt dreads to take a step.*
> *Faith soars on high.*
> *Doubt questions, "Who believes?"*
> *Faith answers, "I."*
> GOSPEL BANNER

It's just as simple as that.

"No, no," I hear people say. "It can't be that simple."

Yes, it is. It's a choice of attitudes. Doubt sees the obstacles; faith sees the opportunities. Doubt and faith are patterns of thinking formed over a long period of time.

Now doubt has many disguises. It doesn't always come out like a doubt thing; it operates undercover. You have to pull back the disguise to see that the real problem is doubt. So, what does doubt use for a disguise? Here are five (but there are more):

- *Fear.* "God won't protect me." Do you remember what doubt is? Doubt is a lack of confidence or assurance that God will keep His promises. So one of the disguises of doubt is fear.

- *Anxiety.* "Oh! What's up ahead? What's going to happen to me? Will I be OK?" That anxiety is doubt—that's what it is.

- *Frustration and anger.* "God won't solve this problem on my agenda in my time!" Right . . . You're doubting God.

■ *Withdrawal.* That's pulling back from others or putting up a wall. Not willing to draw close to the Lord. Pulling back spiritually. Why? A growing attitude of doubt.

■ *Bitterness.* "God won't heal this hurt in me." You're so bitter and unforgiving. You're doubting the goodness of God. You've taken that on yourself, and you're keeping your heart all stirred up about it because you don't believe that God can really heal that thing that was done to you. But He can. And He wants to. Just let Him.

Did you know . . .

Thomas Gets a Bum Rap!

"God won't answer my questions." Yes, He will. Just check in with Thomas (John 11:16; 14:5; 20:24–29). He's called a doubter, but a little unfairly. Sure, he had doubts and questions, but his heart was willing to believe. God will go a long way in revealing Himself to a person who honestly wants answers. Do you really want answers? God has made some promises. Would you agree? And if we have confidence in God, we're going to have Promised Land living. But if we're filled with doubt, we're going to live in the wilderness. In fact, *those who choose doubting as their lifestyle will spend their lifetimes in the wilderness.* God was getting ready to send a whole bunch of them into the wilderness back in Numbers, partly because of the doubt that they expressed by murmuring.

"Fine," you say. "You nailed it—I have a lot of doubts. Fine, you blew their cover as fear, anger, and stuff. *But* if you were in my situation—if you could come this week and be with me where I live . . ."

Don't Miss This . . .

Those who study human experience agree that life is really not about the difference between our circumstances. The details may vary, but we all live with highs and lows. Advice columnist Ann Landers gets this when she says, "Opportunities are often disguised as hard work. Most people fail to recognize them." Those who study human experience agree almost universally that life is 10 percent what happens to you and 90 percent how you choose to respond. Seminary president and author Charles Swindoll, one of the most gifted Bible teachers in our generation, wrote:

> Words can never adequately convey the incredible impact of our attitude. . . . I believe the single most important decision I can make on a day-to-day basis is my attitude choice. It's more important than my past. It's more important than my education or my bankroll or my success or my failures. My attitude choice is more important than my fame or my pain or what others think or say about me or my position or my circumstances. Attitudes keep me going or cripple my progress. Attitude alone fuels my fire or assaults my hope. When my attitude is right, there is no barrier too high nor valley too deep nor dream too extreme nor challenge too great for me.[2]

Now that's not some possibility, positive-thinking nonsense message. That's the message of genuine biblical attitudes.

You may say, "But I don't want to doubt. I know I'm a doubter. But why do I doubt?" Consider principle four:

PRINCIPLE FOUR:
WHEN SURROUNDED BY DOUBTERS,
DOUBTING COMES EASILY

What a night of victory that could have been, after those spies came back from the land. The people should have been whooping it up. "We're taking the land!" They should have been singing, "All things are possible! All things are possible!" They should have had the campfire going. They should have been rejoicing, "This is going to be the greatest thing in the world! We're going to take the land God has promised! He has never let us down before! Do you remember the plagues? Remember the Red Sea? Remember Mount Sinai?"

They should have been going crazy with confidence in God because of all that they had seen. But they weren't. You say, "Why?" When surrounded by doubters, doubting comes easily.

"Then all the congregation lifted up their voices and cried, and the people wept that night" (Numbers 14:1). Now that ought to make *you* cry. Then what? **"All the sons of Israel grumbled . . ."** (verse 2). Attitude problems spoke up. **"All the sons of Israel grumbled against Moses and Aaron; and the whole congregation said to them, 'Would that we had died in the land of Egypt! Or would that we had died in this wilderness!'"** Notice that this wasn't a few doubtful people. "All the congregation," (verse 1) and "all the sons of Israel" (verse 2)—the whole congregation doubted in unison. When surrounded by doubters, doubting comes easily.

Doubt catches some people by surprise.

Christians are sometimes genuinely puzzled, asking, "Why do I find it so hard to trust God? God's been faithful to me. God's provided for me. He's done a lot of good things in my life!" I find the reason usually is this: Instead of talking often about God's grace and recalling His miracles and thinking about all that He has done, people choose to focus on the obstacles, and they welcome doubt. Once you get that wave going in a group, everybody rides it.

This doubting comes easily when all my best friends, my coworkers, and my neighbors are people who don't love the Lord Jesus and are not filled with faith, or I'm continually surrounded by doubters.

This is true at every age, but it is especially critical in the junior high and high school years. One of the reasons Christian parents need to give special attention to their students spending time with other students in a biblically age-appropriate environment is that they spend so much time in school with people who will not encourage their faith. You're kidding yourself if you're thinking that your child is going to grow up to be a kingdom kid when he's surrounded by people whose lives are filled with doubt and rebellion against God.

I don't understand why parents who won't let their kids choose their diets, their study habits, or what they're going to watch on television, *do* let their children choose what music they listen to, who their friends are, and what their extracurricular activities are going to be. If he or she listens to the wrong music, has the wrong friends, and spends extra-curricular time with doubters, you've got a world of hurt up ahead.

You think, "What difference does it really make to get my kid over to the church to have some fun with other Christian kids?" The clue phone is ringing! It's all about the relationships—not just the biblical content! Those primary relationships with other believers are foundational to faith. Let's wake up to the reality that our kids are hemorrhaging in the world, because we have not clued in to the influences that are stealing their hearts from God.

Why does doubt come so easily?

Here are four reasons doubts come so easily:

1. *Doubting is contagious.* It's easier to catch than the common cold.

2. *Doubting is passive.* Faith requires action; doubting does not. Nobody ever wakes up in the morning and says, "I bet today's going to be a great day for doubting. I'm going to doubt God all day today." Doubting is what takes over when you do nothing. Faith requires doing something; doubting is doing nothing, and it takes you nowhere good. If you aren't busy and involved, you are doubting. You have to get focused and active to be filled with faith.

3. *Doubting satisfies our tendency towards self-protection.* Nobody likes to be wrong. "What if we go all the way up into the land and we trust God for great victories and we don't get it? We're going to look really dumb. Aren't we? There's going to be egg on our faces. We're going to end up in the cemetery outside Jericho. It's just easier not to trust God. I'll just lower my expectations. Then I won't be disappointed." But you are disappointed. Aren't you? Because of your doubt.

4. *Doubters are easier to find than friends of faith.* How many real, genuine friends of faith do you have—I mean people who speak the Word of God into your life and fire you up spiritually? That's why I'm so grieved for our students who are trying to build a foundation for their life spiritually, but they don't have any friends of faith. It's absolutely critical that we cherish those people in our lives and develop those relationships, because friends of faith are absolutely critical.

PRINCIPLE FIVE:
IT'S A SHORT JOURNEY
FROM DOUBT TO DESPAIR

Doubt never stands still. It's always sliding somewhere worse. It's a short journey from doubt to despair. It's not weeks, nor months; it's just a matter of a few days. A crisis can make the trip very short. In the case of the children of Israel, who were really good at doubting, reaching despair was a matter of only a few hours. Notice what started to come forth from their lips, **"The whole congregation said to them, 'Would that we had died in the land of Egypt! Or would that we had died in this wilderness!'"** (Numbers 14:2). They're going to get their wish on that pretty soon. Then they said these tragic words: **"'Why is the Lord bringing us into this land, to fall by the sword? Our wives and our little ones will become plunder; would it not**

be better for us to return to Egypt?' So they said to one another, 'Let us appoint a leader and return to Egypt'" (verses 3–4).

They're saying in effect here, "We're going back to Egypt! God will not give us victory. He will allow us to be killed in battle. He will allow our wives and children to be brutalized. We would be better off as slaves in Egypt, and mutiny against Moses is a good first step in that direction." That was just like spit in the face of God and all of the faithfulness that He had provided for them.

Is that thinking messed up or what? Talk about a bad plan! Here's why:

First, it was totally contrary to their amazing experiences. They had forgotten God's provision: a pillar of cloud by day, a pillar of fire by night, dividing the Red Sea, daily manna, and on and on. Had God not provided for them every step of the way?

Second, if they did turn around and go back to Egypt, would God continue to provide manna for them on the way back across the Sinai? I think not.

Third, what if by some chance they did get back to Egypt? They had drowned all of Pharoah's army in the Red Sea. Now would they walk back into Egypt saying, "Sorry about all of that. We want to make up now"? Yeah—sure!

But here's the main reason it was a bad plan. It rose from desperation. Write in the margin of your Bible there beside verses 3 and 4 the word "desperate." *Desperate plans come from despairing hearts.* I've heard some pretty desperate plans from some people in my time. "You're going to do what?" It's a short journey from doubt to despair, where the future is not bright like the promises of God. They made desperate plans because, like a tumor growing out of control, their doubt had ballooned into despair.

UP CLOSE AND PERSONAL

I have never, *ever* trusted God and regretted it. Sometimes the challenges have been huge, like Landon's birth. Others have been momentary choices when I've decided to trust God and keep on going. I have never trusted God and regretted it. But I can think of many times when I have chosen doubt and missed incredible opportunities to prove the faithfulness of God. Today I need faith more than ever. I have a church of more than four thousand people to care for, two daughter churches, and radio and writing ministries that place many demands for leadership, material, and financial support. I have a wife, and three children at or approaching the teen years. Like you, I have my own issues of faith and discipline and self-control. All that is to say that I have much today about which I need to be on my knees and trusting God for. I know you could come up with a similar list. I'm guessing that as you read this chapter you have seen the danger of doubt not only in the children of Israel but also in your own life.

LET'S TALK SOLUTION

Time again for some soul-searching questions. We need to determine the extent of this wilderness attitude in our lives.

1. *Am I a doubting person?* This is where the Word of God needs to intersect an honest heart. That's how change happens. Am I a doubting person? Maybe the answer is yes. Maybe the answer is sometimes. Maybe the answer is too often. In spiritual matters, doubting is death.

2. *Am I reaping the consequences in my relationship with God?* You say, "Well I'm not a faith person. I'm a 'see it to believe it' person. I've always been that way. I am a realist. You can have your church thing, but I only believe what I see." You're not going to see very much then. Jesus said in John 11:40, **"If you believe, you will see the glory of God."** In spiritual matters, it's not I'll-believe-it-when-I-see-it, it's I'll-see-it-when-I-believe-it. That's how we came to Christ. We didn't have all the promises in the bank when we trusted Christ. It was a step of faith. Every step with God has that same pattern.

3. *Am I willing to repent?* Am I willing to turn from the pattern of unbelief that has produced this wilderness heart of mine? We must ask God to grow a heart of faith, because we cannot do it on our own. Remember that faith is a gift (see Ephesians 2:8); we can't cultivate this ourselves. But we can go to God humbly as the disciples did and say, "Lord, increase our faith." Are you ready to pray that prayer right now?

Look Up

Lord, thank You today that You are a good and a faithful God. Oh, God, increase my faith! Give me this day and this week a greater capacity to trust You, to rest in Your promises. Lord, help me to see You related to the very circumstances I face. Might I see how all that comes our way and how we handle it is directly related to our willingness to rest in Your promises and walk closely with You. Grant that kind of victory to me. May this day be different because of what I've prayed and acknowledged before You in this moment. And I promise to give You thanks and praise and glory for Your care and compassion for my life. In Jesus' name I ask these things. Amen.

NOTES

1. As quoted in Paul Lee Tan, *Encyclopedia of 7,700 Illustrations* (Rockville, Md.: Assurance, 1979), 404.

2. Charles Swindoll, *Strengthening Your Grip* (Waco, Tex.: Word, 1990), 38.

8

. . . WITH AN ATTITUDE OF FAITH

HEBREWS 11

SAY IT IN A SENTENCE:

Only when faith replaces doubt in the life of a believer can the joy of knowing God become a reality.

Wow, you're still reading, excellent! You must be really serious about changing your attitude. Know that an incredible blessing awaits if you persevere. I have been working on my attitudes, too. And I've found an increased sense of joy and the Lord's presence as I put off the attitudes that make life like a wilderness and put on the attitudes that bring peace and satisfaction regardless of my momentary circumstance.

Yes, great blessings await as we begin this important chapter. I encourage you to pray even as you read: "Lord, increase my faith!"

Remember that faith is an attitude—it's Promised Land attitude number four—and that each attitude is a pattern of thinking formed over a long period of time. We may *decide* to change during a crisis, but we *actually change* moment-by-moment in the process of living. Every decision we make contributes in some way to the pattern of thinking that becomes your attitude. That includes the attitude of faith.

WHAT IS FAITH?

Now let's learn how to develop this great Promised Land attitude—faith. We begin by ridding ourselves of the faulty notions of faith:

- Faith is not an ostrich, head-in-the-sand and denying the obvious or the inevitable. It's not pretending that something is real when deep down you really don't believe it. That's fear, not faith.

- Faith is not anti-intellectual, either. Faith is not a warm feeling that requires you to check your intellect at the door. That's feeling, not faith.

- Faith is not a stained-glass and dreamy sort of *Little-House-on-the-Prairie* escapism. I cannot stay in church again, hiding from reality, ignoring the world around me. That's fluff, not faith.

- Faith is not some motivational seminar, with some high-powered guru calling for breathing exercises or self-relaxation and self-confidence, telling you to picture a better future. That's fad, not faith.

- It's not some stupid positive mental attitude, a you-have-to-keep-believing thing. It's not ignoring the pain and embracing optimism regardless of the evidence in front of you. That's foolishness, not faith.

Now hear this:

Faith is rooted in a God who is real!

Faith finds itself founded on a person—the creator God of the universe. The one who created the universe is with you this moment! He loves you. Faith is active confidence in the God who has revealed Himself, not some presumptuous uncertainty about a someone, somewhere out in space. God has proven Himself real again and again, and if you've not experienced His reality, you can.

Everyone has faith—the capacity to trust. We don't stay alive long without it. But what we base our faith on is ultimately what makes the difference. The faith I'm talking about here is the faith that turns away from placing our trust in circumstances or our own abilities, which always fail us. We're saying, "My life goes much better when I place my deepest faith and confidence in a sovereign God." That's the faith that Jesus invites us to place in Him. That's the faith that is so powerfully illustrated by Hebrews 11.

THE PRESCRIPTION OF FAITH

What does faith mean, exactly? Hebrews 11:1 gives us an excellent definition of faith. I like the *New King James Version:* **"Now faith is the substance of things hoped for, the evidence of things not seen."** I love those two words—*substance* and *evidence*. They comprise the prescription of faith. Let's look at them.

First of all, *faith is substance.* Most people don't look at it that way. They look at faith as very ethereal. It's not; faith has substance. We practice such faith often in the physical world. Pick up the phone and call a department store to place an order, and they'll ask for your credit card number. Then they'll probably mail you a receipt. You don't have the product; you only have a receipt. But with it in hand, you wait confidently for the product you ordered to come. That receipt in hand—

that's the substance that you hold on to while you wait for the thing that you've ordered.

Same thing with a hotel reservation: They give you a confirmation number, and with that number, you have faith a room is reserved and waiting for you. Or you pay a bill over the Internet. The first time I did that, it was so scary. What's going to happen? The money came out of my account. They gave me this long number with seventy-four digits and said, "This is your order number." As I waited to see if the money I sent made it, I hung on to that number. The number is the substance that I hang on to while I wait to see if the transaction is completed.

Now the spiritual world operates under similar principles. I take a need before God in prayer. My faith, my active confidence in God, is the thing that I hold on to while I wait to see how the Lord is going to answer what I've brought before Him. If I have a painful circumstance in my life and I'm asking God to change that or to change me, my faith is the substance that I hold while I wait upon God to do the things that I've asked Him to do. So faith is substance.

Faith is also evidence. The reason that I know the product that I ordered is going to come to my front door is because I've done it before. So I don't feel like a fool every time I walk to my front door and check to see if they have delivered the product yet. I don't feel stupid, or presumptuous, or even silly, because I've done this before and I know how it works. So my past experiences are the evidence that I hold on to while I wait for the doorbell to ring.

Now, in the same sense, faith is the evidence that God is faithful. Did you know that we're not the first people to trust God? Psalm 90:1 says, **"Lord, You have been our dwelling place in all generations."** People have been trusting God for thousands of years. This is not a foolish thing to do. The faithfulness of God—not just in generations past, but in my own life—provides me with evidence.

I'm sure you can think of specific times and places where God has come through for you, showing Himself faithful. He has met your needs in the past. That's the evidence of things not yet seen for the future. We know how He works—we've seen it before—so we don't feel foolish waiting upon God to meet our needs again. Faith is active confidence in God. Faith is substance and evidence.

STATEMENT OF FAITH

Faith is so integral to the Christian life that over the years we've boiled it down to a very practical definition. This is our definition of faith: *Faith is believing the Word of God and acting upon it, no matter how I feel, because God promises a good result.*

Let's break that definition down, so you can see how it will work in very practical ways in your life.

Faith is believing the Word of God.

That word *believing* is not "I hope so" as in, "Wouldn't it be nice if . . ." It's much more than that. Believing is a lot more than just shallow hope. Believing is, "I have all my eggs in that basket. I've got all my dreams in that place. I'm 100 percent in, and I don't have an escape route." That's faith.

But faith is not believing in a vacuum; it's *belief based on the Word of God.* That's the key. Faith in *what?* My faith is in the Word of God! I'm not believing the newspaper or the television or my neighbor or my boss. God wrote a Book! I believe in a God who wrote a trustworthy Book.

I know the Bible is trustworthy because God cannot lie. The apostle Paul wrote in Titus 1:2, **"In the hope of eternal life, which God, who cannot lie, promised long ages ago."** Think about that: God cannot lie! Not *won't* lie, like the promises we always hear. Not *doesn't* lie, as in could but hasn't yet. *Cannot* lie! Everything God has said is true, and it will happen exactly as He said. So it's not foolish at all to put your confidence in a God like that. Faith is believing the Word of

God. You say, "Well, if I *think* I believe—is that faith?"

Here's how you'll know for sure:

By *acting* upon it. Faith without works is dead.

Genuine faith always downloads into life. There are all kinds of things that we *say* we believe—but must not really believe them because they don't show up in the way we live. A physics professor who was teaching his class about pendulums and expended energy decided to prove a point with a demonstration. He had told his students that an untouched pendulum will always swing in an ever-decreasing series of arcs. If you start a pendulum swinging from a certain height, it never swings as high on the return trip. The teacher wrote out the mathematical formula, and he drew the picture for the whole class. He asked for questions and encouraged the class to tell him if they had any doubts about the principle. Then he asked, "How many people believe that this is actually true—that a pendulum swings in an ever-decreasing series of arcs?"

The class responded unanimously, "Oh, we believe that!" "Yes, of course, we believe that."

"Well, that's perfect," said the teacher. "You're now ready for the demonstration." He walked over to a large steel ball hanging from a chain that was attached to one of the ceiling joists and reaching almost to the floor. To one side was an empty chair.

"This is how the demonstration will work," he said. "Someone will sit in this chair. I'll move the ball up to barely touch their chin and then I'm going to let it go. It's going to swing away, down, across the room, and then back toward you. How many people believe that this ball will swing in ever-decreasing series of arcs, so there is no danger of getting hit as it swings back?" They all put their hands up.

"Who will be first to sit in the chair?" Guess how many people sat in the chair? Nobody.[1] Clearly, there's a difference between saying you believe something and really believing it.

Now that's a critical point, because it's only when you sit in the chair—it's only when you're willing to put yourself at risk—that faith is active with God. Only when you come to the place where you say, "I know God's grace is my only option—I've cut off all other backup plans. I have thrown myself upon God's mercy."

"Nothing in my hands I bring, only to Your cross I cling," is the way the old hymn writer put it. That's saving faith, and nothing short of that is making it with God. Faith is how we come to God and faith is how we grow in Him, too. Faith is believing the Word of God and acting upon it. The litmus test of genuine faith is "Do I act upon what I say I believe?"

ACTING UPON OUR FAITH MEANS . . .

Acting upon our faith will impact every area of life, including our families, our finances, and even our sense of fulfillment. Let's start with the family need. Let's say that you're a wife, and maybe your husband is not a believer. As a follower of Christ, you want more than anything for your home to be centered on God. Yet your spouse isn't following the Lord. Maybe he goes to church with you sometimes—or maybe never. You're like, "What should I do about this? How should I handle this? How can I influence him?"

God's Word tells you how to handle it. In 1 Peter 3:1–5, the Scripture says that the unbelieving husband can be won through the conduct of the wife *without her speaking a word*. Now if you always shove taped sermons at him, give him Christian books to read (even this one), and plead with him to come to church, you are following your own well-meaning plan. But if you follow God's plan in 1 Peter 3:1, you will **be submissive to your own husbands so that even if any of them are disobedient to the word, they may be won without a word by the behavior of their wives.**

If you start the evenings with, "You've got to watch this video with me," and continually hassle him by saying, "When are you going to accept the Lord?" you have a problem, and it isn't your husband. You can say what you want to say about whether you believe the Word of God, but your actions say that you don't. When we believe the Word of God and act upon it, that's real faith.

In family matters, an active faith means we will trust God to work through a wayward child or even an unbelieving spouse. In finances, we will trust God to meet our daily needs, while giving tithes and offerings; we believe the Scripture that says, **"God is able to make all grace abound to you, so that always having all sufficiency in everything, you may have an abundance for every good deed"** (2 Corinthians 9:8).

What about the need for fulfillment? Maybe you're reading this with an overwhelming sense of loneliness. Maybe you're just discouraged about your life and your direction. You're not sure where to turn, and you're not sure what to pursue. What will be the answer for you?

Sadly, many who claim to be Jesus' followers don't turn to Him to meet their deepest life needs. They turn to a particular substance, or relationship. They expect things or experiences to fill that emptiness inside. But that's actually a lack of faith in our Savior who said, **"Come to Me, all who are weary and heavy-laden, and I will give you rest"** (Matthew 11:28). As you pursue the answer to the longings of your heart, faith determines where and to whom you turn.

Where do you believe the answers to life's deepest perplexities are really found? Faith is believing the Word of God and acting upon it.

The next phrase in our definition of faith is: *no matter how I feel.*

That's critical. Like the woman I just described who wants like *anything* just to talk to her husband about Christ. She's having a hard time believing that she can't be a big part of the solution by telling him some stuff! She feels that she has to say some things or he will never change. But faith discounts how we feel and boldly acts upon the Word of God.

Maybe you're at a place of real financial hardship, and you feel giving a consistent tithe or offering to your church is unrealistic. I can understand the fears that limited funds can bring. When Kathy and I were in Bible college, we didn't have two dimes to rub together. We had $180–$200 per week of expenses, and I was making $150 a week as a youth pastor. I can remember writing that little tithing check for $15 and thinking to myself, "What am I doing this for? I'm just getting further behind."

Those were real feelings of fear and frustration, but they were nonsense compared to God's faithfulness. God was teaching us some very important lessons about life. I learned that God is true to His Word and can be trusted to meet all of our needs if, by faith, we choose obedience and refuse to be guided by emotion. Here's the best part of faith: We can act upon our faith, no matter how we feel, because . . .

God promises a good result.

Here are four questions I've heard from those struggling with faith:

- "Why would I do what God tells me?"

- "Why would I wait on God to bring my husband to Christ?"

- "Why would I give of my finances when I have so many debts?"

- "Why would I invest my energies in following hard after the Lord when I feel like my life is so empty and meaningless?"

The answer to each question is the same: *Because God promises a good result.* That's faith—believing the Word of God and acting upon it no matter how I feel, because God promises a good result.

THE BIBLE'S GRAND VIEW OF FAITH

I have a long-established habit of preaching from one passage of Scripture. We go through it carefully; we give attention to the details of God's Word. But I also know that sometimes it helps to do a flyby of a Bible section to get that sort of overview feel. Sometimes you can study the details of God's Word in such a way that you can't see the forest for the trees. I'm telling you the forest, in the Bible, is faith. I usually want to walk up to one tree and describe it in detail. In the next few paragraphs, I want you see the flyby—the big picture.

Hebrews 11 offers a great landscape of faith to fly over. That chapter is full of what I call the "redwoods of faith," the giants of the Old Testament. Their lives illustrate the prominence of faith. Hebrews 11:2–3 gets us airborne with a powerful challenge about the way faith looks at everything: **"For by it the men of old gained approval. By faith we understand that the worlds were prepared by the word of God, so that what is seen was not made out of things which are visible."** Have you ever read a clearer answer to the lie of evolution than that statement, **"What is seen** [in the universe] **was not made out of things which are visible"**?

Catch a glimpse of the forest of faithful ones!

Now let's enter the forest of faithful ones, as recorded in verses 4–39. The trees are majestic, and remain as reminders for us of a faithful God to those who trust Him.

In verses 4–7, we're reminded of the faith of Abel, Enoch, and Noah. Consider Noah, who **"by faith . . . prepared an ark"** (verse 7). Everybody was laughing at him. "What a fool you are! Dumb boat. What are you going to do with that? You're miles from a lake." Those comments must have hurt, but Noah ignored his feelings (remember, "no matter how I feel") and kept building by faith, because God had promised a good result. I am sure he became very discouraged at times, but he trusted God, and kept on keeping on. Verses 8–31 recount the faith of Abraham, Sarah, and other Old Testament believers, including the prostitute Rahab. Consider the list of these members of the Faith Hall of Fame in Hebrews 11:

- **"By faith Abraham . . . went out, not knowing where he was going"** (verse 8).

- **"By faith even Sarah herself received ability to conceive"** (verse 11).

- **"By faith Abraham, when he was tested, offered up Isaac"** (verse 17).

- **"By faith Jacob, as he was dying, blessed each of the sons of Joseph"** (verse 21).

- **"By faith Moses . . . refused to be called the son of Pharaoh's daughter"** (verse 24).

- **"By faith the walls of Jericho fell"** (verse 30).

- **"By faith Rahab the harlot did not perish"** (verse 31).

Beginning with verse 32, the author picked up speed in naming those people of God who were victorious by faith, including, **"Gideon, Barak, Samson, Jephthah, of David and Samuel and the prophets, who by faith conquered kingdoms, performed acts of righteousness, obtained promises, . . . escaped the edge of the sword, from weakness were made strong. . . . All these . . . gained approval through their faith"** (verses 32–34, 39).

It's clear the Bible commends and urges faith. The Old Testament word *barach* is translated *trust*. When you see *trust* in the Old Testament, that's the equivalent of *faith* in the New Testament. The word for *trust* (*believe* or *be faithful*) is found more than three hundred times in the New Testament.

For example, let's look briefly at the gospel of Matthew. As we do a "flyover" of Matthew, notice the prominent way that *faith* serves as the message of Scripture. Every good thing that God brings to us comes through the funnel of faith. Look at these quick references from the first of four Gospels:

- *Matthew 6.* Jesus teaches His followers that their lives should not be marked by anxiety nor concern about the matters of life but by faith in the God who provides for every need.

- *Matthew 8.* Jesus heals a leper who exhibits faith in Him. **"Lord, if You are willing, You can make me clean"** (verse 2). What a great prayer! In the same chapter, Jesus heals the servant of a centurion and marvels at the soldier's expression of faith: **"I have not found such great faith with anyone in Israel"** (verse 10). Later, Jesus rebukes the disciples for their lack of faith in the midst of a great storm: **"Why are you afraid, you men of little faith?"** (verse 26).

- *Matthew 9.* Seeing the faith of a paralytic and his friends, Jesus heals the man and forgives his sins. A little later, a woman who had been suffering from a hemorrhage for twelve years touches Jesus' cloak in faith and Jesus heals her instantly and says to her, **"Daughter, take courage; your faith has made you well"** (verse 22).

- *Matthew 13.* Jesus returns to His hometown but does not do many miracles there because of the people's unbelief.

- Matthew 14. Seeing Jesus walking on the sea, Peter gets out of the boat and walks toward Him. Then he starts to get frightened, and he sinks down. The Lord questions his faith and says, **"You of little faith, why did you doubt?"** (verse 31).

■ *Matthew 15.* A Canaanite woman implores Jesus to heal her demon-possessed daughter. Jesus answers her request, saying to her, **"O woman, your faith is great; it shall be done for you as you wish"** (verse 28).

■ *Matthew 16.* The disciples quietly discuss their lack of bread. Jesus questions their faith, saying again, **"'You men of little faith'"** (verse 8).

■ *Matthew 17.* The disciples are unable to cast a demon out of a young man. Jesus informs them that the reason they cannot is because of the little-ness of their faith.

■ *Matthew 21.* Jesus causes a fig tree to wither all at once and tells His disciples that they will be able to do even greater things **"'if you have faith and do not doubt'"** (verse 21).

CAN YOU SEE IT?

The message of faith permeates the New Testament; it's somewhere on every page and in every story. Every step with God is a step of faith. Every lesson learned is a lesson of faith. Every victory won is a victory by faith. That's the prominence of faith in the New Testament. It's on that basis that I say this: *Faith is not a part of the Christian life.*

Say what? That's right; faith is not a part of the Christian life. It's not like patience and kindness or other character traits. It's not one part among many other assorted components that may or may not be lacking in our lives at any one time. It's not like teaching or showing compassion or ministering or other Christian activities. It's not like worship or prayer or meditation or other actions that we take toward God. Those are all parts.

Faith, however, is not a part of the Christian life; *it's the whole thing.* Let me repeat that:

Faith is not a part of the Christian life; it's the whole thing.

The Christian life is a life of faith. Genuine believers trust God and exercise active confidence in God. They believe the Word of God and act upon it no matter how they feel, because God promises a good result. When I'm doing that, I'm going forward in a phenomenal way spiritually. When I'm not doing that, I'm backing up and losing ground and falling away from Him.

THE LOVE QUESTION

When I say that faith is the whole thing, Christians will often reply, "Well, what about love? I thought love was the whole thing." Usually they're thinking of or even refer to 1 Corinthians 13:13, **"Now abide faith, hope, and love, these three; but the greatest of these is love"** (NKJV).

If you study the context of 1 Corinthians 13:13, it is talking about the greatest element in our relationships with people. Love is the greatest thing relationally—the greatest thing as we would seek to impact and influence others. In that sense—as it relates to influencing others—love is greater than faith. But keep in mind that love builds on the foundation of faith. We can't even begin to love as Christians until we believe—until faith in Christ has bridged the gap between us and God. So in this way—as it relates to our basic relationship to God—faith is the greatest thing. The book of 1 John makes it very clear that if you say that you have a relationship with God, that you love God, but you don't love other people, you're lying (see especially 2:9; 4:20). So in reality, love for others flows out of our relationship with God.

No doubt about it. Faith is the greatest. That's why I say, "Faith is not a part of the Christian life; it's the whole thing." That's why Hebrews 11:6 says, **"Without faith it is impossible to please [God.]"** That's why the cry of the Reformation was *sola fide,* "by faith alone." Every good thing that God wants to bring to our lives comes through faith.

BEYOND PRESCRIPTION
AND PROMINENCE—POWER!

The last two verses of Hebrews 11 talk about *the power of faith.* We've defined faith and discovered its prominence in Scripture. Now we need to see faith's power. Hebrews 11:39 says, **"All these** [the people he's just listed], **having gained approval through their faith, did not receive what was promised."** In other words, they didn't understand the gospel the way we do. Verse 40 goes on, **"because God had provided something better for us."** We know about the Cross; we understand what Jesus did. The Cross had to happen, and the salvation God accomplished there covered all humanity past, present, and future.

The Old Testament believers looked forward to something by faith. We look back to something by faith. For them it was a promise; for us, what Christ did in dying and rising again and paying the penalty for our forgiveness is an established fact. Faith allowed all those people to be converted to God before the Cross. It allows all of us to be redeemed by looking back. Faith is a powerful force!

In fact, 1 John 5:4 says, **"This is the victory that has overcome the world—."** What is it? **"—our faith."** That's a great verse—one you want to get on the tip of your tongue.

How on earth does faith give us victory?

The apostle John had it right: "Faith is the victory." When I look at what I see, I am filled with doubt. But when I disregard what I see and focus my thoughts on a God who has promised to ultimately triumph; a God who said, **"'Vengeance is Mine, I will repay, says the Lord'"** (Romans 12:19), my small circumstances suddenly fit into a much bigger picture! Faith trusts a God who has promised to balance all the books of justice.

Maybe you're carrying a hurt or an injury or an injustice with you right now. Our faith is in a God who says, "I see that. I know that. You just sit still for a moment. Flip a few pages on your calendar by faith. I'll be on the scene, and I'll take care of that." So we wait on God by faith. *Faith* is the victory. It's not man's ingenuity, or argumentation. Ultimate victory in this world comes by faith.

Regardless of our political persuasion, we saw immense cracks in the integrity of American leaders and some of their supporters during the presidential election of 2000. We could easily despair when we see the immense capacity of human nature to organize opinions around what they want to be true. Whether one yearned for George W. Bush or Al Gore to become the forty-third American president, we saw rational people, including senators, congressional representatives, and lawyers on both sides, organize the facts around what they wanted to be true.

That's the deceptiveness and the deceitfulness of the human heart. That's why we need a Book that wakes us up and makes us say, "Forget about what I think and forget about what you think. What does God have to say about that?" As I watched the controversy over the Florida presidential vote unfold on the television news day after day, it became really depressing. I mean, there is just no way you can walk in victory looking at that. You have to have another place to put your eyes. Our eyes are upon the Lord, and His eyes are upon us! The Republican candidate eventually won, but the election of President Bush is not the answer, anyway. The answer is not in political victories or power. If we put our eggs in that basket, we're going to be disappointed. Instead, pick up your hopes and lay them before the Lord. God is the One whom we're trusting. Faith is the victory that overcomes the world. There is no other way.

How to Build Your Faith:
With the Word, a Witness, and a Walk

How many people would say that our land is the land of promise? As great as it is, it isn't our eternal homeland! Don't live like a citizen; live like an alien. Our citizenship and hopes are elsewhere. Abraham **"lived as an alien in the land of promise . . . looking for the city which has foundations, whose architect and builder is God"** (Hebrews 11:9–10). Like Abraham, we should also look to the city whose maker and builder is God.

Here's a practical, three-step plan for building your faith. First, study the Word; that is how you . . .

Cultivate your faith.

Paul pointed out that **"Faith comes from hearing, and hearing by the word of Christ"** (Romans 10:17). That's what grows your faith: the Word of Christ—His holy Scriptures. If we could stick a spiritual thermometer under your tongue and measure the level of your faith, the thing that would cause your faith-temperature to go up measurably is the minutes and hours and days that you've spent with your nose in God's Word. "Well, my faith is very low right now, and my heart is cold towards God," you say. Then I know something else about you too; you haven't been in the Word. Faith grows by hearing the Word of God.

It's discouraging to me sometimes when I hear people say, "James, I wish I had your faith." Actually, I have thought the same about others, but there is no mystery about how to close the gap we perceive between our faith and that of others. Log more time in God's Book! Faith comes by hearing, and hearing by the Word of God. Is this a difficult concept? I don't think so. If I find myself Thursday morning filled with anxiety and trouble and "What's going to happen?" kinds of thoughts, I must remember that faith comes by hearing and hearing by the Word of God. You can cultivate your faith.

I spoke recently at Chicago's Moody Bible Institute during their spiritual enrichment week. I didn't know the students at all, but the campus auditorium was filled with young people. I spoke on Jonah and went home the first day kind of discouraged. I didn't think the students were all that open and receptive. But I went back the next day, opened the Scriptures again, and saw its power begin to change hearts. The third morning, in Jonah 3, I pointed to the principles of continuous revival.

During those three days of extended exposure to the Word of God, their faith and spiritual focus seemed to build. So I told the MBI president, Joe Stowell, "I think we should have a special meeting, one that hasn't been planned." He was great with that, so we invited the students—anyone who wanted to come. I didn't know if fifteen or twenty would come, but almost five hundred students came back that third night.

I brought our church worship team and spoke on repentance, again sowing the Word of God into their lives. At the end, we gave an invitation, and almost every student came forward and got on his or her face before God. It was phenomenal and God was working powerfully!

Where did all of that come from? To what can you attribute their incredible responsiveness and humility? "Faith comes by hearing, and hearing by the Word of Christ." As the Word of God is sown increasingly into our lives, we find our faith growing and flourishing. If your spiritual diet for the whole week consists of what you take in each Sunday, don't be confused about the lack of faith. You're starving yourself spiritually!

Second, have a witness; that is,

Confess your faith.

Romans 10:9 says, **"If you confess with your mouth Jesus as Lord . . ."** There is great power in what we say from the heart. God wants what's in us to come out. That's why Paul asked the Ephesians (6:19–20), **"Pray on my behalf that . . . I speak boldly, as I ought to speak."** If you want your faith to grow, confess your faith. Throughout church history, the power of confessing faith was understood, and so they recorded their beliefs in creeds. Everyone would say those creeds aloud as part of corporate worship. Somehow this has been lost in the modern church, and we need to get back to this, confessing our faith. There is power in confessing your faith in the church—as well as to the world outside.

Have you ever had an experience where you were somewhat discouraged spiritually until all of a sudden God gave you an opportunity to speak for Him and share your faith? So you opened your mouth and spoke about Christ and what He means to you! Then as you walked away, you realized how much it fired you up to speak for Christ. Why? Because when we confess our faith to others and say, "Christ means so much to me," and "I'm trusting the Lord in this situation," our own faith grows. Jim Cymbala, pastor of New York's Brooklyn Tabernacle and author of *Fresh Wind, Fresh Fire,* is such an encouragement to me. Recently we were talking on the phone about faith. I picked up a little line and recalled how many hundreds of times he has said this to me, "Let's just believe God for that."

I would say, "Well, what about . . . ?"

"Let's just believe God for that," he would answer. He was gently pointing me to faith as the answer. There is such power in speaking out, "I'm trusting the Lord. I'm waiting on God. I'm believing God for that!" Confess your faith.

Third, walk daily in your faith; that is . . .

Corner your faith.

Someone has said that we should live our lives in such a way that if God is not who He said He is, we'll fall flat on our face. I would encourage you, under the leadership of the Holy Spirit—not testing or presuming upon Him (Matthew 4:3–7)—to look for opportunities to trust God. Choose to live your life in such a way that God has to come through for you. Make decisions that will cultivate and build your faith during tough times.

During a recent visit to my alma mater, Trinity Seminary, I listened to John Piper, a Minneapolis pastor I greatly respect, speak to fellow pastors. He talked about suffering and how we need to trust God during suffering.

One pastor raised his hand and said, "I'm not suffering at all. My life is just going so perfectly wonderful. Everything is great at my church. Everything is great at home. I'm not suffering in any way. I just . . . " He couldn't quite formulate a question.

Well, John Piper is a very gracious man. It took him a couple of minutes to get to the bottom line. He basically said, "Do you know what? Too many Christians, including pastors, are living on wimpy faith. They're not putting themselves in a position to trust God." Then Piper got serious. "Do you want to suffer? Just go share Christ with every person on your street, and press it to the point where he knows that he's going to go straight to hell if he steps out of this world without Christ. You'll suffer.

"Just call up all of the apostate pastors in your area who aren't preaching the gospel of Jesus Christ," he continued. "Challenge them to get on the biblical program. You'll suffer.

"If you're not suffering in this world," he concluded, "it's because you're not choosing to walk to places where you have to trust God."

I took John's words to heart! They challenged my faith. Now I pass them on to you. Do you want your faith to grow? Make a decision to "corner" it—to live it out in the hard challenges of life. I don't mean through presumption or any fleshly putting God to the test. But allow God to lead you, then willingly go by faith into situations where you have no way out but with God. Corner your faith, and it will grow for sure.

You may wonder, "But during those tough times, can I hang in there?" and "Can Jesus sustain me in faith?" Remember Jesus' admonishing words, "'If You can?' All things are possible to him who believes" (Mark 9:23).

UP CLOSE AND PERSONAL

Contrary to popular opinion, pastors struggle with faith too. Now I no longer wonder about the reliability of the Bible or the historicity of Jesus Christ, but I do wonder about other matters of faith. I struggle at times to wait for God to balance the books of justice. I have seen and experienced at least my share of harsh treatment in this world, and it is not in my nature to sit quietly by and wait on God. When falsely accused, I want to lash out, say what I know, and set the record straight. I am aware of the axiom "truth and time walk hand in hand," but I often feel like truth takes too long to make itself heard. The answer? I keep going and commit my reputation to God.

Moving from ministry issues to family, I find it hard sometimes to trust God with my children. I become anxious about their futures in this dark world and want to protect them from every evil influence that would seek to capture their minds. And sometimes I get very disappointed with Christians. I don't see how people can live with such a gaping cavern between what they profess to believe and what they actually live. I see too many people harboring bitterness when we are clearly commanded to forgive. I see too many people living for the here and now. But the bottom line is: I see too many *people* and need to get *my eyes back on the Lord*. Like Peter walking toward Christ on the water, the moment that you and I take our eyes off the Lord, we begin to sink. I could tell you in detail how I resolve each of these issues, but the answer for me is always the same: *faith*.

LET'S TALK SOLUTION

Here are three questions to ask as you develop faith, the fourth Promised Land attitude:

1. *Can you describe the last time you actually and specifically trusted God about something?* Have you told anyone about that? If you have not, try to do so this month.

2. *How would you rate yourself in the three keys to growing your faith: (1) focusing on the Word, (2) having a witness, and (3) walking daily in your faith?* In what ways has your life become like a wilderness because you have been choosing doubt and unbelief over the power of trusting God by faith?

3. Look back at the three steps to faith just above. *What practical steps could you commit yourself to just now that would grow your faith and all the joy and blessing that comes with it?*

Look Up

Father, thank You for giving me Your Word. Thank You for ordaining that the way to You is by faith. Forgive me for wishing that everything about You could be seen and known as a fact. Forgive me for preferring the ways of this physical world to the spiritual realities that You have chosen to create. Teach me deeper lessons about what it means to walk by faith. Give me spiritual eyes to see this world as You do. Help me to embrace by faith the brevity of life and the nearness of eternity. Give me strength to guide those I love toward faith in You, and help me to be a good example of what it means to really trust You. Lord, my needs are great, but You are a great and faithful God. I pray that You would, by Your Word and through my witness and walk of faith, increase my capacity to rest in and trust You. Might it be said of me before my days are through that I am a man/woman of faith. Keep this goal ever before me, I pray in Jesus' precious name. Amen.

NOTE

1. Michael P. Green, ed. *Illustrations for Biblical Preaching* (Grand Rapids: Baker, 1989), 137.

9

REPLACE A REBELLIOUS ATTITUDE . . .

NUMBERS 16

SAY IT IN A SENTENCE:

Rebellion against proper authority reveals a deeper rejection of God's authority, which brings devastating consequences to our lives.

Rebellion! What do you picture when you hear the word? Some Fonzie-like tough with the collar up on his black leather jacket and an attitude that will not quit? Maybe you picture a sixteen-year-old standing up to parents and resolutely refusing to do what is asked. Or do you think of people resisting government authority and marching in the streets to demand their rights?

Rebellion has many faces, and all are not equally bad. Certainly the American Revolution had elements of rebellion in it, as did the women's and civil rights movements of the now-past century. But when rebellion is against God and His ordained authority structure, the consequences can be devastating.

That's rebellion in a nutshell. It's knowing what God wants me to do and refusing to do it. Like Saul, like Samson, like Jonah . . . wait, like me. We all have rebellion in our hearts. All of us have areas in our lives where we have chosen not to do what we know to be right. All of us know more than we are doing. That is rebellion.

In this chapter, we want to look at the rebellion of the children of Israel, find out where they went wrong, and see if we can avoid a similar peril in our own lives. Let's begin with this thought:

Rebellion is serious.

This is no small matter or trifle that we're talking about. Lives are at stake. There is no heart that God has a harder time dealing with and changing than a rebellious heart. By the time Numbers 16 happened, Moses and Aaron had led the children of Israel—two million of them—on a journey from Egypt to the borders of the Promised Land. Actually it wasn't much of a journey. Did you know that it was only three hundred miles? And did you know that it took them, minus the wandering, only sixteen months, with a year of that time being spent at Mount Sinai camped in one place? Their rebellious attitudes, however, extended a short trip into a lifelong journey—forty years of wandering —that they would never finish.

KORAH GOES CRAZY

Your Bible probably subtitles Numbers 16, "Korah's Rebellion." As with the other events from this section of Scripture, the apostle Paul says that what happened is recorded "for our instruction" (1 Corinthians 10:11). Let's remember that during the events recorded in Numbers 16, Moses was more than eighty years old. He was a proven leader, though certainly not perfect. We see some of his faults, but he's humble and he has been successful. Clearly, the people's murmuring was often against Moses, but their failure wasn't his fault.

A group of men, led by Korah, got together and began a revolt. They wanted to carry out some kind of mutiny against Moses and Aaron. So they got in Moses' face about what they felt was wrong with his leadership. In truth, they resented Moses and Aaron because of their prominence as leader and priest to the people. God's anger at their rebellion was so strong that Moses had to plead with God not to wipe out everyone because of the rebellion of a few. God responded, and Moses warned the people to back away from the rebels (verses 21–24). Then Moses told the rebels, in effect, "Do you guys want to be priests? Do you want to be me? Do you think you can do what I do?" He told them to pick up the censers, as a way to claim their new roles. A censer, in case you're wondering, is a pole with a pan on the end, covered by a lid. It was used to carry coals in worship. The priests would scoop coals out of the fire and then bring them into worship, where different fragrant herbs and spices would be placed in the censer as a fragrant offering before God.

Now only the priests were allowed to use censers in worship. Through Moses, God told all these wanna-be priests, "Go get a censer. Do you want to be a priest? Let's do this right now." God allowed them to pretend to be priests so He could clearly indicate who was and was not really on His program. Second Timothy 2:19 says, **"The Lord knows those who are His."** The bottom line: In the midst of all of this, the ground opened up and swallowed all the rebels. Those with the censers fell alive down into hell itself. Then other rebels were burned alive by a fire from God (see verses 28–35).

Amazingly, the people who watched all of this actually began to complain *against* Moses and Aaron. They blamed their leaders for Korah's rebellion. So God sent a plague, and eventually more than fifteen thousand people died in the rebellion of Korah (see verses 41–50).

That has got to be one of the most tragic stories in all of the Old Testament. These people knew the truth. They had no excuse—yet they chose rebellion, so God had to choose judgment. In case you didn't catch it: *Rebellion is serious.* The Bible says that **"rebellion is as the sin**

of witchcraft" (1 Samuel 15:23 NKJV). Think about that for a moment: all of the horrific animal sacrifices and cruel, perverse activities that are connected with witchcraft. You say, "Well, I would *never* do something so sick and idolatrous as witchcraft." No, I believe that you wouldn't. But God says that from His perspective, rebellion is like the sin of witchcraft. Rebellion is very serious.

WHO'S IN CHARGE?

Romans 13 tells us that the powers that be are ordained of God. So what are these powers? What authorities has God established?

- Human government.

- Church leadership—elders and pastors—and other recognized church leaders.

- Husbands in the home as leaders of the family.

- Husbands and wives together as leaders of their children.

- Our bosses at work and the people who are over us. You may say, "You don't know where I work." No, no, listen; that relationship is established by God for a reason.

- The whole criminal justice system and the court system, which can be seen as part of human government.

The powers that be are ordained of God. And to make a choice to rebel against authority that God Himself has established is a very serious choice.

Now we could talk about different kinds of rebellion. We could talk about knowing what God wants me to do in His Word and not doing it. But the primary focus of Numbers 16, the wilderness attitude we're trying to put off, is rebellion against people, not rebellion against truth. We're not talking about rebellion against the Word. This whole chapter is about the people that God has placed in authority in your life and how you handle them. In thinking about them, this is the first principle to remember: Rebellion is serious.

Here's a second truth about rebellion from Scripture:

Rebellion exists in every human heart.

Numbers 16 vividly pictures how rebellion exists in every human heart. Take note of verses 1–2: **"Now Korah the son of Izhar, the son of Kohath, the son of Levi, with Dathan and Abiram, the sons of Eliab, and On the son of Peleth, sons of Reuben, took action."** The two names that are really important in there are *Levi* and *Reuben,* founders of two of the twelve tribes in the nation of Israel. Verse 2 says that these descendants **"rose up before Moses, together with some of the sons of Israel, two hundred and fifty leaders of the congregation, chosen in the assembly, men of renown."** Who are these rebels? They're not outcasts. They're not known troublemakers; not the untrained and uneducated, on the fringe of the nation of Israel. These are noble men of the Israelite society. They're responsible leaders gone bad.

Korah was a descendant of Levi, the tribe that was given the responsibility of tabernacle worship. Only the Levites could lead worship, so Korah had a significant place in the tabernacle worship. In addition to Korah and his Levites, we also meet Dathan and Abiram among the Reubenites who helped lead the rebellion.

With them were two hundred and fifty men from almost every tribe in the nation of Israel. Talk about strange bedfellows! But when the word of the day is rebellion, you would be amazed at the people who will get together.

We've seen this right here in our own church. All of a sudden, "Who's talking to who? They don't even like each other!" Surprise,

surprise; people who would hardly talk to one another and would have nothing to do with each other will come together on the basis of their mutual desire to resist the authority that God has placed over them. Rebellion does exist in every human heart.

Before we're too hard on the people here in Numbers 16, we need to look at ourselves. Are we guilty of the same attitude? Keep in mind that by *rebellion*, I do not mean ignorance (when I don't know and I need to be taught) nor discouragement (when I know, but I'm discouraged and I'm struggling). No, rebellion is knowing but not doing. Rebellion is not the pain of trying and failing and repenting and trying again. Rebellion is, "I won't—I know I should—but I won't! You can't make me!"

Are those the thoughts behind your attitude? Remember, rebellion is a lip-out, arms-folded, back-turned attitude. "Don't look at me like that! Get away from me! I'm going to do what I want to do!" It's a choice. It's a pattern of thinking formed over a long period of time. Those who choose rebellion as their lifestyle will spend their lifetimes in the wilderness.

REBELLION GOES WAY BACK!

A propensity to rebel thrives in every human heart. It's as old as the Garden of Eden. What did God say to the original couple? "Here's the whole world I've created and put under your care—99.9 percent of all of the things. Do what you want; only here's one thing you can't do." And what did they do? They rebelled. They did the one thing God commanded them not to do.

The book of Proverbs says, **"Foolishness is bound up in the heart of a child"** (22:15). Foolishness—rebelliousness—is bound up in our very being. It's part of our nature! There's a desire to go my own way. It's in the heart of every kid—each little baby who comes into the world. They sit in the nursery and you think everything is innocent perfection. All of a sudden, they get to age one or two and you see they have a will. They didn't learn it; it came from within.

Kathy and I received the grand tour at my brother Todd's new house during a recent visit. Kathy and I were being led by our two little nephews, Josh (eight) and Tanner (six). As we walked around the basement, I complimented their house: "Oh, this is so nice, your new house," and "That is so nice." Later I said, "Oh! What's this door? I really like this door." I was pointing at a heavy door with a big deadbolt.

"That's the door that goes outside!" one of my nephews said. I said, "Oh, let's open it and see . . ." "No, no! Dad doesn't want that door opened! Don't open that door!"

"Well, no problem," I said. "We won't open the door because Dad's the boss." I looked at them and asked, "Your dad's the boss, right?"

Then little Tanner said, "Yeah, he is, but we wish he wasn't!"

That's it, isn't it? We laughed about it. But do you know what? That is in every single human heart, the desire to rebel. You say, "Well, why? Where does it come from?"

The answer is found in our third biblical truth about rebellion:

Rebellion has many sources.

You don't wake up in the morning and say, "I think I'll be a rebel today. I think I'm just going to be in everybody's face all day." Rebellion is where you end up. Other attitudes push you to that place.

Notice that verse 3 begins, **"They assembled together."** This was a conspiracy—an organized, well-thought-out coup. Allow me a brief word of caution here: Don't ever be the person who gets on the phone and pulls together the group. There is a huge accountability before God if you are the instigator and organizer of rebellion, as Korah was in this circumstance.

Notice how they approached their leaders: **"They assembled together against Moses and Aaron, and said to them, 'You have**

gone far enough, for all the congregation are holy, every one of
them, and the Lord is in their midst; so why do you exalt yourselves above the assembly of the Lord?'" (verse 3). This was Korah
talking to Moses on behalf of his rebellious group. Look at Korah's
half-truths, " . . . All the congregation are holy." True or false? Well,
in the sense that all of them were set apart by God and belonged to
Him and that each one had equal access to holiness, there's some truth
to that. "And the Lord is in their midst." Is that not right that the Lord
was with every one of His children? Sure, it is. Most rebellion is based
upon half-truths. But then comes this last part, the accusation hidden in
a question: "Why do you exalt yourselves above the assembly of the
Lord?" There's the lie. Far from self-exalting, Moses was self-abasing.
Moses was the guy who God had to basically knock down and drag
into this role. Remember the burning bush in Exodus 2 and Moses'
reluctance to lead? We've also learned in Numbers 12:3 that Moses was
more humble than any man on the face of the earth. He was the guy
saying, "I don't want this job. Does anyone else want it? Come on, you
can have it." Moses did not exalt himself.

WE'RE ALL EQUAL, BUT . . .

If you don't know the whole story, it's easy to get carried away.
After all, Moses was uniquely called by God, powerfully used by God,
and clearly appointed by God. While these rebels were right in saying
that they were equal with Moses on one level, they were wrong in what
they meant. They confused equality with sameness. They assumed that
their equality as children of Israel made them the same as Moses in
every way. But equality does not equate to sameness. Moses was the
ordained-by-God leader. They were not.

This principle is true in the body of Christ. Are we not all equal?
We are all equal, but all are not the same. You are equal with your boss,
but you are not the same as your boss. Wives are equal with their husbands, but they are not the same as their husbands. If we are students,

we are equal with our teachers in our personhood before God, but we are not the same as them. Similarly, we are equal as followers of Christ, but we are not the same as our elders. God appoints and places people over us. Some are leaders, and some are followers who should submit.

Korah and his little club were way off base on this one. They were equal with Moses, but they were not the same. To suggest that they were was rebellion.

SIX SOURCES OF REBELLION

So where did their rebellion come from? There were six sources, and they can appear in our lives today. The first source of Korah's rebellion was *jealousy*. It's so clear when they say, "Why do you exalt yourselves above the assembly of the Lord?" Like most rebellions, this one was about control. Korah and his agents wanted to be in authority over Moses or at least equal with him in authority. "I don't want to submit to you because you have a position that I think I should have."

Several years ago, I had a lunch meeting with a man in our church. I sat down with him, just trying to encourage him and care for him. All of a sudden, he began a series of questions. "How come *you* get to be the pastor at Harvest? How come *you* get to be in charge of such a cool church? I've known the Lord longer than you! I've been serving Christ longer than you! How come *you* get to . . . ?"

His questions surprised me. In fact, I almost choked on my food. I thought, "Where did this come from?"

Well, a few months later, this person got bent—really upset—and injured a lot of people in his own version of "Korah's Rebellion." And I knew the entire time that the source problem was jealousy.

Whether it's in the home or in the marketplace or in the church, if you set your eyes upon those whom God has placed in authority over you and begin saying, "*I* should be the one—that should be my place!" That's jealousy, one of the sources of rebellion.

Here's another source: *delusions*. Look at verse 4, **"When Moses**

heard this, he fell on his face." Now if that's not a confirmation of the good-heartedness of Moses, I don't know what is. If he had lashed out and attacked the people who were rebelling against him, it would have been a confirmation that there was a big problem on his part. Instead, Moses humbled himself and got on his face before God. Clearly, Korah and his club had delusions of grandeur about Moses. How could they think Moses had any grand schemes? Notice Moses' response. He called up Korah and the others to assemble the next day with the censers. **"Then Moses said to Korah, 'Hear now, you sons of Levi'"** (verse 8). He was saying, "Do you all think you want to do what I do? Do you all think you want this responsibility? You don't know what you're talking about!" They had said to him, "You've gone too far," in verse 3. Now he's like, "No, *you've* gone too far!"

Moses was saying, in effect, "Do you think you want to be me? Well, let me just ask you: Where were you when I was forty years out in the wilderness? Where were you when I stood trembling before Pharaoh in Egypt? Where were you when all the ten plagues were going on? Where were you when the Egyptian armies were coming behind us, and I held out my arm to cross the Red Sea? Where were you when I was up trembling before God on a mountain for how many days and bringing down the Ten Commandments? And *now* you want my job?"

A rebellious attitude is sometimes rooted in not seeing ourselves clearly.

Often people desire a position, but they don't respect the process. They want the opportunity, but they don't realize the work and energy that's gone into getting to that place. They covet the results without recognizing the requirements. You don't roll out of bed some morning and become a leader in any sphere in society. Leadership requires a lot of work and a lot of apprenticeship. There's a lot of brokenness and a lot of trying, failing, and trying again.

Before you set your sights on your boss's job or your husband's job or your teacher's job, and before you have some coldhearted cynical attitude toward the police officers in your area, consider the real picture. Today's police officer, for example, gets no respect, no appreciation, and certainly no pay compared to the risk that goes with the job. I thank God for the men in our church who do this work. And God forgive us for our rebellious attitudes toward people that He's placed in authority. You don't get to those places easily. Those who covet the positions of others are often, in my experience, a little bit delusional, not really recognizing all that they involve. So Moses said, "You've gone far enough." Sometimes you have to stand up to a rebellious person and say, "Do you know what? Enough is enough! You're jealous, you've got delusions, and you're downright rebellious."

A third source of rebellion is *ungratefulness.* In verse 9, Moses said, **"Is it not enough for you that the God of Israel has separated you from the rest of the congregation of Israel, to bring you near to Himself, to do the service of the tabernacle of the Lord, and to stand before the congregation . . . ?"** What a privilege and opportunity! Korah was serving in the tabernacle. He had a job as one of the special separated ministers. Yet he wasn't grateful for this special position as a Levite. Why? He just didn't think he had a big enough job.

He wasn't getting to do as much as he *wanted* to do.

Moses continued: **" . . . and that He has brought you near, Korah, and all your brothers, sons of Levi, with you? And are you seeking for the priesthood also?"** (verse 10). Moses was saying, "Isn't this enough for you? Do you want to be a priest too?"

If you have a position of authority, don't ever forget that first of all it comes from God. The Scriptures tell us that promotion doesn't come from the east or the west. God is the Judge, the One who sets up one person and puts down another (see Psalm 75:6–7). Second, if you have a position, it came from God but it came through people. People allow people to function in positions of authority. Don't ever forget that a position of authority is a trust, given by people in the church, in the home, in the marketplace. If you start to think that you deserve it, or can demand it, then you have forgotten how you got there. And you're ungrateful. That's a source of rebellion.

Another root of rebellion can be found in verse 12: stubbornness. *Stubbornness* fuels rebellion. **"Then Moses sent a summons to Dathan and Abiram, the sons of Eliab; but they said, 'We will not come up.'"**

Notice this amazing audacity. The ruler of two million people sends for these two mo-jos, and they're like, "We're not coming!"

Very few people would identify themselves as rebellious, but let me ask you:

Are you hard to agree with?

Are you hard to reconcile with? If someone injures you, is it hard for them to get that worked out? Is it easy to lead you or is it hard to lead you? Are you an easy person to influence? Do you have a flexible spirit? If you have prided yourself on, "I'm stubborn. I don't—", that's not good. You have a rebellious heart.

"Well, my mom told me that's a strength." Sorry about your mom's confusion, but stubbornness is a weakness. It will hurt you. Don't confuse strength of character with stubbornness—they're not the same. Stubbornness will definitely take you a long way, but you'd better bring some food and water, because the road of stubbornness leads to the wilderness.

Disappointment is the fifth source of rebellion. Verse 13 reveals this aspect of the rebellion, **"'Is it not enough that you have brought us up out of a land flowing with milk and honey . . . ?'"** Their twisted view is laughable! Look at how they describe Egypt. How would you respond? Moses could have correctly responded, "But you were slaves! You made *bricks* in Egypt! You've hardly been gone a year but you forget what you were!"

Notice how rebellion distorts the picture and leads to accusations. **"'Is it not enough that you have brought us up out of a land flowing with milk and honey to have us die in the wilderness, but you would also lord it over us? Indeed, you have not brought us into a land flowing with milk and honey, nor have you given us an inheritance of fields and vineyards'"** (verses 13–14). Do you see what's going on here? They are expressing disappointment. Now what the rebellious person feels is real. It's not right, but it's real. What happened?

They were disappointed, and disappointment often leads to rebellion.

Maybe there has been a church leader in your life who didn't live up to some of what he professed, and the person disappointed you. Have you used that as an occasion to rebel? It's wrong (both what he did and how you have responded)! Or maybe your boss has done some dishonest things. Now you've disqualified him and have said, "I don't have to be under his authority. I don't have to respect him because he did some things that aren't right." You're wrong. God has placed you there, and you need to find God's purpose in that place. As long as the person is not asking you to sin, you need to find a way to be under that authority.

I wonder how many wives I speak to each week whose husbands have disappointed them so that they think, "Well, I don't have to live under his authority." No, they're wrong. I know there are children who say, "Well, my parents aren't perfect. I know their inconsistencies, so I'm going to do what I want." All those are very bad decisions. Disappointment with others is one of the things that fuels rebellion.

Here's the final source of rebellion: *distrust*. Notice what verse 14 says: **"'Would you put out the eyes of these men? We will not come up!'"** When Moses told Dathan and Abiram, "You all get up here," they said as part of their answer, "Would you put out the eyes of these men also?" They're saying, "Hey, do you know what, Moses? The only people who really support your leadership—they're blind. They are a bunch of yes-men. The only people who can really support you are the people who you've duped into blindness. They don't see your faults. But we see them, Moses! We know what you want to do. You want us to come up there and meet with you, so you can brainwash us like you have the others." So the way they say it is, "You're going to poke out our eyes, too."

Wow, how distorted can you get? They distrust Moses—his judgment and his supporters.

The headlines of the daily news might have read:

Moses Not Perfect, But God On His Side.

Of course, Moses may not have been perfect. But wait 'til you see how God feels about the critics' attitude. Korah's group felt like Moses had disappointed them and let them down. So they built up a lot of things in their minds, and they decided, "We're not trusting you anymore, Moses." Once they stopped trusting him, once they stopped believing in Moses' heart despite his weaknesses, whatever they were, once trust was gone, rebellion was on the way. There is a fourth biblical truth about rebellion in this passage:

Rebellion has many consequences.

At least four consequences await those who rebel, according to this portion of God's Word. After Moses told Korah and his company to meet with Aaron and him the next day with censers, the rebels returned to learn of God's displeasure and the consequences of their murmuring.

And the glory of the Lord appeared to all the congregation. Then the Lord spoke to Moses and Aaron, saying, "Separate yourselves [there's the first consequence] from among this congregation, that I may consume them instantly." But they fell on their faces and said, "O God, God of the spirits of all flesh, when one man sins, will You be angry with the entire congregation?" (verses 19–22)

God's impending judgment is just, yet the compassionate Moses pleads with God on behalf of the people. And God showed mercy. **"Then the Lord spoke to Moses, saying, 'Speak to the congregation, saying, "Get back from around the dwellings of Korah, Dathan and Abiram"'"** (verses 23–24). Get back from around their dwellings. It's too late to change attitudes; God is about to judge.

WHERE HAVE ALL THE LEADERS GONE?

Before we see how God judges them, let me make this point: One of the consequences of rebellion is *leadership withdrawal*. God commanded Moses and Aaron, the elders of the nation, to pull back: "Separate yourselves," he said. Often people wonder why those in authority seem to have little interest in them. This could be one of the reasons. If you are continuously difficult to lead, leaders will often pull back and not lead you anymore. In every sphere—in the home, in the church, in the marketplace—if you become difficult to lead, leaders will pull back from you. That can make your life very lonely and unprotected, kind of like a wilderness.

I first heard Bill Gothard, founder of the Institute of Basic Life Principles, teach that authority is like an umbrella. It's a protection. There are a lot of hurtful things in this world, and God allows some of them into our lives. But God also protects us from many of the things that would injure us by placing us under authority. Now no authority is perfect, but the powers that be are ordained of God. Unless they're asking you to sin, you need to do the things that you're asked to do. When you choose not to do that, you place yourself in a position of great risk. Those under proper authority can count on safety;

Those out from under authority can count on danger.

I'm amazed at how many people's lives are nothing more than the sum total of the decisions that they've made to get out from under worthy authority—bad choices and the consequences that follow, often for the rest of their lives.

I often remind the young people at Harvest to stay under the authority of their parents. They need to embrace the protection that God has provided. The vast majority of the young people I know have parents who love them and are giving themselves for their kids. Unless what their parents are telling them to do is sin, unless they are deeply wounding and injuring them, those students would be wise to obey and honor their parents.

Whether you are a teen or an employee, it's better to submit to authorities—even when you don't understand all their reasons—than to go your own way and maybe make a decision that you will regret for the rest of your life. When young people, wives, or employees, or anyone under authority chooses to rebel and become difficult to lead, they will eventually reap the consequence of leadership withdrawal.

ANOTHER CONSEQUENCE OF REBELLION

Imagine the tension as the showdown began. Moses warned **"the congregation, saying, 'Depart now from the tents of these wicked men, and touch nothing that belongs to them, or you will be swept away in all their sin'"** (verse 26). The people did so, and then the Scripture indicates, **"Dathan and Abiram came out and stood at the doorway of their tents, along with their wives and their sons and their little ones"** (verse 27). At least three generations were standing there, including grandchildren.

Moments later, the ground opened up, and they fell straight down into hell—not just Korah and all those men—but other innocents with them. Later in Numbers we learn that Korah's children did not die

(26:11), but there is not mention of any of the other children, let alone wives and other relatives—all innocent but swept away in God's judgment upon the rebels. You say,

"That's terrible!"
You're right; it is.

Rebellion not only results in leadership withdrawal; it creates a situation where *innocent people are injured*. And that *is* terrible—the terrible second consequence of rebellion. Korah led an insurrection out from under Moses' authority, but he couldn't provide for or protect those who followed him. Korah said, "Hey, you all, come with me! We know what we're doing! Come on, everybody!" But in the end he only led them into a deep hole in the ground that became their grave. Be careful about joining a rebellion. Korah led his rebels to a place where he couldn't protect them. When rebellion is pursued, innocent people always suffer.

REBELLION WILL BE JUDGED

The third consequence of rebellion is that the *guilty will be condemned*. Moses explained as everyone watched,

> "By this you shall know that the Lord has sent me to do all these deeds; for this is not my doing. If these men die the death of all men, or if they suffer the fate of all men, then the Lord has not sent me. But if the Lord brings about an entirely new thing and the ground opens its mouth and swallows them up with all that is theirs, and they descend alive into Sheol, then you will understand that these men have spurned the Lord." As he finished speaking all these words, that the ground that was under them split open; and the earth opened its mouth and swallowed them up, and their households, and all the men who belonged to Korah with their possessions. So they

and all that belonged to them went down alive to Sheol; and the earth closed over them, and they perished from the midst of the assembly. And all Israel who were around them fled at their outcry, for they said, "The earth may swallow us up!" Fire also came forth from the Lord and consumed the two hundred and fifty men who were offering the incense. (verses 28–35)

When it was too late, the judgment was shocking and swift.

"Then the Lord spoke to Moses, saying, 'Say to Eleazar, the son of Aaron the priest, that he shall take up the censers out of the midst of the blaze'" (verses 36–37). God then gave the direction to pound the metal from the censers into thin sheets and nail them in place on the tabernacle altar as a reminder of the lesson that they had learned.

The rebels were judged for their rebellion. They could have given a lot of excuses, but it was too late for excuses. God condemned their rebellion.

A Spreading Infection

Here's the last consequence: *The infection spread*. Hebrews 12:15 points out that *a root of bitterness will defile many people*. Rebellion is like spiritual AIDS: It spreads rapidly and can infect many people.

Notice verse 41: **"But on the next day all the congregation of the sons of Israel grumbled against Moses and Aaron, saying, 'You were the ones who have caused the death of the Lord's people.'"** The rebels died; the infection lived on. You say, "Do you mean they saw those people fall down in the depths of the earth—a divine act for sure—and the very next day they were complaining against the person who said, 'this is not my doing'? No way!" Way! I know. I've seen it. I've seen the exact thing happen in my lifetime.

Good people, wonderful people, become bent because they started listening to a rebel. Rebellion is a contagious disease.

There is a final biblical truth about rebellion.

Rebellion is ultimately against God.

Make no mistake about it: Rebellion is ultimately against God. You can't miss that here. Verse 30 clearly indicates they rebelled against the Lord, but the key verse is verse 11, which says, **"'Therefore you and all your company are gathered together against the Lord.'"**

God didn't see this as a rebellion against Moses. If He's the One who puts the person in authority, rejecting the authority is rejecting God. That's why He takes it so seriously.

If the powers that be are ordained of God, then to resist and rebel against the established authorities is to resist and rebel against God. "God, You don't know what You're doing. He shouldn't be in charge. Why do I have to do what she says?" That's ultimately a rejection of God, and it brings huge consequences for our lives.

UP CLOSE AND PERSONAL

I had a lengthy story written here, but I am going to save my personal disclosure for the next chapter. Suffice it to say that rebellion is something that God has done a lot of work on in me. I have been through many painful seasons of growth and change as I make progress in this wilderness attitude, which has at times been deeply rooted in my human heart. Much more on that in chapter 10.

LET'S TALK SOLUTION

Maybe you clearly recognize the sin and dangerous consequences of having a rebellious attitude. The tragic end of Korah and his company is a warning you want to heed, and you wonder, "How much am I a rebel, and how can I abandon this wilderness attitude?" Here are three sets of questions to ask that will help you do both.

1. *Am I a rebel?* Don't answer this question without praying about it first. Ask the Lord to bring to your mind the faces of specific people whose rightful authority you have resisted. Invite the Holy Spirit to examine each of the relationships in your life: family, marriage, work, the body of Christ. Are you playing the rebel's role in any of those places? This ought to be a prayer with fear and trembling. The example of Korah in your mind should be enough to help you see how close rebellion comes to inviting destruction. Remember that every instance of rebellion toward a human authority is also an attitude of rebellion against God.

2. *Am I reaping the consequences in my relationship with God?* Have you realized reading this chapter that your heart has been like a wilderness because your life has the undeniable symptoms of rebellion? Could you prove your persistent rebellion with specific stories from your life? Those memories are God's gift to help you put off that attitude. Let the weight of the garbage that our rebellion creates motivate us to put it off.

3. *Am I willing to repent?* Again, the key in all of this is a willingness to repent. A recognition of where your sin has taken you and a free admission of responsibility is where the transformation always begins. Agree it is sin, and tell God you wish to turn from it. He will quickly grant His forgiveness. When the vertical work is done, it's time to get to work on the horizontal. In fact, doing the work with God sincerely automatically produces a desire to make things right with the people our rebellion has affected. The relationships God brought to your mind above need healing. In most cases, that will have to start when you confess and ask for forgiveness. I know that will be hard for you, but it will help you entrench your decision to go in a new direction.

Take some time to read the next chapter as you prepare for those conversations, because you need to have a clear understanding of submission as you approach the authorities that God has placed in your life.

Look Up

Lord, I understand that rebellion is easy; humility and submission are very hard. I want to take the hard way because it's the best way, and it's Your way. Lord, please forgive all of my rationalizations.

In the relationships where I'm wrong, Lord, bring the face of that person to mind in this moment that I might acknowledge my sin and turn from it. Especially in my church, Lord, if I've resisted the counsel of a leader or made some wrong decisions and pulled back, or even participated in rebellious conversations, forgive me. Create in me a clean, submissive heart, oh, God! Teach me, Lord, what joy You have in humility and gracious submissive attitudes.

Lord, as I read the next chapter on submission, help me put off this heavy load of rebellion and put on the light load of submission. I believe that this is the road to joy and peace, and I choose to pursue it for Your glory, in Jesus' name. Amen.

10

. . . WITH AN ATTITUDE OF SUBMISSION

1 PETER 2:13–25

SAY IT IN A SENTENCE:

Submission, when properly understood and applied, replaces the pain and strife of rebellion and greatly increases human happiness.

We're all natural-born rebels, so we have a built-in resistance to submission. On top of that, submission has been hijacked by some selfish-minded, even cruel, authoritarians who have twisted and distorted the truth for their own purposes. Submission has a terrible reputation right now, so it's hard to get even sincere people to consider it seriously.

In the next few pages, open your mind in a fresh new way and think, "Well, maybe what I've heard about submission isn't really what God's Word says. Maybe there is more treasure to be discovered in that word *submission* that I ever thought." We don't want to abandon a subject that's in God's Word simply because it's been misunderstood and misused. If you read on with an open mind, you will see that submission, when properly understood and applied, replaces the pain and strife of rebellion and greatly increases human happiness.

One crucial truth to learn before we get into our main text in 1 Peter 2:

Submission is not just for a few people.

Romans 13:1 makes it very clear that **"every person is to be in subjection to the governing authorities . . . established by God."** Every single believer is to be practicing, on a regular basis, the principle of submission. It's not just for children; it's also for parents. It's not just for church members; it's for pastors. It's for everyone. In fact, Ephesians 5:21 says, **"Be subject to one another in the fear of Christ."** So before we're ever asking wives, children, employees, or church members to submit, we're to be submissive—all of us—to one another. The apostle Peter gave five principles on submission in his first epistle. These five truths in 1 Peter 2:13–25 will guide and encourage you as you replace a rebellious attitude with a submissive one. It's the final step in putting off wilderness attitudes. You've done well to make it this far, so let's finish the task.

PRINCIPLE ONE:
SUBMISSION IS DUTY TO GOD

First, *submission is duty to God.* That's really the focus point: God is the One to whom we're submitting. As verses 13 and 14 say, **"Submit yourselves for the Lord's sake to every human institution, whether to a king as the one in authority, or to governors as sent by him."**

Submit is a military term that means "to place yourself in order under established authority." It means "to operate within the chain of command." Notice the word *yourselves* in verse 13. You might circle that if you're looking carefully at your own Bible. No one is to force you to submit; God's Word says "submit yourselves."

Don't miss the principle Peter was applying: Forced submission from the top down is not taught anywhere in the Bible. Nowhere do we see the person in authority demanding, "You submit to me!" The person in authority does not *command* submission. A leader receives that from those under his or her authority. That leader is called to win the favor of those who are under him through serving and selflessness. That's servant leadership.

Submission is a choice—not top down, but bottom up.

If you're in a role where you need to submit, that's a choice of heart that God asks you to willingly make, for His sake. Husbands are not to be demanding that their wives submit. Pastors are not to be demanding that their people submit but lovingly serving and giving themselves to them. A godly response to that servant leadership is the choice of submission.

You ask, "Well, who exactly is supposed to be doing the submitting? Who exactly am I supposed to be under?" Actually, it's quite a list. Let's skim through the end of 1 Peter 2 and into 1 Peter 3. Verses 13 and 14 say we are to submit **"to every human institution, whether to a king as the one in authority, or to governors as sent by [the king]"** (and ultimately sent by the King of Kings). Verse 17 tells us to **"honor all people."** Verse 18 says, **"Servants, be submissive to your masters."** The modern context of that is the marketplace. Do what your boss asks or tells you to do, even if he's not a very good boss.

Further on, 1 Peter 3:1 says, **"In the same way . . ."** In what way? In the same submissive way that we've been talking about. Concerning the home, Peter writes, **"In the same way, you wives, be submissive to your own husbands."** Now men seem to get that verse down but then they miss verse 7, which says, **"You husbands in the same way . . . "** In what way? In the submissive way that's being talked about:

"In the same way, live with your wives in an understanding way." Verse 8 sums up the thought, **"All of you be harmonious, sympathetic, brotherly, kindhearted, and humble in spirit."** In a word, *submissive*—finding your place of humility and cooperation under the influence of others.

But notice the key phrase back in 2:13, **"Submit yourselves for the Lord's sake to every human institution."** We submit for the *Lord's* sake. Our true citizenship is in heaven, but God is trying to get some things done in this world. Everyone who resists the established authorities is resisting God. Everyone who submits to the established authorities—whether they're right or wrong; whether one agrees or not—is assisting with what God is trying to accomplish in this world.

The problem is with that "for the Lord's sake." I don't think I've met a Christian who, if Jesus Christ were to walk up and to stand before him in all of His glory and ask, "Could you do this for Me?" would hesitate. He would say, "Not a problem. Let me get that done right now. Let me spend the rest of my life getting that done for You!"

The problem is that it's not the Lord we see. He's behind the scenes. The ones we see—our boss, our parents, our elders—are humans. They're frail, not perfect. So we use the imperfections of human authorities to dismiss our responsibility to be submissive. Our attitude is not right, and God doesn't bless it. That's why this text says, "Submit for the Lord's sake."

We see the speed limits posted and think how unfair they are. We conclude, "Well, the police don't even obey the speed limits. When I drive the speed limit, I have police cars passing me. *They* don't obey the speed limits, so *I'm* not going to obey them, either!" As my wife often reminds me, that excuse doesn't work, especially with officers who have pulled me over. We are to submit, not because of the people we see with all of their inconsistencies, but for the Lord's sake.

Your boss seems unfair and demanding. Maybe she's easy on herself and hard on you. She leaves early, but she expects you to work late. You *know* that's not right. So you decide, "Once she's gone, I'm going to leave, too. I'm going to take matters into my own hands. I'm not going to be submissive." That's a mistake, because the One whom you're really refusing to submit to is not your boss, but the Lord. You're saying, "God, I won't *do* what You want me to do." That's a very bad decision. We submit for the Lord's sake, not the boss's.

PRINCIPLE TWO :
SUBMISSION IS PROTECTION BY GOD

Here's the second principle: *Submission is protection by God.* Notice verse 14: These **"governors [are] sent . . . for the punishment of evildoers and the praise of those who do right."** What a phenomenal statement about our judicial system! If only our government would turn to God's Word, how much they could understand! What is the purpose of a judicial system? The Scripture indicates it is to punish wrongdoers and honor "those who do right." Did you know that the escalating crime in our society over the last fifty years is almost directly related to the decision our government made to move away from a punitive judicial system and toward a rehabilitative judicial system? Instead of seeing criminals as wrongdoers who should be punished, we now see them as sick people who need help. Of course, criminals should be helped and treated with respect, but above all, God's Word says they are to serve time for their crimes.

Part of God's purpose for authority is to "praise . . . those who do right." Blessing and favor come to the person who lives in submission. Why? **"For such is the will of God"** (verse 15). God's will is for us to display lives of submission, not of rebellion against authority. Do you think God isn't watching? He is. When recognized authority makes a decision and you don't like the choices that they're making, God is very aware of how you respond. God's will is **"that by doing right you may silence the ignorance of foolish men"** (verse 15). Yes,

People in authority can be foolish.
But God's desired response from us is "doing right."

Are you in a situation where you're being unfairly treated? Do right and silence the ignorance of foolish men. That word *silence* actually means *to muzzle*. You say, "There are some people I would *love* to muzzle." Great! God's all for putting a muzzle on them. But you have to know how to get that done. It's by doing right, trusting God, waiting upon Him, and living a life of biblical submission.

We are to "do right" no matter what.

- Are you struggling with injustice? Do right and silence the ignorance of foolish men.

- Have you been passed over for a promotion at work, something you deserved and should have gotten? You're angry about it. It's not right and it's so political. What should you do? Do right and silence the ignorance of foolish men.

- Has someone turned against you in a relationship and injured you? Do right and silence the ignorance of foolish men.

- Have you experienced a marriage breakdown and people think they understand what happened? Even though you know what really happened, maybe people have harsh opinions of you, and now you're reaping the consequences of all of that. You say, "How do I get out of this? I have to defend myself!" Do what's right and silence the ignorance of foolish men. Whether you've been maligned or rejected or ignored, do right and silence the ignorance of foolish men. As I explained in the last chapter, submission to authority is like having an umbrella. When we choose to submit, what we're really choosing to do is to put ourselves under God's protection. That is a wonderful place to live your life. You might feel like there are some bad things that are falling, but submission is a covering. It's your place of protection. When you get out from under that, you are very vulnerable. The promises of God do not extend to you when you choose to live as a rebel. However, when you choose to live under the umbrella of God's protection by submitting to His plans and doing what's right, all the promises and blessings of God are yours in abundance.

The choice between submission and rebellion affects every part of life. Think about this little list of contrasts:

Protection	Danger
Submission	Rebellion
Humility	Pride
Love ("You before me")	My rights
Waiting on God	Acting on my own
Trust and obey	Doubt and disobey

Turn for a moment to 1 Peter 5. The people to whom Peter was writing were suffering Christians in the early church. They were being very harshly treated, more than most of us have ever experienced. So submission to authority comes up quite often in 1 Peter. First Peter 5:5 says, **"You younger men, likewise, be subject to your elders; and all of you, clothe yourselves with humility toward one another, for God is opposed to the proud, but gives grace to the humble."** That is a phenomenal truth: God is opposed to the proud. In this context, the proud would be the unsubmissive.

Why do we get bent and rebellious? Because there is someone in control and we're not. There are things that we want to happen and they're not happening. So we get rebellious and say, "I'm going to make it happen. I'm going to get what I deserve, and you're not going to stop me!"

That's rebellion. But here's the underlying problem: You're too focused on the human authority. Behind that person is God, and if you pridefully resist that person's authority, God Himself will oppose you. He's going to make sure that attitude of rebellion never takes you to a good place. Bottom line: God's team always wins.

If you submit to God's established authority, God is on your team, but if you rebel, He joins the other team.

When He's with the other team, you will lose for sure. It's pretty clear, isn't it? God is opposed to the proud. He gives grace to the humble. **"Therefore humble yourselves under the mighty hand of God, that He may exalt you at the proper time"** (1 Peter 5:6).

But you say, "You don't see my situation. What's happening to me is so unjust. And the way I'm being treated and the opportunity I'm being given and the place where I am being ranked is not fair! It's not right!" The answer: "Humble yourself under the mighty hand of God, that He may exalt you at the proper time." Clawing your way to some position of success or opportunity may seem appealing, but it is far more exciting to wait and trust God and see Him put you in that place. Then you know that He wanted you there. He can get you there and keep you there.

Maybe you're feeling it will be so hard to wait on God, and you are right. Waiting is very hard.

That's why verse 7 is here, **"Casting all your anxiety on Him, because He cares for you."** You say, "But I worry. What if He doesn't come through?" Cast your anxiety upon Him. "But I've worked so hard, and I'm so discouraged." Cast all your anxiety upon Him. Get before the Lord on your knees and lay this matter before the throne of grace. Then wait upon and trust Him. He will *not* disappoint you. Submission is protection by God.

Principle Three:
Submission Has Limits Under God

You say, "Wow, this submission thing is getting radical. Are there any limits at all? This could be really dangerous."

Yes! There are some limits to the principle of submission. Once when I spoke on this subject, a tall, articulate young lady came up after the message. She was ticked off at me. She said, "How could you tell women to submit to their husbands? Do you know how many abused women are out there? They need courage to leave and not be reinforced to stay in those brutal situations."

She needed assurance that submission had limits, and I encouraged her to come back the next Sunday when I would talk about them. As usual, the Bible itself acknowledges the tensions and the difficulties of trusting God in a fallen world, and sets the limits on submission very clearly.

Look at 1 Peter 2:16. After Peter wrote, **"For such is the will of God that by doing right you will silence the ignorance of foolish men,"** he added this, **"Act as free men."** See, you are not locked in. Submission is not slavery or giving up personal responsibility. God does not want His children living or acting like slaves.

But some like to argue, "The apostle Paul said he was a slave!" (citing 2 Corinthians 4:5 and Philippians 1:1). My answer is a question: to whom? Paul was a slave to Christ (Ephesians 6:6). We are not slaves to human authorities. We're not to act like slaves. Wives are not to act like slaves—except to Christ. Employees are not to act like slaves, except to Christ.

When Christ says "Jump," I say, "How high?"

Other than that holy servitude, we are free people. The obedience that we give to human authorities, we give freely. We offer it when we voluntarily submit. If we begin to act like slaves in human relationships, or people try to make us feel like slaves, that is not righteous.

It deeply grieves me to see women wither in homes where an overbearing, unbiblical version of submission is applied. Here's my challenge to husbands: If your wife is not flourishing—if she is not blossoming like a rose—under your leadership, it's not righteous leadership. That's part of the balance. Submission does have limits under God. Husbands who think a lot about submission aren't thinking enough about their own duties toward their wives! I know too many husbands who can quote Ephesians 5:22 by heart, but they have no idea of the huge responsibility God gives them in Ephesians 5:25. Husbands who get passionate about Ephesians 5:25—loving their wives as Christ loves the church—usually discover their wives have a lot less trouble with Ephesians 5:22! Indeed, the knife of submission cuts both ways.

People who are trying to submit biblically will often ask,

"Well, then, how much submission is too much?"

There are certainly some levels of injustice that we need to bear up under, and there are some levels of injustice that are abusive. The question, then, is when is submission abusive, and how much abuse should a person bear up under? A second and equally important question is this: When a person can't or shouldn't bear up under it anymore, how does he or she get out of that situation? Here are three guidelines to help you decide when enough is enough. *First, it depends upon the source.* There are some things you can tolerate in your marriage from your spouse that you would never tolerate from your employer. A greater amount of grace is given at home because of the lifetime commitment that has been made. So it depends on where the abuse of authority is coming from.

Second, it certainly depends on the severity of it. If the abuse you are experiencing is merely passive, if it's neglect as opposed to aggression, you can bear up under it much longer with God's help. As tough as a neglectful situation might be, that is hardly grounds for getting out of the commitments that you've made before God. However, if it's aggressive and active in verbal and physical ways, I remind you that you are not a slave.

Here's one aspect of severity to consider: Is the abuse just involving you? Sometimes you can bear up under things in the Lord's strength for a season to give Him an opportunity to work. But if it's spilling over to your children, then there is a responsibility to protect that extends beyond your own capacity to endure.

Third, your response will depend upon the frequency. Once a month or once a year or once in a lifetime is no excuse for you to jump out and say, "Good! I'm free from this commitment! I wanted to be free! Now I'm out of here!"

Again, if your boss has said some awful, hurtful things to you and you just started working there this week, you might start looking around. There's more of that coming. But if you've been working there for fifteen years and this has happened only two times, I think your response is obvious; you can endure.

It depends upon who is the source and what is the severity and the frequency. Those are appropriate limits to consider under submission, knowing that God wants His children to live as free people, not as slaves.

AVOIDING THE EXTREMES

One extreme is using abuse as an excuse to escape commitments when difficulties aren't frequent or severe. The second extreme is using submission as an excuse to stay, using a misunderstanding of what the Bible teaches about submission. The biblical teaching on submission does not encourage staying in a relationship that's destroying you and others you love.

"Well, how do you get out from under an ungodly, repeatedly abusive authority?"

If that's your question, look at 1 Peter 2:21—look at Christ. Verse 21 indicates Christ is to be our example. Peter says, **"For you have been called for this purpose, since Christ also suffered for you, leaving you an example for you to follow in His steps."** The context is submission. Our example is Christ and how He bore up under injustice. **"Who committed no sin, nor was any deceit found in His mouth"** (verse 22).

It's surprisingly easy for an abused person to claim, "I've never committed any sin in this situation. No deceit is found in my mouth. I'm not part of this problem in any way." No, I don't think anyone can say that but Christ. He was unjustly treated. Notice, however, His response: **"While being reviled, He did not revile in return; while suffering, He uttered no threats."** That's pretty clear. **"But kept entrusting Himself to Him who judges righteously"** (verse 23).

Who is the "Him who judges righteously"? God, the Father. Christ, the second person of the Trinity, kept entrusting Himself to the Father. He only had one above Him in authority, the Father. We have a lot more up-lines than Christ did. Here's the biblical principle: When Christ was ridiculed, He kept entrusting Himself to Him who judges righteously. When Christ was harshly treated and finally crucified, He kept entrusting Himself to Him who judges righteously. Christ appealed to the highest authority. He went above.

AUTHORITIES CAN HELP

If the authority structure in the home is failing, the next level of authority needs to be involved. Children or abused spouses need to know that if there are things going on in their home that are sinful, bringing them hurt and abuse, the authority above the authority of their home is their church. They should talk to a pastor or elder. They need to get their problem out in the light, and let the authority structure help. The church leader will offer biblical counsel and, if necessary, can recommend other, outside authorities.

Remember, the church is over the home. If you are not placing yourself or your family under any church, then you're out from under the protection. The authority structure of the church exists to help when the authority structure in the home fails.

What about abuse occurring outside the home? I think you understand how it works in society. Christians don't take other believers to court. Just read 1 Corinthians 6. If I have a problem with another believer, and the relationship structure has broken down and failed, I appeal to the elders in my church and ask them to intervene and work that out. But if it's someone in society who has wronged me—engaged in a legitimate, significant wrongdoing—it is not wrong to go to court to ask for justice. Remember, God *loves* justice. That's why He has established that system. That's why we have municipal courts, appellate courts, and supreme courts. You appeal to the higher authority.

That's what Christ did, but He only had one option. We have many options. If it's a criminal activity, what do you do? You call the police. You call the local child welfare agency. (In Illinois, we have the Department of Child and Family Services.) Those are not wrong decisions. Those are the authority structures that God has established. If the authority structure over you is failing you and injuring you significantly over an extended period of time, it is not right to remain in that situation. That is not biblical submission. It is right to appeal to the next higher authority as a way of allowing God to accomplish the transformation that He wants to bring.

Christians who overlook these principles often help bad situations go on that could have been healed. God desires wise, proactive submission, not slavery or ignorance from us. But having said that, let me add this: The vast majority of Christians who are struggling with issues of submission are not in abusive situations. I have dealt with the terrible situations reflected in the previous paragraphs, because I'm not oblivious to the kind of sinful people that we all are. But for most of us, the struggles that we're having in our lives are not abusive situations. Our difficulties are just the basic relational hardships of "I am tired of that person telling *me* what to do." In those contexts, we need to remember that submission is duty to God. Submission is our protection.

In summary, Peter says we are free, not slaves, but we are not to use our freedom to do whatever we want. **"Act as free men, and do not use your freedom as a covering for evil, but use it as bond-slaves of God"** (2:16). Do not use your freedom as an excuse to do what you want. Remember that as one who is free, you are not to be enslaved to any person—but you are to be slaves to God's will.

Principle Four: Submission Is Favor from God

Here's the reason submission takes us out of the wilderness: *Submission is favor from God.* This is the phenomenal truth of this text. God loves heartfelt, willing humility.

Some of the most powerful worship songs that we sing at Harvest Bible Chapel focus on humility. When we raise our voices, I know God is pleased. I sense His presence moving through our congregation. It's like, "Look at My brother over here. Look at My daughter over there. Look at My son over here. He is so humble. Look at the way he bears up under—." God *loves* a gathering of humble, submitted hearts. He's there!

When God sees you bearing up under injustice with a submissive spirit, get ready to get blessed, because God loves that! God invites us to submit, and honors us when we do. **"Servants, be submissive to your masters with all respect, not only to those who are good and gentle, but also to those who are unreasonable"** (1 Peter 2:18). Most of us, sooner or later, have to work or live with someone in authority who is unreasonable. Peter explains why we do: **"For this finds favor, if for the sake of conscience toward God a person bears up under** sorrows when suffering unjustly" (verse 19). If you bear up under unjust suffering, you get favor from God. How great is *that* promise? But Peter's not done. **"For what credit is there if, when you sin and are harshly treated, you endure it with patience?"** Remember, if the problem is *your* fault, God is not up in heaven saying, "Look at him hanging in there." He's going, "Boy, I wish he would stop doing that."

But there is favor with God when we endure for the right reasons: **"But if when you do what is right and suffer for it you patiently endure it, this finds favor with God"** (verse 20).

PRINCIPLE FIVE:
SUBMISSION IS INTIMACY WITH GOD

Lastly, and I think most wonderfully, 1 Peter 2 offers this truth: *Submission is intimacy with God.* There is a unique fellowship with Christ that comes through submission to suffering. **"For you have been called for this purpose, since Christ also suffered for you, leaving you an example for you to follow in His steps"** (verse 21). What steps? The steps of suffering. The steps of submitting to ungodly authority and finding God's favor through it. Suffering is not incompatible with biblical Christianity; it's part of it. Notice Christ's example: **"While being reviled, He did not revile in return; while suffering, He uttered no threats, but kept entrusting Himself to Him who judges righteously; and He Himself bore our sins"**— how unjust is that?—**". . . so that we might die to sin and live to righteousness; for by His wounds you were healed. For you were continually straying like sheep, but now you have returned to the Shepherd and Guardian of your souls"** (verses 23–25). If, in fact, you have returned to the shepherd of your soul, make no mistake about what it means to follow in His steps. To follow in His steps is to embrace suffering.

For most of us, the challenge, almost all the time, is to embrace suffering, to submit to it, knowing that there is a God who loves us and is watching. God is so capable of pouring favor into our lives if we live in submission to Him. This means submitting even when we don't see His actions on our behalf, even when submitting brings suffering and heartache. God is opposed to the proud, but He gives grace to the humble.

UP CLOSE AND PERSONAL

What is the greatest injustice that you've ever suffered? In the past or maybe in the present? Maybe someone in authority just jerked you around, really badly. Think about it for a minute. It happens to all of us, doesn't it? It's part of life. I remember three times when I experienced great abuses of authority. Each time God taught me a submissive response, and used it to bring blessing (though once He had to show me the hollow victory of resisting the person in authority).

THE DEATH OF ONE DREAM . . .
AND THE BIRTH OF ANOTHER

During my high school years, basketball was everything to me, and in my senior year I encountered a great disappointment. Leading in every statistical category, I should have been the person on my team picked for the league's all-star game. It's just a fact. I should have been there, but I wasn't. I could give you all the reasons that the person in authority did not choose me. (Some, no doubt, were my own fault.) But, bottom line, in that moment I was deeply hurt and felt so unjustly treated.

I remember going to the game, sitting in the stands, watching the other players, and thinking, "I should be *out* there! This isn't right!" It was so hurtful to me at the time. Now it's laughable. I'm embarrassed to even bring it up. But maybe someone will relate to it.

What I felt in my own heart was, "This is death of my basketball dream." Of course, I was at the end of high school, and thought maybe college ball awaited. But I look back now and realize it was the birth of my ministry dream. "I'm not going to be the person I thought I was going to be. I'm going to go in a very different direction instead." My response brought favor with God, as I didn't make a big scene or say a lot of things that I would regret. That ill treatment by a God-established authority was used by God to bring favor and blessings that I simply could never have imagined at the time.

MAKING THE GRADE

Later, during Bible college, I had a professor who taught preaching but didn't like me at all. I'm sure it was partly my own fault. You don't see these things about yourself when you're younger. But, for whatever reason, he didn't like me. Every time I would preach a message in front of all of the other students, he would get up and criticize me and belittle me. He made me feel so lousy, like I had no ability at all to speak for God! It was such a hard thing.

I didn't handle this one very well. I got so troubled about it one day that I borrowed a paper from one of my buddies in school. I recopied and improved it a little, and put my name at the top to prove a point. We both turned in the exact same paper. My buddy got an "A;" I got a "D." I was upset! I took both papers to his office and laid them down right in front of the professor. I challenged his authority, and on a human level I was 100 percent in the right. But you know what? I didn't win; I lost. He didn't back down. My actions injured my reputation, and I didn't get favor from God in that instance.

It was only later, through submission, that God's blessing rested upon me, when I realized nothing good was accomplished by taking things into my own hands. I was right, but I was wrong!

HARD EARLY DAYS

I think of some of the early days at Harvest when twelve of the eighteen people that we started the church with turned their backs on Pastor Rick and myself and walked out and said some awful things about us. I tried to leave and Rick tried to leave. It was *such* a hard time. I can remember just weeping before the Lord, but God broke us during that and we submitted to the hardship.

None of the favor and blessing that have come since could have happened apart from submission. It seems to me that the history of my life has been seasons of struggle under difficult authorities involving choices of submission, followed by abundant favor and blessing from God.

What if in any of those opportunities I would have said, "I'm out of here! I don't want to put up with this! I don't care anymore"? I would have missed the favor of God. If there is anything in my life that will stand at the judgment seat of Christ, I trace it directly to those choices of submission and the favor of God that followed abundantly those seasons of hardship.

LET'S TALK SOLUTION

I asked you at the beginning of this chapter to set aside, for a time, your understanding of submission. I pray you now understand the critical way that submission affects your relationships with others and your relationship with God. Here are three questions to measure this attitude in your life and three action steps to develop this Promised Land attitude.

1. *Do I practice submission?* Here's an easy way to find the answer to that question. Make a list of the primary authorities in your life. On a scale of 1 to 10, with 1 being total rebellion and 10 being total submission, what has been your attitude of submission to each of them? Put the number after the person's name. Then list next to each authority what you plan to do as a way to improve your attitude of submission toward them.

2. *Am I experiencing the results of submission?* Can you illustrate submission in your life by decisions that have cost you? It's easy to submit to a caring and gentle leader. How have you done with authorities who have placed unpleasant demands on you? When you examine your life, can you see the difference in past situations between the results of submission and the results of rebellion?

3. *Am I ready to submit to those whom I am resisting?* Consider that some of the authorities in your life may have withdrawn and will not reengage with you unless you confess and state your willingness to recognize their rightful role. As you pray the prayer below, open yourself for direction from God regarding relationships that need rebuilding through submission, and those that need to be deepened by a new appreciation on your part of your role as someone who willingly submits for God's sake.

Look Up

Father, at this moment, I would just say without apology that I desire Your favor. I have lived my life long enough to know that at the end of the day what really matters is the favor and the blessing of almighty God. Lord, Your Word says, "If God is for us, who can be against us?" I realize, God, that You are for me, and You're for my highest and best. You don't use me or abuse me. You make my life something phenomenal and great and praiseworthy. And so I choose the path of submission for my lifestyle.

Lord, I know there is enough relational conflict in this world to stifle any person's joy. There are enough selfish, sinful people in positions of responsibility who take advantage of others and think only of themselves. But, Lord, I want my eyes to be on You. I choose by faith to walk in obedience to Your Word. I anticipate already in my home, my church, and where I work and in my neighborhood the blessing and the favor that come only from a God who is watching and who knows. So I ask You, Lord, to help me. Help me to put off my pride and rebelliousness and to put on submission and grace and forbearance and hard work in the midst of hardship. Lord, help me wait and rest and live in obedience to You. Give me strength to live in submission, not ultimately to human authorities, but to You and to You alone. I offer myself to You afresh for those kinds of victories. I pray all of this in Jesus' precious name. Amen.

CHANGE . . . BEFORE IT'S TOO LATE

I just sent Luke, my fifteen-year-old son, to basketball practice, and before I did I gave him the "attitude speech." He'd been feeling pretty frustrated with his coach recently, thinking his efforts were not being rewarded as quickly or as fully as he would like. So I called him in and gave him the speech. He knows it so well he could give it word for word himself.

"Attitude is everything," I said. "Work hard, encourage others, do your best! Basketball is not your life. Set your eyes upon the long-term goals, and in time you will be rewarded. You have so much to be thankful for; focus upon the positive. Attitude determines outcome, so make sure yours is good. God will honor that in His time and in His way."

He nodded knowingly, set his jaw as one who is choosing his attitude, and rushed out the door into the cold winter air.

The world is a very cold place and will do all it can to push and pressure you into a miserable attitude. There will always be enough injustice and irritation to keep you in the wilderness if you choose to murmur and complain and criticize and covet and doubt and rebel. On the flip side, though, life also has plenty of people and situations to generate thankfulness and love and faith and submission and contentment—attitudes that cause life to flow with the "milk and honey" of God's blessing and abiding presence. The choice is truly ours.

Of course, some of our choices are limited. At different times, we reach forks in the road of our lives where we really cannot control very much. I've heard people tell me:

"I can't control where I work."

"I can't control where I live."

"I can't control who my authorities are or how they treat me."

Sound familiar? *The only thing we can always control is our attitude.* As we said much earlier in this book, you can *choose* your attitude. Sometimes it is the only thing you can choose. We all face those times when we have little control. During those times, the only thing that will separate us for good or bad is our attitude. We can choose to respond with Promised Land attitudes.

WHAT HAPPENED?

Do you ever find yourself down and you don't know why? Does that ever happen to you? It's like, "Everything is going great! I love living here and I love being with these people and I love what I do!" All of a sudden, it's like, "I don't love any of that anymore." Unexpectedly, you find yourself down in the dumps and discouraged and confused! "What happened!"

Has that ever happened to you? Is it the weather? Is it a relational thing? "What's bothering me exactly?" Well, I used to wonder about that a lot. What's bothering me? But I don't wonder anymore. I know what it is. And I hope after reading this book you know it too! It's an attitude that I've chosen.

As we draw this book to a close, may we never forget how God feels about bad attitudes and why He feels so strongly.

TRUTHS ABOUT OUR ATTITUDES

First of all, *the attitude reveals the true person.* **"The things which proceed out of the mouth come from the heart,"** Jesus said (Matthew 15:18 NKJV). Your attitude reveals the person you truly are. You can get your external behavior in order, but *inside* you're still a mess. God is not just interested in soldiers that look the part; God wants us to be the part! He looks on the heart because that is where the true person resides. The goal is not a makeover but real heart transformation, and that requires us to work on our attitudes.

Second, God is fired up about attitudes because *attitudes predict the future.* **"As [a person] thinks in his heart, so is he"** (Proverbs 23:7 NKJV). Attitudes are patterns of thinking formed over a long period of time. You can't think in critical, negative, faultfinding, complaining ways without becoming that person! People say, "You are what you eat." Well, to some degree that's true, but in a deeper, more spiritual and eternal way, you are what you think! God is very concerned about our attitudes, because you become what you *think* about; your attitudes predict the future.

Third, God is focused upon heart attitudes because *they are primarily vertical.* There's a horizontalness to most sin; stealing and lying definitely affect personal relationships. Ultimately, those actions are against God as well, but attitudes are definitely vertical. In every passage we have studied, there is a phrase that links the attitude to God. "Why have you done this against God? Why have you rejected the Lord your God?" God considers our attitudes directed against Him. That's why He takes them so seriously.

We can see this clearly in another murmuring recorded in Numbers 21. Forty years after the wilderness rebellion at Kadesh Barnea, the children of those who died in the wilderness finally were on the edge of the Promised Land. Most scholars agree that Numbers 21 records an event that took place after all of the original murmuring generation had died. The children, now adults, knew the whole story;

they had an incredible opportunity to learn from their parents mistakes and inherit God's favor instead of judgment. But they didn't, and God had to deal with them accordingly.

The land of Edom was in their way and they wanted to cut through, but the Edomites, descendants of Esau, opposed the Twelve Tribes of Israel, who were the descendants of Jacob, Esau's younger brother. And the descendants of Jacob (Israel) "became impatient because of the journey" (Numbers 21:4). And they complained.

"The people spoke against God and Moses. 'Why have you brought us up out of Egypt to die in the wilderness? For there is no food and no water. We loathe this miserable food!'" (verse 5). What's going on here? Yes, more murmuring, this time in the form of complaints.

Notice how aggressively God dealt with the attitudes in wilderness generation number two: **"The Lord sent fiery serpents among the people and they bit the people, so that many people of Israel died"** (verse 6). The words "fiery serpents" literally mean *snakes that produced burning*. These snakes apparently had a venomous bite that produced a burning in the bodies of the people. Now *serpent* in the Bible is a picture of sin and, in the Garden of Eden, Satan and the serpent. And so it's not surprising that God sent these fiery serpents as a consequence of the people's sinfulness.

After all this, there came an excellent response to the Lord's chastening. **"So the people came to Moses and said, 'We have sinned'"** (verse 7). Now that's repentance. With all five wilderness attitudes, we have emphasized the need for repentance. Every good step with God begins with the humility of saying, "Do you know what, God? I'm wrong; You're right." In this case, "My attitude is wrong, God. I have no excuse for it. All my rationalizations—I'm done with them! I shouldn't be the critical person that I am. There is no reason for me to be covetous the way I am."

THE POINT OF REPENTANCE

If you have read this whole book and not had an honest point of repentance with God and said, "God, *that's* why I've been so troubled! That's why I've been so discouraged! It's my attitude, Lord! Right there!" If you haven't done any specific business with God, then you have sort of wasted your time. But it's not too late! If God has been faithful to speak to your heart—repentance from murmuring will bring access to God's provision for victory.

The people of Israel couldn't get the grace that they were about to get without that sentence, **"'We have sinned, because we have spoken against the Lord and you; intercede with the Lord, that He may remove the serpents from us.' And Moses interceded for the people"** (verse 7). The people were very specific with Moses, and no doubt Moses was the same with God; they wanted the serpents gone. God answered Moses' prayer, but He didn't remove the serpents. Sound like your life? Is God letting you feel the weight of all the garbage you create by not trusting Him? God seldom removes the hard thing in our lives that brought us to our knees. Instead He gives us the grace and the strength to endure in daily doses and keeps us at the place of dependence.

God's not quick to take that off our shoulders because He knows "no serpents = no sense of need. No sense of need = no coming to God."

So we go to God and we're like, "God, get that out of here!" and God's like, "No way! That's the thing that brought this moment about! That's the *last* thing that I'm going to take out of your life at this point! That's the thing that brought you to see how much you need Me!" God seldom removes the serpents, but in His grace He provides relief and healing from their effect. That's what He did for repentant Israel. Look again at Numbers 21.

The Lord said to Moses, "Make a fiery serpent and set it on a standard; and it shall come about, that everyone who is bitten, when he looks at it, he will live." And Moses made a bronze serpent and set it on the standard; and it came about, that if a serpent bit any man, when he looked to the bronze serpent, he lived. (verses 8–9)

Moses had a craftsman make this bronze serpent, and he stuck it up on the top of the pole in the middle of the camp. So everyone was getting bitten by these snakes, and God's deal was, "Do you know what? If you'll just *look* you'll be healed." I doubt if they needed any training workshops; God always makes His provision simple and available. If a snake bites you, what do you do? Look and you will be healed. How simple is that? But the text clearly seems to imply that some people didn't look, and some people weren't healed.

IGNORING THE REMEDY

You say, "No way!" Way! There were people, I believe, right in that camp who understood the plan, needed healing, but they would not look.

You say, "Why would people not look?"

First, they may have been denying their need for help. They were like, "I can heal myself. I don't need God's remedy; I don't like God. I don't like His authority in my life. I'm going to handle this my way!"

Second, maybe they denied the goodness of God. "Well, maybe God *won't* heal me. Maybe it's a trick. Maybe it won't be best for me. I'm going to keep control of things myself."

And, third, maybe they denied the problem. They were like, "I'm not really sick."

"But, dude! What are those teeth marks on your leg?"

"Oh, that? I scratched myself. That's not a serpent bite. I don't really have a problem." Just like today with so many denying their true need.

CHANGE . . . BEFORE IT'S TOO LATE

It would be wrong to assume that you will always be as open to the message of God's Word as you are in this moment. The call to change is one you should act on now. If you are a Christian, heed the warnings of the Scriptures in Numbers 11–16, and begin, with God's help, to change your attitude. If you do not know Christ, realize fundamental change can only take place through a relationship with Him.

In John 3:14 we are told that the bronze serpent is a picture of Christ. I'm not one of those people who likes to turn the Bible into an allegory, but when the New Testament says that something in the Old Testament is a picture—it is! In this context, Jesus Christ Himself was talking with Nicodemus, a man who was searching to find the truth.

He came to Christ and asked, "How does this work, exactly?"

Jesus answered, "You have to be born again."

Nicodemus was like, "What? How can I enter into my mother a second time?"

Jesus was like, "No, no. Not born twice physically. You have to be born spiritually just like you were born physically." (See John 3:2–7 for the actual dialogue.) Later Jesus looked to the events in Numbers 21 and told Nicodemus, **"As Moses lifted up the serpent in the wilderness, even so must the Son of Man be lifted up; so that whoever believes will in Him have eternal life. For God so loved the world, that He gave His only begotten Son, that whoever believes in Him shall not perish, but have eternal life"** (John 3:14–16). If we turn from our sin and look to Christ by faith as the only basis for our forgiveness, we can have eternal life. As someone has said: "Born once, die twice. Born twice, die once."

Do you have assurance that your sins are forgiven? If you were to die in this moment, step into eternity, and stand before a holy and righteous God, what you would say? If God asked you, "Why should I let you into heaven?" what would you say? Can you look to a time in your life where you turned from your sin and embraced Jesus Christ by faith as the only basis for your forgiveness? Have you simply heard about that, or have you made that choice yourself?

This is something you want to be sure about. Maybe today it's time for you to decide.

Just like the Israelites did with the bronze serpent on the pole, if we look to Christ, we can be healed of our sin problem and know that our sins have been forgiven. These are my final paragraphs in the "attitudes" study. There is an urgency to this message. I hope you will never think that this book is about *trying harder* to have a good attitude. Christ is the answer! If you're not turning to Him and walking intimately and personally with Him, you will never escape the wilderness. Even if you are a Christian, but are trying to do it yourself, it won't work. Resolutions like, "I'm going to try to be more thankful. I'm going to try to be more loving," simply won't work. If you don't allow Christ to live His life through you, if you don't allow the Lord to accomplish what He wants through your yielded heart, your efforts will surely fail. **"Christ in you [is] the hope of glory"** (Colossians 1:27), the Scripture says. It also affirms, **"I have been crucified with Christ; and it is no longer I who live, but Christ lives in me"** (Galatians 2:20).

A personal, intimate, daily walk with Christ is the only thing that can fuel the fire of your spiritual victory. If you don't have it, you won't experience it. Period. Looking to Christ is the only way to come to God, and looking to Christ is the only way to walk with God. He alone can lead us out of the wilderness of our own murmuring attitudes and lead us into the joy and fullness of God's abiding presence.

LOOK UP

Maybe as you were reading this epilogue, you were acutely aware that you're in that first group: You're not sure that you've ever made a commitment of your life to Christ. You can do that right now. This could be your day of decision. It's simple, but not easy:

Accept the fact that you're a sinner and that you deserve the judgment of a holy God.

Believe in your heart that Jesus died to pay the penalty for your sins.

Confess Him as your Lord and Savior. We commit our lives to Christ by doing the above, and we can affirm these steps by praying to God, which is simply calling out to Him. Here is a prayer to receive Christ that I commend. Let's look up now, and do that.

> *God, I believe that You love me and sent Jesus Christ,*
> *Your Son, into this world to die and to pay the penalty for*
> *my sin. I acknowledge that I'm a sinner and have failed*
> *You in many ways. I know that I stand in need of Your*
> *forgiveness. Right now, by faith, I repent of my sin. I turn*
> *from that pattern of living that says, "You don't matter,*
> *God." I confess all the wrong that I have done, and I*
> *embrace Jesus Christ by faith as the only basis for my*
> *forgiveness. I'm not trying to earn Your favor. I'm not*
> *trying to work my way into heaven anymore.*
>
> *Lord, I thank You for the promise that as many as receive*
> *You, to those you give the authority to be called the*
> *children of God, to those who believe in Your name [see*
> *John 1:12]. I thank You, Lord, in this moment by faith*
> *for allowing me to make the choice to trust in Christ alone.*
> *Thank You that in Jesus' name I can pray. Amen.*

Finally, here's a prayer for those who have received Jesus and want a change of attitude *through Him.*

> *Lord, I do not have the strength to follow You. Forgive me*
> *for thinking that while I needed You to save me, that I was*
> *going to change myself. I'm asking You to flow*

Your grace and strength into my life.
Every week of failed attempts reinforces
to me how desperately I need Your help.

I invite You to fill me with Your Spirit and give me the
strength that I need for every difficult circumstance and
person I encounter. I ask that Your grace would help me
put off all sinful attitudes and put on righteous ones in
their place. I declare with gratitude that I trust You will
change my attitudes, and that it's definitely not too late!
In Your name, Jesus, I pray. Amen.

STUDY GUIDE

LORD, CHANGE MY ATTITUDE
Before It's Too Late!

INVITATION AND INTRODUCTION

Objective: As a result of this study, participants will grasp the central theme of the book and begin to identify the "wilderness experiences" in their lives.

Welcome to this study of the book *Lord, Change My Attitude Before It's Too Late*. It may come as some surprise to you, but half this book is based on the Old Testament book of *Numbers*. As you will discover, this much neglected book deserves closer attention.

The book of *Numbers* records a startling and troubling occurrence among the population of Israel. Within a relatively short time span, an entire generation disappeared. During forty years, everyone over the age of twenty died. The book of *Numbers* tells us how and why this tragedy occurred. And it offers us a vivid picture that explains certain key lessons in our own lives. It literally helps us "do the math" in our relationship with God!

If you haven't read the Invitation and Introduction of the *Lord, Change My Attitude* (pp. 13–29), take a few minutes to do that right now.

#1—Prelude and Judgment: Read *Numbers* 13–14

The concept of ***murmuring*** is defined and subdivided into five distinct attitudes in the book. Each of these negative attitudes has a positive, identifiable counter-attitude, and these five positive outlooks can be summarized in a single term "contrastable" with *murmuring*— ***Praising***.

Suggested remedy:

> If *murmuring* is a demonic dissonance of destructive negative attitudes (complaining, coveting, criticizing, doubting, and rebelling),
>
> Then *praising* is a holy harmony of Promised-Land attitudes (gratitude, contentment, love, faith, submission).
>
> When we murmur, we turn any circumstance and surrounding into a wilderness; when we praise, we allow God to transform our circumstances and surroundings into hints of paradise.

#2—Five Invitation Questions: (pp. 14–17)

Read the five questions again and mark your answers below.

1. ____ yes ____ no

2. ____ yes ____ no

3. ____ yes ____ no

4. ____ yes ____ no

5. ____ yes ____ no

The Central Theme/Application Point of this book:

> *Those who choose murmuring as their lifestyle will spend their lifetimes in the wilderness.*

#3—Write a brief definition for each of the following terms that expresses your current understanding:

Choose—

Murmuring—

Lifestyle—

Wilderness—

#4—Based on what you have read so far, describe below at least one (or more) short or lengthy period in your life you would identify as a "wilderness experience":

I was in a wilderness experience during the time I was _____

_____

The Central Question of the book:

Why did God decide to wipe out an entire generation of His chosen people?

#5—As you begin this study, what is your present answer to this key question?

Crucial References to the event:

Psalm 95:7b–11

1 Corinthians 10:5

Hebrews 3:7–18; 4:1–3

#6—Read each of the above passages. If you are in a group study, discuss their significance in your understanding of "wilderness". Otherwise, note their significance below:

LOOK UP! (p. 29)

Use or adapt this prayer as you apply the challenges of this lesson.

Next assignment:

Read Chapter 1 of *Lord, Change My Attitude Before It's Too Late.*

LORD, CHANGE MY ATTITUDE
Before It's Too Late!

Those who choose murmuring as their lifestyle
will spend their lifetimes in the wilderness.

Chapter 1
REPLACE A COMPLAINING ATTITUDE . . .

Objective: As a result of this lesson, participants will identify areas in their lives where *complaining* has a destructive effect and will decide to seek a replacement.

SAY IT IN A SENTENCE:

Complaining is an attitude that if left unchecked will wither my capacity to experience joy and genuine thankfulness.

WILDERNESS ATTITUDE ONE = COMPLAINING

#1—Key Passage: Read Numbers 10:11–11:3

The people of Israel were on the move. God gave them supernatural guidance. Yet after three days' journey, the people complained.

What clues can you find in this passage about what motivated the people's complaints?

How would you have responded (how do you respond) to complaints?

What phrases or expressions most represent complaining in your life?

How does James explain his admission, "I like complaining" (see p. 32)?

#2—We choose our attitudes and train them into habits (see pp. 33–34).

Why is it important to acknowledge the fact that we choose our attitudes?

In what sense would you agree that complaining can become a habit?

#3—Defining Attitude (see pp. 34–36)

How does James combine "patterns of thinking" and "time" to develop a definition of "attitude"?

What is the definition of attitude and how accurately does it describe your experiences with "attitudes"?

#4—Defining Complaining (see pp. 38–40):

Complaining is expressing dissatisfaction with circumstances that are not wrong and about which I'm doing nothing to correct.

How does James explain the addition of two qualifications to the definition of complaining: 1) circumstances that are not wrong, and 2) circumstances about which I am doing nothing? Why are these qualifications important?

In what senses does a persistent attitude of complaining equal wilderness living no matter what our actual circumstances?

What characteristics put complaining into the sin category?

What kind of complaining does this chapter describe as the worst kind of complaints?

#5—How God Responds to Complaining (see pp. 44–45):

How did complaints affect God (see Numbers 11:1)?

What did God do as a result?

How should that response affect our view of God today?

How does the laundry room story help you identify with God's response to complaints (p. 46)?

#6—The Principle of Replacement: Matthew 12:43–45

How would you state in your own words Jesus' point about cleaning out but not filling up in this passage?

Which of the three questions on p. 50 presented the hardest challenge for you in the area of complaining?

LOOK UP! (pp. 51–52)

Use or adapt this prayer as you apply the challenges of this lesson.

Next Assignment:

Read Chapter 2 of *Lord, Change My Attitude Before It's Too Late*

LORD, CHANGE MY ATTITUDE
Before It's Too Late!

*Those who choose murmuring as their lifestyle
will spend their lifetimes in the wilderness.*

Chapter 2
...WITH A THANKFUL ATTITUDE

Objective: As a result of this lesson, participants will focus on deliberate expressions of thanksgiving in those areas where they are habitual complainers.

SAY IT IN A SENTENCE:

Thankfulness is the attitude that perfectly displaces my sinful tendency to complain and thereby releases joy and blessing into my life.

PROMISED LAND ATTITUDE ONE = THANKFULNESS

#1—Key Passage: Luke 17:11–19

Luke (the doctor) alone describes this event. A group of lepers presented Jesus with a class-action request for mercy. He sent them to do what healing required. On the way, they realized they were healed. What happened next is a profound lesson in uncommon gratitude.

Ten were healed; what do we know about the one who turned back to say, "Thanks"?

What does Jesus point out by His response to the man's gratitude (pp. 55–56)?

What lesson can we take from the man's response to God's grace?

#2—God, Our Gracious Provider (see pp. 56–57)

According to Romans 1:19-21, what do all of us instinctively know about God?

What four negative results followed from humans failing to acknowledge their awareness of God (see Romans 1:21)?

#3—More Than Words (see p. 58)

How can we express gratitude in ways other than words?

Why do you think social scientists are noting connections between thankfulness and people's mental and physical health?

Based on the definition, gratitude involves actions and words that "show that a kindness received is valued," how did you do on the gratitude test (pp. 60–61)?

#4—Levels of Gratitude (pp. 62–63):

Describe why and how each of the verses below identifies a level of gratitude we can learn.

Elementary (Hebrews 13:15)

High School (1 Thessalonians 5:18 KJV)

Graduate Level (Ephesians 5:18, 20 NKJV)

#5—Three Lessons from Psalm 107:8

Under each of the three "lessons" below, note an area (1) of your life or experience where you've discovered that truth. Then record an area (2) where you need to apply that truth more consistently.

Thankfulness is a decision/choice—not could but would (pp. 63–66).

1.

2.

Thankfulness is a decision based on reality (pp. 66–68).

1.

2.

Thankfulness is life-changing (destination & journey-altering decision) (pp. 68–69).

1.

2.

Crucial Insight from this chapter:

The same capacities and skills we use to complain we can use for practicing gratefulness.

#6—Reflect on the Insight above and then answer the following questions:

What skills and capacities do you use each time you complain?

Think of several examples that illustrate how those same skills or capacities could be used to express gratitude.

#7—Review the Let's Talk Solution section and apply the personal analysis questions to your life (pp. 71–73).

LOOK UP! (p. 73)

Use or adapt this prayer as you apply the challenges of this lesson.

Next assignment:

Read Chapter 3 of *Lord, Change My Attitude Before It's Too Late.*

LORD, CHANGE MY ATTITUDE
Before It's Too Late!

*Those who choose murmuring as their lifestyle
will spend their lifetimes in the wilderness.*

Chapter 3
REPLACE A COVETOUS ATTITUDE...

Objective: As a result of this lesson, participants will identify areas in their lives where coveting has a "blocking" effect and will decide to seek a replacement.

SAY IT IN A SENTENCE:

Covetousness, rampant in the Western world and the evangelical church, blocks the flow of God's fullness in our lives.

WILDERNESS ATTITUDE TWO = COVETING

#1—Key Passage: Read Numbers 11:4–35

Very quickly the miraculous daily manna became the taken-for-granted boring routine.

Who were the original spokespeople for an expanded diet and how did their "movement" spread (verses 4–6)?

How did Moses react to this fresh set of problems (verse 10–15)?

What did God do to deal with a) Moses' problem, and b) the people's demands for meat?

Describe at least one significant lesson each of the following individuals/groups learned through these events:

Moses—

Joshua—

Eldad and Medad—

Those who hoarded meat—

#2—The Problem: We've met the enemy and he is us.

How do the statistics quoted on pages 78–79 develop of picture of rampant coveting in our society today?

In what specific way does coveting parallel the physical experience of being stranded in a desert wilderness?

#3—Four-Part Definition of Covetousness: (pp. 80–81)

1) Covetousness is wanting wrong things.

Check Exodus 20:17. How does the tenth commandment define basic covetousness?

What are some of the obvious coveting traps in your life?

2) Covetousness is wanting right things for wrong reasons.

What example(s) of this kind of coveting can you identify in your life?

3) Covetousness is wanting right things at the wrong seasons/ time.

What example(s) of this kind of coveting can you identify in your life?

4) Covetousness is wanting right things in the wrong amount.

What example(s) of this kind of coveting can you identify in your life?

What do these four expressions of coveting have in common that characterizes this wilderness-living mentality?

#4—Bible Study in Three Acts

P R E L U D E — Acknowledging the Problem

Why is it so difficult to acknowledge coveting?

A C T 1 — Numbers 11:4–10 (pp. 82–87) Yielding to covetousness and why God hates it

How does the term "yielding" help us understand the difference between awareness of desire and acting on desire?

What does covetousness express about God?

A C T 2 — Numbers 11:16–20 (pp. 87–91) A gift from God you don't want

How does Psalm 106:15 explain God's answer to the people's demand for meat?

Respond to this caution: Beware of begging God for nonessentials. In time you may hate what you had to have.

A C T 3 — Numbers 11:31–35 (pp. 92–96) Consequences of Covetousness

How does covetousness destroy the concept of "enough"?

What are the telltale signs of cactus country?

#5—Solution

Reread each of the probing questions on pages 96–97. What personal decisions were provoked by those questions?

LOOK UP! (pp. 97–98)

Use or adapt this prayer as you apply the challenges of this lesson.

Next assignment:

Read Chapter 4 of *Lord, Change My Attitude Before It's Too Late.*

LORD, CHANGE MY ATTITUDE
Before It's Too Late!

*Those who choose murmuring as their lifestyle
will spend their lifetimes in the wilderness.*

PROMISED-LAND ORIENTED LIVING = PRAISE:
A Holy Harmony of Healthy Attitudes
WILDERNESS-ORIENTED LIVING = MURMURING:
A Demonic Dissonance of Bad Attitudes

Chapter 4
... WITH AN ATTITUDE OF CONTENTMENT.

Objective: As a result of this lesson, participants will practice contentment in several new areas of life.

SAY IT IN A SENTENCE:

A consistent attitude of contentment can bring lasting joy and lead you out of the wilderness of covetousness.

PROMISED-LAND ATTITUDE TWO = CONTENTMENT

#1—Key Passage: 1 Timothy 6:6–10

What points does this passage make about contentment?

Put the following definition from the book into your own words.

> *Contentment is satisfaction with God's provision. It means resting in what one already has and seeking nothing more.*
>
> *Contentment is a settled sense of adequacy.*

#2—Contentment's Partner (pp. 101–102)

Why must we never be content with who we are; only with what we have?

It what sense is a desire for godliness the ideal partner for contentment?

#3—Spiritual Equation (p. 102)

Why can we be confident that the following spiritual formula provides the antidote to coveting:

Godliness + Contentment = Great Gain

#4—False Formulas (pp. 104–106)

Consider each of the following popular formulas for living.

Godliness + Prosperity = Great Gain—Not

Why can't prosperity substitute for contentment in our lives?

Godliness + Poverty = Great Gain—Not

How does poverty fail as an adequate defense against covetousness?

Godliness + Power or Influence = Great Gain—Not

Although control of circumstances and people seems to offer an effective strategy for living, why does it fail miserably?

Godliness + Family Harmony = Great Gain—Not

What shortcomings disqualify the perfect family as a source for a "great gain" life?

Godliness + Ministry Success = Great Gain—Not

Like the previous successes (wealth, influence, family), how does even ministry success fall short of replacing contentment in life's formula?

#5—Practicing Contentment (1 Timothy 6:7–10)

STEP ONE: Look to Eternity (verse 7)

How do we see the unseen when there are so many visual distractions?

STEP TWO: Let Enough Be Enough (verse 8)

What is your definition of "enough"?

How would you describe your present "room and board"?

STEP THREE: Learn By Example (verse 9–10)

Who is your most powerful example of someone who knows and lives by the principle of "enough is enough"?

How do the thoughts on pages 109–112 help you understand better the phrase, "For the love of money is a root of all sorts of evil"?

#6—Let's Talk Solution (pp. 113–114)

What are you seeking?

What are you saying?

What have you settled?

How did you respond to the three examination questions on pp. 114–116 ?

LOOK UP! (p. 116)

Use or adapt this prayer as you apply the challenges of this lesson.

Next assignment:

Read Chapter 5 of *Lord, Change My Attitude Before It's Too Late.*

LORD, CHANGE MY ATTITUDE
Before It's Too Late!

Those who choose murmuring as their lifestyle
will spend their lifetimes in the wilderness.

Chapter 5
Replace a Critical Attitude . . .

Objective: As a result of this lesson, participants will identify the presence and effects of critical attitudes in their lives.

SAY IT IN A SENTENCE:

A continuous critical attitude toward those around me will consume all that is healthy and joy-producing in my life.

WILDERNESS ATTITUDE THREE = CRITICISM

#1—Key Passage: Numbers 12:1–12

This passage illustrates a significant point. Complaining relates to situations; criticism relates to people. Criticism is dwelling upon the perceived faults of another with no view to their good. Despite all they had accomplished as a team, Miriam and Aaron began to take Moses to task about his life.

What were Miriam and Aaron's two criticisms against Moses?

At what point did they get in trouble? What did God do?

Describe Moses' responses while others were criticizing him.

#2—Defining Criticism

Criticism is dwelling upon the perceived faults of another with no view to their good.

How does this definition capture the "double blows" of pain caused by criticism?

In what situations have you experienced the destructiveness of criticism?

What tends to bring out a critical attitude in you?

#3—Bible Study Application

PRINCIPLE ONE: Criticism is wrong—why? (pp. 127–131)

—it ruins our fellowship with God.

—it hurts us.

—it destroys our fellowship with others.

How do the results of Miriam and Aaron's critical attitude illustrate the above three sub-points?

PRINCIPLE TWO: Criticism is petty—why? It camouflages three deeper problems. (pp. 131–134)

—a blend of unforgiveness.

—envy, jealousy, or resentment.

—personal failure.

How did Miriam and Aaron exhibit each of these problems as they criticized their younger brother?

PRINCIPLE THREE: Criticism is self-exalting (p. 134).

In what ways does criticism create a subtle elevation of the one making the criticism?

PRINCIPLE FOUR: Criticism is painful (pp. 134–136).

What would happen if we applied every critical statement we are about to make to ourselves before we applied it to anyone else's life?

PRINCIPLE FIVE: Criticism is often inadvertent (p. 136).

How do you keep from making thoughtless comments?

What do you do when you realize you've just made a thoughtless comment?

PRINCIPLE SIX: Criticism plugs the flow of God's blessing (pp. 136–137).

If criticism given or received blocks our relationship with God, what must we do to resolve the problem?

#4—Let's Talk Solution (p. 139)

Based on the first evaluation question, in what areas are you most prone to practice a critical attitude?

How has your relationship with God been affected by criticism?

What moments of repentance have you experienced in the past?

As a result of this session, in what relationships do you realize you need to repent of a critical attitude? How will you do that?

LOOK UP! (p. 140)

Use or adapt this prayer as you apply the challenges of this lesson.

Next assignment

Read Chapter 6 of *Lord, Change My Attitude Before It's Too Late.*

LORD, CHANGE MY ATTITUDE
Before It's Too Late!

*Those who choose murmuring as their lifestyle
will spend their lifetimes in the wilderness.*

Chapter 6
. . . WITH AN ATTITUDE OF LOVE.

Objective: As a result of this lesson, participants will seek to substitute the practice of love in situations where they habitually criticize.

SAY IT IN A SENTENCE:
The only attitude big enough to replace a critical attitude is an attitude of love.

PROMISED-LAND ATTITUDE THREE = LOVE

#1—Key Passage: 1 Corinthians 13:1–8a

The apostle Paul interrupted a major section in his letter to the Corinthians where he was detailing the logistics of life together (Chapters 11–14). He inserted an emphatic parenthesis in chapter 13 to point out that every aspect of spiritual life must be permeated with genuine love or it will have little value.

> Given what you know about the relationship between Paul and the Corinthians, why is the placement of this love chapter so important?

> Of the three primary words for "love" in Greek, which one does Paul use in this chapter? Why?

#2—When Love Is Missing (pp. 146–149)

Before Paul describes love in these verses, he notes three impressive areas of "spiritual achievement" which he concludes are meaningless without love. What are these areas and how does the absence of love affect them?

1. 1 Corinthians 13:1—

2. 1 Corinthians 13:2—

3. 1 Corinthians 13:3—

How are each of these areas transformed when they are saturated with love?

#3—The Paradigm Shift (pp. 149–150)

Why is there a natural tension between practicing truth and practicing love?

How does MacDonald describe the usual way people try to handle both truth and love in their relationships?

Summarize the paradigm shift involved in truthful loving (see p. 150)?

In what ways would the three guidelines for loving action (p. 150) help you in a present relationship?

How do you see the difference between majors and minors (pp. 151–156)?

What "minors" tend to rear their ugly heads when you examine your critical reactions?

What have you learned in this chapter about handling minors?

Which of love's sixteen or so traits in this passage do you most desire in greater quantity in your life?

#4—Big Enough!

The "Say It in a Sentence" feature for this chapter is, "The only attitude big enough to replace a critical attitude is an attitude of love." Based on what you have learned in this chapter, why is this true?

#5—Let's Talk Solution (p. 163)

What specific personal changes would make it easier for you to be able to answer that question, "Am I a loving person"?

List at least five benefits of love that are part of your life right now.

How will you remember to let love overrule in areas and relationships where criticism has become a habit?

LOOK UP! (p. 164)

Use or adapt this prayer as you apply the challenges of this lesson.

Next assignment:

Read Chapter 7 of *Lord, Change My Attitude Before It's Too Late.*

LORD, CHANGE MY ATTITUDE
Before It's Too Late!

Those who choose murmuring as their lifestyle
will spend their lifetimes in the wilderness.

Chapter 7:
REPLACE A DOUBTING ATTITUDE . . .

Objective: As a result of this lesson, participants will learn how much the habit of doubt undermines their faith.

SAY IT IN A SENTENCE:

Those who make doubting their lifestyle will spend their lifetimes in the wilderness!

WILDERNESS ATTITUDE FOUR = DOUBTING

#1—Key Passage: Numbers 13:1–14:11

What begins as an exciting recon mission by handpicked men from Israel rapidly turns into defeat "before the first shot is fired!" A virus of doubt infected ten of the twelve spies and made them more eloquent spokesmen for the power of the enemy than for the power of God.

> What do you think the atmosphere was like back in the camp of Israel while the spies were carrying out their mission?

> Look again at the assignment given to the spies by Moses (Numbers 13:17–20). In what way did they miserably fail their mission?

#2—Defining Doubt? *A lack of confidence or assurance that God will keep His promises.*

Note at least one example from you own life or an acquaintance's that illustrates this definition.

Of the four wilderness attitudes we've examined so far (complaining, coveting, criticizing, and doubting), which presents the greatest difficulty for you? Why?

#3—Irrevocable Promises (p. 168)

Besides the three major promises from God described in this section, what other promises of God immediately come to mind?

#4—How God Destroys Doubt (pp. 169–184)

PRINCIPLE ONE: God places regular tests of faith before His children.

—meant to bring about success, not failure.

—when the bucket is bumped, what's inside spills out.

How do you respond to the claim that tests ultimately help us clarify what we actually know beyond what we casually think we know (see Deuteronomy 1:20–32)?

In what sense is faith the defining core of the Christian life?

PRINCIPLE TWO: The circumstances of life will either shrink or stretch your faith.

—people can see the same thing and come to opposite conclusions (p. 173).

—story of Landon.

Why is it crucial to remember that Christians face all the same setbacks and disasters in life that non-believers experience? If life's blows aren't going to be all that different, why be a Christian?

PRINCIPLE THREE: Doubts sees obstacles; faith sees opportunities.

—the facts of life

The majority committee (ten spies) and the minority committee (two spies) had the same collection of evidence upon which to base their response. Why did Caleb and Joshua urge the people to take the land?

PRINCIPLE FOUR: When surrounded by doubters, doubting comes easy (p. 180).

Doubting is contagious—Doubts love company!

Doubting is passive.

Doubting satisfies our tendency toward self-protection.

Doubters are easier to find than friends in faith.

Illustrate each of the points above from this lesson's key scripture passage.

PRINCIPLE FIVE: It's a short trip for doubt to despair.

Doubts lead to desperate, bad plans (p. 183).

In what four ways did the people demonstrate their doubt-driven despair by their response to the majority report?

#5—Let's Talk Solution (p. 185)

Read the three self-examination questions in this section of the chapter, along with the explanation. What do your answers to these questions tell you about your struggle with doubt?

LOOK UP! (p. 186)

Use or adapt this prayer as you apply the challenges of this lesson.

Next assignment:

Read Chapter 8 of *Lord, Change My Attitude Before It's Too Late.*

LORD, CHANGE MY ATTITUDE
Before It's Too Late!

*Those who choose murmuring as their lifestyle
will spend their lifetimes in the wilderness.*

Chapter 8:
. . . WITH AN ATTITUDE OF FAITH.

Objective: As a result of this lesson, participants will reaffirm the central role of faith in their relationship with God.

SAY IT IN A SENTENCE:

Only when faith replaces doubt in the life of a believer can the joy of knowing God become a reality!

PROMISED LAND LIVING ATTITUDE FOUR = FAITH

#1—Key Passage: Hebrews 11

Often called The Great Hall of Faith in Scripture, Hebrews 11 surveys Old Testament history to highlight men and women of outstanding faith. And yet the stunning point of the chapter is the lesson that those examples of faith lived their entire lives "in the dark" about what God would actually do to reward their faith. In comparison, we have the cross and the resurrection to remind us that God's plans are eternal and dependable.

Whom would you call a personal hero in this chapter? Why?

In what ways does Hebrews 11 challenge, encourage, and clarify your own faith?

#2—Defining Faith (p. 191)

**Christian faith is an attitude of trust rooted in the God
who has revealed Himself in Jesus Christ and His Scriptures.**

How does someone demonstrate faith or trust?

How does God know you trust Him?

#3—What We Learn from Lives of Faith

PRINCIPLE ONE: Faith is substance.

How does MacDonald explain the "substance" aspect of faith?

What can you say about the substance of your faith?

PRINCIPLE TWO: Faith is evidence.

What are the differences between faith in evidence and faith as evidence?

PRINCIPLE THREE: Statement of Faith: Faith is believing the Word of God and acting upon it, no matter how I feel, because God promises a good result.

What role does God's Word play in your day-to-day faith?

Why is it so hard to get the feelings out of faith?

When have you acted in faith despite the feelings you had?

PRINCIPLE FOUR: Faith is not a part of the Christian Life—it's the whole thing.

Explain this principle as you understand it.

PRINCIPLE FIVE: How to build your faith—

1. Cultivate your faith with the Word.

2. Confess your faith with your mouth.

3. Corner your faith with trusting action.

How would you prioritize these three steps according to the need to build your faith these days?

What is one area of your life where you can practice "cornering" your faith?

#4—Let's Talk Solution (pp. 209–210)

Prayerfully read through the three questions in this section of the chapter. As you consider your answers to this probing self-exam, decide what actions you are going to take to follow through on your discoveries.

LOOK UP! (p. 210)
Use or adapt this prayer as you apply the challenges of this lesson.

Next assignment:
Read Chapter 9 of *Lord, Change My Attitude Before It's Too Late.*

LORD, CHANGE MY ATTITUDE
Before It's Too Late!

*Those who choose murmuring as their lifestyle
will spend their lifetimes in the wilderness.*

Chapter 9
REPLACE A REBELLIOUS ATTITUDE . . .

Objective: As a result of this lesson, participants will identify strong-holds of rebellion in their lives that can be surrendered to Jesus Christ.

SAY IT IN A SENTENCE:

Rebellion against proper authority reveals a deeper rejection of God's authority, which brings devastating consequences to our lives.

WILDERNESS ATTITUDE FIVE = REBELLION

#1—Key Passage: Numbers 16

Murmuring is like a pot of liquid heating up. Complaints, coveting, criticism, and doubts gradually bubble through a group, gathering energy. Eventually the toxic mixture boils over into an attitude of rebellion. When Korah gathered his fellow murmurers to confront Moses and Aaron, they intended to carry out a coup. The murmuring in God's sight had reached a boiling point.

> When Korah's group stated their case, what arguments did they use to challenge Moses and Aaron's authority?

> How did Moses respond?

> What line did Korah use that Moses gave back to him (vs. 3, 7)?

After God dealt with Korah and his team, how did the people respond (verse 41–50)?

What wilderness attitude did the people fall back into despite God's swift punishment of Korah's rebels?

#2—Defining rebellion:

Rebellion involves knowing what God wants me to do and refusing to do it.

Complete the following two sentences.

Most Christians know that God wants them to _____ but refuse to do it.

I know that God wants me to _____ but I refuse to do it.

Which of the four other wilderness attitudes (complaints, coveting, criticism, and doubt) tend to contribute most when rebellion is an issue in your relationship with God?

#3—Bible Study Application

PRINCIPLE ONE: Rebellion is serious (pp. 214–217).

How does this section combine Korah's story with the teaching of Romans 13 to bring the issue of rebellion into everyday settings?

PRINCIPLE TWO: Rebellion exists in every human heart (pp. 217–219).

In what ways is rebelliousness a universal problem for us?

PRINCIPLE THREE: Rebellion has many sources (pp. 219–222)

How do the following sources express aspects of the four other wilderness attitudes that lead to rebellion?

Jealousy—

Delusions—

Ungratefulness—

Stubbornness—

Disappointments—

Distrust—

PRINCIPLE FOUR: Rebellion has many consequences (pp. 226–230).

As you review each of the sections below, note an example from your life that illustrates the point.

Leadership withdrawal—

Innocent people are injured—

Guilty will be condemned—

The infection spreads—

PRINCIPLE FIVE: Rebellion is ultimately against God (p. 231).

Which of the personal examples you just listed above do you now realize may have resulted from rebellion against God?

#4—Let's Talk Solution (pp. 231–232)

The people who backed up Korah refused to recognize the three issues in this self-exam. Before you review the questions and your answers, ask God for the wisdom and courage to respond in truth.

LOOK UP! (p. 233)

Use or adapt this prayer as you apply the challenges of this lesson.

Next assignment:

Read Chapter 10 of *Lord, Change My Attitude Before It's Too Late.*

LORD, CHANGE MY ATTITUDE
Before It's Too Late!

*Those who choose murmuring as their lifestyle
will spend their lifetimes in the wilderness.*

Review:

PROMISED-LAND ORIENTED ATTITUDE = PRAISE/WORSHIP:
A Holy Harmony of Healthy Attitudes

WILDERNESS-ORIENTED ATTITUDE = MURMURING:
A Demonic Dissonance of Bad Attitudes

Chapter 10
... WITH AN ATTITUDE OF SUBMISSION

SAY IT IN A SENTENCE:

*Submission, when properly understood and applied, replaces the pain
and strife of rebellion and greatly increases human happiness.*

PROMISED LAND ATTITUDE FIVE = SUBMISSION

#1—Key Passage: 1 Peter 2:13–25

The average person who heard Peter's letter read during the First Century was probably a slave. His or her human bondage was often twofold. They were not only someone's possession, they were also part of a conquered people. Rome ruled the world. The empire did not exercise her authority gently. Peter's audience was at least as resistant to the idea of submission as we are today.

Based on this passage, what kinds of people did Peter have in mind as he wrote?

What areas of submission did he include?

Why is submission a difficult subject to discuss and a hard attitude to practice?

#2—Defining Submission:

Any time we chose not to complain, covet, criticize, doubt or rebel, we are practicing submission.

If rebellion is at the heart of murmuring in Wilderness living, why is submission at the heart of praise and worship that characterizes Promised Land living?

#3—The Target of Submission:

Submission is for everyone (Romans 13:1; Ephesians 5:21)

According to these passages, who are the candidates for submission?

How do these two passages shed light for you on the significance of submission?

#4—Bible Study Application

PRINCIPLE ONE: Submission is duty to God (pp. 236–239).

Why is it crucial that we understand submission as ultimately part of our response to God rather than simply part of our role in human relationships?

How does the Bible teach healthy rather than unhealthy forms of submission?

PRINCIPLE TWO: Submission is protection by God (pp. 239–242).

Explain the phrase "Do right and silence the ignorance of foolish men" in the context of submission.

How does 1 Peter 5:5–7 point out the value of submission?

PRINCIPLE THREE: Submission has limits under God (pp. 243–248).

How does the key passage (1 Peter 2:13–25) include a standard for determining the limits of submission?

MacDonald includes three guidelines and two significant notes to deal with limits of submission. What are they?

PRINCIPLE FOUR: Submission Is Favor from God (pp. 248–249)

What does it mean to have favor with God?

On the things which you desire from God, how high do you list having favor with Him?

PRINCIPLE FIVE: Submission Is Intimacy with God (pp. 249–250)

Why and how can submission (at times a difficult undertaking) lead to intimacy with God?

In what ways have you found this principle true personally?

#5—Let's talk solution

Prayerfully read again the three probing questions in this section. Remember that how you answer them will ultimately affect your application of all the other principles in this book. How did you answer each question?

How would sharing your answers with others who can pray for you and encourage you be in itself putting submission into practice?

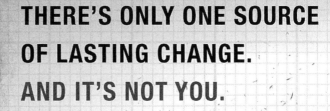

THERE'S ONLY ONE SOURCE OF LASTING CHANGE.
AND IT'S NOT YOU.

LORD CHANGE ME

JAMES MACDONALD

I KNOW, LORD.
I NEED TO CHANGE.
HELP ME.

JAMES MACDONALD

MOODY
Publishers™

From the Word to Life